CAVE-IN-ROCK
From an original oil painting by J. Bernhard Alberts, made in 1916

The Outlaws of Cave-in-Rock

Historical Accounts of the Famous Highwaymen and River Pirates who operated
in Pioneer Days upon the Ohio and
Mississippi rivers and over the
old Natchez Trace

Otto A. Rothert

With a Foreword by Robert A. Clark

Southern Illinois University Press
Carbondale and Edwardsville

Foreword by Robert A. Clark copyright © 1996 by the Board of Trustees, Southern Illinois University
Printed in the United States of America
Production supervised by Robyn Laur Clark
99 98 97 96   4 3 2

Library of Congress Cataloging-in-Publication Data
Rothert, Otto Arthur, 1871–1956.
    The outlaws of Cave-in-Rock / Otto A. Rothert ; with a foreword by
Robert A. Clark.
        p.   cm.—(Shawnee classic)
    Originally published: Cleveland, Ohio: A.H. Clark Co., 1924.
    Includes bibliographical references and index.
    ✓1. Cave in Rock (Ill.)—History.   2. Brigands and robbers—
Mississippi River Valley—History.   3. Brigands and robbers—Ohio
River Valley—History.   4. Brigands and robbers—Natchez Trace—
History.   5. River Valley—Mississippi River—History. ✓6. River
life—Ohio River—History.   7. Mississippi River Valley—History.
8. Ohio River Valley—History. ✓9. Natchez Trace—History.
I.Title. II. Series.
F549.C37R8   1996
977.3´98–dc20
                                                                        95-21812
    ISBN 0-8093-2034-7 (pbk.)   CIP

The paper used in this publication meets the minimum requirements of
American National Standard for Information Sciences—Permanence of
Paper for Printed Library Materials, ANSI Z39.48-1984. ∞

TO MY FRIEND
YOUNG E. ALLISON

Contents

Illustrations

Foreword

At first glance the title of Otto A. Rothert's 1924 study of outlaws is deceiving. Time has reshaped our impression of the "outlaw." You won't find the gun-toting, bank-robbing criminal of the Wild West in this book. The subtitle, in the verbose style of the period, better describes the criminal type: "Historical Accounts of the Famous Highwaymen and River Pirates . . . "

The Harpes and their ilk who preyed on vulnerable flatboats and overland travelers in the Mississippi and Ohio valleys during the late eighteenth and early nineteenth centuries were a very different sort of criminal from the gunmen of the late 1800s. To stumble into such evildoers in the wilderness was the great fear of the western trader or traveler.

In 1915 Rothert visited the notorious Cave-in-Rock for the first time. He became enamored of its history and began researching original documents dealing with its criminal inhabitants. In the spring of 1922 he queried the Arthur H. Clark Company of Cleveland, publishers of historical studies, regarding its interest in publishing the manuscript he had prepared on the subject. "I have an idea it will be interesting to those who 'dearly love the excitements of the criminally audacious,' " he opined.

Rothert was secretary, 1917–45, of the Filson Club, a historical society in Louisville, Kentucky. He had written and published several other books with Morton and Co. of Louisville: *A History of Muhlenberg County* (1913); *A History of the Unity Baptist Church, Muhlenberg County, Ken-*

tucky (1913); *Picturography of Madison Cawein* (1921); *Story of a Poet; Madison Cawein* (1921); and The Filson Club and Its Activities, 1884–1922 (1922).

Sale of his previous books had been only marginally successful. In a letter to Milo Milton Quaife, former superintendent of the State Historical Society of Wisconsin, he confided, "Financially my books are dismal failures, and time may classify them as 'bunk.' " Research and travel were expensive, and he had underwritten the production expense of several earlier titles. In *Outlaws* he hoped for some commercial success. His letters to the publisher detailed promotional ideas and included lists of prospective buyers. In November 1923, just a few weeks before the release of the book, he wrote to Clark, "Here's hoping The Outlaws will out-do anything you have published."

But his letter to Quaife expressed a pessimism not evident in his correspondence with the publisher: " . . . if my Outlaws is a failure I will simply have to give up trying to compile history, for the failure of this book will convince me that I am a failure. I would like to write a book on Early Flatboat Life. . . . I have much material on that subject; the outcome of the Outlaws will decide what I'll do about it."

Clark published an edition of one thousand copies of the book. Sales were slow. In 1942, eighteen years after publication, eighty-six copies remained of the original thousand, and they were sold as a remainder to Barnes and Noble.

Though not commercially successful, Rothert's *Outlaws* was in fact a valuable contribution to regional history, and it remains a source book sought by historians, amateur and professional. We applaud Southern Illinois University Press for again making the book available.

Robert A. Clark

Spokane, Washington, May 31, 1995

The Purpose of this Narrative

This book is intended to give the authentic story of the famous Cave-in-Rock of the lower Ohio River, as collected from historic and romantic sources, and to present verified accounts of the most notorious of those highwaymen and river pirates who in the early days of the middle West and South filled the Mississippi basin with the alarm and terror of their crimes and exploits.

All the criminals herein treated made their headquarters at one time or another in this famous cavern. It became a natural, safe hiding-place for the pirates who preyed on the flatboat traffic before the days of steamboats. It came also to serve the same purpose for highwaymen infesting the old Natchez Trace and other land trails north and south.

A century ago and more, its rock-ribbed walls echoed the drunken hilarity of villains and witnessed the death struggles of many a vanished man. Today this former haunt of criminals is as quiet as a tomb. Nothing is left in the Cave to indicate the outrages that were committed there in the olden days.

One state historian of our own times – Parrish, of Illinois – thus describes it: "The gruesome spot, which in those old border days witnessed many a scene of revelry and bloodshed, is today no more than a curiosity, its past victims, white and black, forgotten. Just below it, where, in 1801, there stood one lone cabin, there is today a thrifty village." In a sense the victims have been forgotten; yet they survive in the true stories of such of them as the preserved records can be made to disclose.

The story of the Harpes is more than that of mere criminals. They were arch-criminals among criminals, apparently loving murder for its own sake. There was a time when the whole of Kentucky and Tennessee was terrorized at the possibility of their appearance at any hour in any locality. Samuel Mason (or Meason) the Wilsons, and others, measured up more nearly to the standard of true highwaymen and pirates. If they had lived in England their careers would have closed on Tyburn Hill or at the rope's end on "Execution Dock." The stories of James Ford show that his real classification must forever remain largely a mystery.

Any history of these outlaws would doubtless be looked upon as wild fiction unless the statements were carefully verified by court records and contemporary newspaper notices, and the records of early writers who gathered the facts regarding them when these facts were told by men and women who lived at the time the atrocities were committed. The adage that "truth is stranger than fiction" is exemplified fully in their careers.

The lives and exploits of these men constitute an important phase in pioneer life because their deeds greatly affected the settlement of the new country. Dread of them brought peaceful settlers together in communities and helped to hasten the establishment of law and order. Their histories are therefore a part of the history of the country. The historian who passes them over as mere blood-and-thunder tales misses entirely one of the high lights in the great adventure of the settling of the Mississippi basin.

Owing to the sparse population and the great distances between settlements in the West, the early accounts of these criminals and their crimes were subject to change and to the effects of terrorizing rumor. In time the deeds of one would be attributed to another, and the circumstances of one crime confounded with others. In the main, however, tradition preserved a generally consistent story. Here and there men like James Hall and the editors of early newspapers preserved accounts of them and so blazed the way to court records and approximated the dates for private archives to be consulted. The pages that follow contain the result of years of patient investigation of these records and of archives that have never been published.

Numbers in brackets inserted in the text refer to the authorities as numbered in the bibliography.

OTTO A. ROTHERT

Louisville, Kentucky, March 17, 1923

The Lair of the Outlaws

Nature has set her own seal of wonder and immortality upon some of her works. The cavern of Cave-in-Rock, on the northern bank of the lower Ohio River, bears such a seal. Lacking the adventitious aids of immensity, depth, and remoteness, it was regarded with religious interest in the vague traditions of the aborigines, and has excited the curiosity, aroused the imagination and stirred the fear of white men since they first discovered it. The Cave has been at once noted and notorious, famous and infamous, and it remains today, through all the changing years and diversities of its use, actual or attributed, practically unchanged, still challenging curiosity, surprise, fear, and admiration.

The scenery above and below the Cave attracted the attention of the earliest western travelers. Much deforestation has taken place during the past century, but the landscapes along the banks of that section of the Ohio stand today, as they did in the olden days, unsurpassed by any other along the river's course. The mouth of the Cave is in a high bluff overlooking the Ohio, which is the central link in a chain of majestic landscapes. It seems almost a paradox that a spot so beautified by nature should have been made the headquarters of outlaws, and the scene of much that was hideous in crime.

Pioneers in the West were likely at any time to encounter wild animals or to be forced to battle with plundering or revenge-seeking Indians. Whether traveling overland trails or upon navigable streams, the first-comers in the middle West were always in danger of highway robbers or river pirates. The cruelest of all highwaymen were the Harpes and the shrewdest of the river pirates were the Masons.

Cave-in-Rock's history as a rendezvous of outlaws does not begin until about 1795. The date of the discovery by white men has not been ascertained. The earliest record found is in *The History of New France,* by Charlevoix, in 1744. It includes Bellin's Map of Louisiana presenting the general course of the Ohio, drawn from observations made by M. de Lery. When this explorer came down the river in 1729 he noted the location of the Cave by referring to it as "Caverne dans le Roc." After 1778 it is indicated on many English and American maps. Early travelers designated it by various names, each of which, except "House of Nature," contained the word "cave." Since 1800, Cave-in-Rock has been practically the only name applied.

The early French called the Ohio "La Belle Riviere." In the days of primeval forests it was one of the most beautiful streams in the world. Evidences of its former grandeur are nowhere so well retained as in the neighborhood of Cave-in-Rock. The last of the giants of the forests standing on the bluffs and in the bottoms along the river will some day disappear, but Cave-in-Rock will defy time and its changes, and ever stand as a reminder of the days when wilderness was king.

Cave-in-Rock is in Hardin County, Illinois, about twenty miles below Shawneetown and twenty miles above Golconda, or about eighty-five miles below Evansville, Indiana, and fifty miles above Paducah, Kentucky. It is about two and one-half miles below Ford's Ferry and a half mile above the village of Cave-in-Rock. Its position commands a long view up and down the Ohio River. It has a large and dark tunnel-like opening extending into a gray limestone bluff which is partly hidden by shrubbery and small trees. Whether one sees it while passing in a boat or approaching it from the shore the view invariably stirs the beholder. It has the appearance of a large arched crypt, imbedded in solid rock. It is a "house" built by Nature, and is as solid as Gibraltar. It is sphinx-like in its silence, and bewilders those who enter.

The mouth is an arched opening, semi-elliptical in form, about fifty-five feet wide at the base. The cavern extends back horizontally one hundred and sixty feet with an almost uniform width of forty feet. The walls and roof, which change to more or less of an ellipse near the mouth, again change near the center into a semi-ellipse and retain that curvature to the end. The ceiling is horizontal throughout its length, while the floor, beginning about seventy-five feet from the entrance, gradually inclines upward toward the rear, and at the extreme end comes within a few feet of the arched ceiling. At this end there is a hole large enough to permit a man to climb out into a sinkhole in the surface above. The upward incline of the floor in the rear is due to a deposit of earth, washed there during the past half-century by water coming down through the sinkhole during heavy rains. Near the middle of the ceiling are two perpendicular crevices with an average width of less than a foot, extending across and beyond the Cave, and upward to within about fifteen feet of the surface of the cliff. One of these narrow crevices has, near the center, a chimney-like opening sufficiently large to admit a man. It leads to a rough-walled enlargement about four feet wide and ten feet high. This small place is known as the "upper cave," and has a history and fiction of its own.

In the lower part of what may be designated the lower lip of the mouth-like opening is a large, level, wedge-shaped space about five feet lower than the floor of the Cave. At its outer extremity this wedge-shaped space is almost as wide as the mouth itself, but rapidly tapers inward to a width of about four feet. It then continues back into the mouth about twenty-five feet through the solid rock, in the form of an excavated channel or passage about three and one-half feet wide. This narrow channel, about five feet deep at the beginning, inclines upward until it reaches the general level of the floor of the Cave. The top of the rock on either side of the excavation is level and resembles a platform. These two platforms or stage-like floors extend inward and, like the inclined passage, soon reach the general level of the Cave. This excavated channel and the part of the wedge-shaped space from which it leads may have been made by men, but whether by Indians or early whites is not known. It may possibly be the result of erosion.

At a normal stage of the river the mouth of the Cave is, measured in the perpendicular, about half-way between the top of the bluff and the water's edge. In spring the river frequently comes up to within a few feet of the opening. When the water is extremely high it enters; during great floods there is ample depth to row a skiff the entire length of the Cave.

Such is Cave-in-Rock today, and such it was in pioneer times, except that in the rear a deposit of earth had not been washed in, and that large trees, which stood in front of the mouth and hid or partly concealed it, have long since disappeared. It was an ideal lair for river

INTERIOR OF CAVE-IN-ROCK

showing entire interior of cave and entrance to small upper cave

(From a drawing by J. Bernhard Alberts, made in 1916)

outlaws; it furnished shelter and gave them every advantage over passing travelers.

In March, 1766, John Jennings, a Philadelphia merchant, going down the Ohio with a cargo of goods for Fort de Chartres, Illinois, notes in his *Journal* that he stopped for an hour near "a large rock with a cave in it," some twenty-five miles below the mouth of the Wabash River. The earliest record of a homeseeking pioneer who came to the Cave-in-Rock country and there began an overland trip into Illinois dates back to about 1780, when Captain Nathaniel Hull, of Massachusetts, appeared at what later became Ford's Ferry. "He and several other young men," writes Governor John Reynolds in his *Pioneer History of Illinois,* "descended the Ohio to a point near Ford's Ferry on that river [for a while known as Hull's Landing and later as Robin's Ferry] and came across by land to Kaskaskia . . . At this day the Indians were not hostile as afterwards, so that Hull and party escaped through the wilderness without injury." Nor had any white man as yet practiced piracy on the lower Ohio.

Victor Collot, a French engineer, is one of the first writers who stopped at the Cave and published a brief description of it. He knew of its existence long before he arrived, for his book, *A Journey in America,* shows that he had planned to stop at the "Big Cave," and did so in the summer of 1796 when he went down the river to New Orleans.

A few months later the place was visited by Andrew Ellicott, then on his way to Natchez for the purpose of determining the boundary line between the United States and Spain. An entry in his *Journal,* dated December 15, 1796, shows he "dined at the Great Cave . . . one of the greatest natural curiosities on the river."

On April 16, 1797, Francis Baily, the English astronomer, stopped there. His *Journal of a Tour in the Unsettled Parts of North America* contains a few pages on the "Big Cave." Among other things he says, "its entrance was on a landing-place. It had somewhat the appearance of an immense oven. We entered it and found the sides very damp . . . We beheld a number of names cut in the sides of the cave, which in this solitary place, and cut off as we were from society, gave us a degree of pleasure to look over." Baily apparently heard of no outlaws during his short stay. This probably was due to the fact that his visit was made at a time when the Cave was very damp, as is frequently the case in spring. Had he appeared later, he might not have survived to tell of his interesting travels in America, for during the greater part of the year 1797 the place was occupied by the notorious Mason family.

Perrin du Lac, in his *Travels through the two Louisianas*, writes that he embarked at Pittsburgh, April 22, 1802, "in a pirogue thirty feet long and three feet broad" and that a few weeks later he stopped at the Cave. He says "it is considered one of the greatest natural curiosities in North America."

The first detailed description of Cave-in-Rock ever printed, as far as now known, appeared in one of the earliest editions of Zadok Cramer's *The Ohio and Mississippi Navigator* and was republished in the appendix of *Journal of a Tour,* 1805, by Thaddeus M. Harris without credit to Cramer.

Thomas Ashe, an unreliable English traveler, wrote an account of Cave-in-Rock shortly after the Cramer or the so-called Harris description was published, and at a time when reports of some of the early robberies that had been committed there were still in fresh circulation. His book entitled *Travels in America performed in 1806,* contains a chapter of fabrications headed "Cave in the Rock, Ohio Bank, September, 1806."

In July, 1807, Christian Schultz, then a young man, started from Pittsburgh down the Ohio in a flatboat. He arrived at "The Cave in the Rock" about October 1, continued his trip to New Orleans, and returned, via ship, to New York. In his *Travels on an Inland Voyage* he devotes a few pages to the Cave, saying, among other things:

"It is a very curious cavern . . . I could not help observing what a very convenient situation this would be for a hermit, or for a convent of monks. . . I have no doubt that it has been the dwelling of some person or persons, as the marks of smoke and likewise some wooden hooks affixed to the walls sufficiently prove. Formerly, perhaps, it was inhabited by Indians; but since, with more probability, by a gang of that banditti, headed by Mason and others, who, a few years ago, infested this part of the country and committed a great number of robberies and murders . . ."

Fortesque Cuming, an unprejudiced Englishman, wrote in his *Tour to the Western Country* that the Cave is "one of the finest grottoes or caverns I have ever seen." This interesting traveler, in January, 1807, proceeded to Maysville, Kentucky, by boat, and from there made horseback trips to central Kentucky and Ohio. Returning to Pittsburgh, he started, on May 7, down the Ohio in a flatboat for New Orleans. From old Bruinsburg, a few miles above Natchez, he visited old Greenville. In this town about three years before, one of the Cave-in-Rock outlaws had been convicted under unusual circumstances and hanged and buried in an

unusual manner.   When traveling by boat Cuming always carried a few skiffs in order to get ashore more
easily.   On May 18, 1807, a few minutes after passing
the head of Cave-in-Rock Island, he landed at what is
known as Cave Spring, a cave-like opening a few hundred yards above Cave-in-Rock from which a strong
spring of water constantly flows.   This crevice in Cave-
in-Rock bluff is about nine feet high, three feet wide,
and extends back some forty feet.   Cuming at first mistook it for the famous Cave, as has been done by more
than one traveler since his day.   In his sketch pertaining to his visit to Cave-in-Rock he writes:

"Rowing along shore [below Cave Spring] with the
skiff, we were soon undeceived as to that's being the
Rocking Cave, as a third of a mile lower down, one of
the finest grottoes or caverns I have ever seen opened
suddenly to view, resembling the choir of a large
church as we looked directly into it.   We landed immediately under it and entered it.   It is natural, but it
is evidently improved by art in the cutting of an entrance
three feet wide through the rock in the very center,
leaving a projection on each hand, excavated above to
the whole breadth of the cavern, the projections resembling galleries . . . It is crowned by large cedars,
and black and white oaks, some of which impend over,
and several beautiful shrubs and flowers, particularly
very rich columbines, are thickly scattered all around
the entrance . . . Standing on the outside, the appearance of some of the company at the inner end of the
cave was truly picturesque, they being diminished on
the eye to half their size, and removed to three times
their real distance.

"There is a perpendicular rocky bluff just opposite
the lower end of Cave Island, about two hundred yards

above the Cave, where the river narrows to less than half a mile wide, forming a fine situation for fortification."

Thomas Nuttall probably was the last distinguished traveler who came down the Ohio in a flatboat and commented on the Cave. In his *Journal of Travels into the Arkansa Territory* he states that he and his party left Shawneetown December 14, 1818. After floating a short distance they came up with three other flatboats and, lashing them together, proceeded upon an all-night journey. He further comments: "The river is here very wide and magnificent and chequered with many islands. The banks of Battery Rock, Rock-in-Cave, and other places are bold and rocky with bordering cliffs. The Occidental wilderness appears to here retain its primeval solitude; its gloomy forests are yet unbroken by the hand of man; they are only penetrated by the wandering hunter and the roaming savage."

The early western travelers already cited, and a number of their contemporaries and followers who saw the Cave, published descriptions or references that agree in the main, but each, in his own way, was evidently more impressed by certain of its various features than were some of the others who visited the place. A few speculated upon it as an Indian temple of prehistoric times. Some commented upon it from a geological standpoint. A number were especially interested in the names they found carved on the walls; some in the trees that grew around the opening. Others dwelt upon it as a rendezvous of outlaws.

For what various purposes the Cave may have been used in prehistoric times by Mound-builders and Indians, or even Cave Dwellers, is a question for archae-

ologists and ethnologists. There is far less physical
evidence to indicate a previous presence of robbers and
counterfeiters than there is to prove that the place was
inhabited by prehistoric man. A rusty home-made
dagger blade and a part of a counterfeiter's mold are
the only relics that point toward the outlaw occupancy.
On the other hand, five well-defined mound sites in the
level fields above Cave-in-Rock bluff, and the many
flint and stone implements picked up during the past
century in and near the Cave indicate beyond doubt
the former presence of Indians and Mound-builders.
In April, 1918, Robert L. Yeakey, while spading his
garden on this bluff, unearthed a carved stone image,
six inches high and four inches wide, weighing two
pounds, six ounces, representing a man in squatting
position. The probability that the image is an idol
gives strength to the inference that the Cave was used
as a temple some time in the prehistoric past.

The mounds are additional evidence to this effect.
These were opened many years ago and have since been
plowed over often. Each contained, it is said, from
five to ten human skeletons. The bodies had been
placed in a stone-walled sepulcher that was covered
with flags of stone a few inches thick, over which a cir-
cular mound of earth was thrown. The fact that each
of these mounds contained a number of skeletons, apparently placed there at one time, leads many to the
conclusion that a battle, or battles, must have been
fought in or near the Cave and that all, or some, of the
dead were buried together. Scientists advance a plausible explanation of this: "We know not if these burials
indicate famine, pestilence, war, or unholy sacrifice.
We can only conjecture that they were not graves of
persons who had died a natural death." Because of

the Cave's temple-like form and its proximity to these old mounds, it appears more probable that they were erected in connection with the ceremony of "unholy sacrifice" than for any of the three other suggested causes.

The Harris description of the Cave, written about 1803, refers to it as "the habitation of the Great Spirit." Some thirty years later, Edmund Flagg, in *The Far West,* written after his visit to "Rock-Inn-Cave," says: "Like all other curiosities of Nature, this cavern was, by the Indian tribes, deemed the residence of a Manito, or spirit, evil or propitious, concerning whom many a wild legend yet lives among their simple-hearted posterity. They never pass the dwelling place of the divinity without discharging their guns (an ordinary mark of respect) or making some other offering propitiatory of his favor."

From official records we learn that the section of the country in which Cave-in-Rock is embraced was sold, in 1803, to the United States by the Kaskaskia tribe. In 1818, when the sale was confirmed by the same Indians and the three other tribes then constituting the Illinois confederacy, it became unchallenged government property. Thus, when the Masons, the Harpes, and other early outlaws held forth there, it was still in the Indians' territory.

From a geological standpoint, the Cave is evidently nothing more than a prosaic hole in a limestone bluff. In neither the main cave nor the crevices above are there any stalactites or stalagmites, but an incrustation resembling such a formation occurs here and there on the walls. In 1818, Henry R. Schoolcraft, in his *Personal Memoirs*, says: "The cave itself is a striking object for its large and yawning mouth, but to the geologist presents nothing novel." Collot, in 1796, expressed the opinion that "it is an excavation made in the rocks by the continual beating of the flood." In a *Report* published in 1866, A. H. Worthen, director of the Geological Survey of Illinois, states that "the limestone (St. Louis limestone) is quite cherty and the Cave has probably been formed by the action of water percolating through crevices of the rock and by the eroding influences of the atmosphere." Neither of these explanations is satisfactory. No other has been found. Cave-in-Rock has the appearance of a section of a large cave that was formed by an underground stream in some remote geological age, and later disconnected, by upheavals, from the other parts of the subterranean passage. Some of the other parts may still exist. Sulphur Springs Cave, four miles southwest of Equality, may be one. Bigsby Cave, eight miles north of Cave-in-Rock, may be another. Hardin County is besprinkled with many sinkholes, the outlets of which are unknown. The "Big Sink," four miles north of the Cave, covers about one hundred acres. Cave-in-Rock may have been an outlet for some of these sinkholes until upheavals made such drainage impossible.

In early days the virgin forests retarded, to a great extent, the water of the heavy rains, and as a result floods were less frequent and less severe. It is probable that when Cave-in-Rock and the country about were covered with trees the place was damper than now, for the water then slowly seeped down from the tree-covered surface. Nevertheless, it was sufficiently dry to serve as a good shelter not only for outlaws, who frequently occupied it, but also for men and women going down the river in flatboats.

Today it is comparatively dry, except during the

spring and shortly after a heavy rain. Practically all the water running through the Cave now comes from a narrow crevice in the rear, which drains a small sink-hole in the surface. Through this opening, as already stated, much soil has been deposited in the back part of the Cave during the past fifty years. Nature has made practically no changes in the Cave itself since its discovery by white men, but the landscape has been affected by the removal of the large trees that once shaded its mouth. A decrepit sycamore, an ash or two, a few small maple trees, some scrub cedars, and some Virginia creeper constitute the only vegetation now growing around the opening.

The travelers who visited Cave-in-Rock in flatboat days gave the place more time and thought than did those who appeared after the introduction of steam-boats. The New Orleans, or Orleans, which was the first steam-propelled boat to make a trip from Pittsburgh to New Orleans, passed it in 1811. Not until fully five years thereafter was the practicability of navigating the Ohio by steamboats satisfactorily demonstrated. Local tradition has it that the James Monroe, coming down in 1816, was the first steamboat to land at the Cave. Thomas Nuttall, who appeared on the scene two years later, was, as already stated, one of the last distinguished men who floated down the river in a flatboat and commented on the place. Leisure was an inseparable feature of flatboat travel. With the coming of steamboats the lingering of travelers along the river became a thing of the past. After 1820 comparatively few boats of any kind stopped at the Cave. Boats became more numerous, but whether propelled by steam or oars, they traveled not only faster but through a country rapidly increasing in population, and passengers and crew stopping in this section found better shelter elsewhere. But Cave-in-Rock was ever pointed out as a place that "in days gone by" had been the den of flatboat robbers. Counterfeiters and other outlaws, however, operated in the neighborhood until as late as 1832.

The earliest record of a professional artist making a sketch of the Cave dates back to May, 1819, when Major Stephen H. Long came down the Ohio on the steamer Western Engineer, on his way to his Rocky Mountains exploring expedition. In his notes on "Cave-Inn-Rock or House of Nature" he gives a description of the Cave, and says that Samuel Seymour, the official artist of the expedition, "sketched two views of the entrance." Edwin James's account of this expedition contains many of Seymour's pictures, but none of places east of the Mississippi. Efforts made in Washington to locate his original sketches were without success.

Edmund Flagg, a traveler, journalist, and poet, who lived the greater part of his life in Louisville and St. Louis, spent a short time at the Cave in 1836, while on a steamboat trip gathering material for his book, *The Far West*. He gives some of the history of the outlaws of "Cave-Inn-Rock" and then describes the Cave and the Island. He says the place furnishes "a scene of natural beauty worthy an Inman's pencil" and that "if I mistake not an engraving of the spot has been published: a ferocious-looking personage, pistol in hand, crouched at the entrance, eagerly watching a descending boat."

Maximilian, Prince of Wied-Neuwied, writes May 19, 1833: "We embarked on the Paragon steamboat at Shawneetown . . . and after passing Cave-in-Rock

INTERIOR OF CAVE-IN-ROCK ABOUT 1825

A view from the rear of the lower cave, showing burned embers on floor, notched log (on left) leading to upper cave, and flatboats on the river

(From the original drawing by Charles Alexander Lesueur)

Island, a long wooded island, we glided past Cave-in-
Rock, a cavern which has been drawn by Lesueur."
Lesueur's drawing was made about 1825. It is an interior view looking out over the river and conveys a
good idea of the Cave's size and form. However, the
opening to the small upper cavity and the leaning pole
for climbing into it are placed a little too far to the
left.[1]

Maximilian was accompanied by his artist, Charles
Bodmer, who, during the course of his travels in North
America, made eighty-one pictures, all of which were
published in 1843 in the *Maximilian Atlas*. Most of
these drawings pertain to the life of the Indians of the
Upper Missouri, and stand today as the first and best
record of the costumes of these tribes. Among the subjects presented is his Cave-in-Rock picture, one of the
two early views of the Cave now available. Bodmer
probably drew it from memory. It shows a landscape
interesting in itself, but it is an absolutely misleading
presentation of the actual scene. From no point or
angle does the view appear as drawn by him, or even
suggest such a scene. By the ordinary working of
nature no such changes could have been brought about
in many centuries. The mouth of the Cave is near the
lower end of a long bluff of almost uniform height and
opposite the lower end of Cave-in-Rock Island. A
camera picture of the lower end of this bluff, made in
1917, appears among the illustrations in this book.
Bodmer's view places the opening in a short bluff that

---

[1] Charles Alexander Lesueur (1778-1857) French naturalist and artist,
was a member of Robert Dale Owen's communal colony at New Harmony,
Indiana, forty miles northeast of the cave. His drawing of Cave-in-Rock has
never been published except in a doctoral thesis by Mme. Adrien Loir
entitled, *Charles Alexandre Lesueur, artiste et savant Francais en Amérique
de 1816 a 1839*; issued in 1920 by Museum d'Histoire Naturelle, Le Havre.
In this thesis are reproduced forty of Lesueur's drawings.

is more or less cone-shaped and opposite or above the head of an island. When high water reaches the mouth of the Cave, as is shown by Bodmer, then Cave-in-Rock Island is submerged many feet and its banks cannot possibly be seen. This picture occurs in a number of books, but without any comments on its gross inaccuracy. Some reproducers have taken the liberty of adding a setting sun in the background.

In 1916, J. Bernhard Alberts, of Louisville, made an impressionistic painting of the mouth of the Cave. His painting is true to the scene as it was at the time of his visit. He also drew a pencil sketch showing a general view of the interior with the inner edge of the mouth in the immediate foreground, the artist's point of view being from just outside the mouth.

Piracy and Rough Life on the River

It is not clear when Cave-in-Rock first became the headquarters of the criminals who flourished on the Ohio, and preyed upon primitive commerce and travel between Pittsburgh and the Lower Mississippi. Shortly after the Revolution was under way, renegades from eastern communities, corrupt stragglers from the American army, and villains who had had their brutal training in western wilds, began to seek in the Ohio valley refuge from the more orderly and well settled communities. Samuel Mason, who had been an officer in the Continental army, converted the cavern into an inn as early as 1797. While he occupied the Cave, and a few years thereafter, it was known as "Cave-Inn-Rock." It was ideally located. Every passing boat must reveal itself to those in the Cave who had a long, clear view up and down the river. A lookout could detect boats long before boatmen could perceive the Cave. The bold beauty of the bluff made it pleasant for the boats to run in near the sharply shelving shore, and many travelers were thus simply and easily delivered into the hands of the banditti. As an inn, where drink and rest could be had, it decoyed them; as a scene for shrouded crime it was perfect.

The earliest travelers on the western rivers floated or propelled themselves with paddles and oars in small, clumsy craft. The Indian canoe or pirogue was heavy, but was managed with skill by those accustomed to its use. With the growing stream of settlers and the in-

creasing number of settlements along the Ohio and
Mississippi, there arose a necessity for larger craft that
would bear heavier burdens. This brought the flatboat
era covering the period from 1795 to 1820–that quarter
of a century known as the Golden Age of Flatboating.
During that era river piracy was at its height. The
lighter boats, pirogues, skiffs, and batteaux were to the
clumsy rafts and flatboats bearing heavy cargoes what
submarines and torpedo boats have been to the heavier
ships in later warfare. Inland piracy had its advantage
in using the small craft on dark nights for sudden
descents and escapes.

In the midst of this period the stately steamboat age
began its development. It was inaugurated in 1811
when the first steam-propelled "water-walker" made
its laborious and astonishing way from Pittsburgh to
New Orleans. By 1820 steamboats had become a de-
pendable factor in traffic, and were, to river travel,
what the railroad train was later to become to the slow
stagecoach and freight wagon. It was inevitable that
under steamboat influence flatboats of all types – arks,
broadhorns, Orleans boats, keel-boats, and flat-bottomed
barges – would follow the primitive pirogues, skiffs,
and batteaux into retirement, except for neighborhood
use. River piracy waned with the conditions it preyed
upon, but not until about 1830 did it cease utterly.

In society, as in nature, everything develops with
opportunity and disappears according to necessity. In
the primitive age of river craft many travelers were
captured or killed by Indians bent on revenge or pil-
lage. These marauders were sometimes led by white
renegades. Later, pioneers floating down the Ohio or
Mississippi on flatboats came in contact with comparatively few savages, but were exposed to a far more dar-

ing and dangerous enemy in the form of river pirates – white men, many of them descendants of supposedly civilized European families. These disappeared as the population increased. Then ensued the reign of the more diplomatic river pirates – the professional gamblers who, for a half century, used cards and other gaming devices as instruments with which to rob those who ventured into their society.

Such were the types of craft and men operating upon and infesting the rivers in the early days. The country through which these boats moved was not the country we see today. Changes in the shapes and channels of the rivers have been numerous, only the rock-defined reaches preserving their original contours. Appearances in detail have greatly changed. The wonderful unbroken forests are gone. Where they once stood are now fields and farms or cut-over forests; every few miles there is a town. The river channels once mysterious and uncertain are now carefully charted.

Early voyageurs going down the river had, of course, no guides and there were no known marks to indicate their approach to any of the features of the river as it wound through the wild, uninhabited country. The boatmen who came afterwards carrying maps rudely scratched, found them unsatisfactory because of inaccuracies or lack of detail. Not until a handbook was made available, after some years of careful compilation of river features, could the uninitiated navigate the large rivers with any degree of safety.[2]

The numerous charts in *The Navigator* show the

[2] The first, and in a sense the only standard guide book of this kind ever published, was Zadok Cramer's *The Ohio and Mississippi Navigator*. It made its appearance about 1801 and was followed by a number of revised and enlarged editions until 1824, when the last edition was printed. It was practically the only printed guide for flatboats.

curves, islands, sandbars, eddies, and channels, and
mark the location of towns and many other places of
significance. The accompanying text contains instructions of value to the boatman, and historical data of
interest. It is curious, however, that no section of either
the Mississippi or Ohio is designated as one where outlaws were likely to be encountered – not even Cave-in-
Rock nor the mouth of Cache River, which were long
considered the most dangerous resorts on the Ohio. In
every edition of *The Navigator* about a page is devoted
to a description of the Cave and instructions to boatmen
passing it, but there is no reference to its grim history.
Zadok Cramer was evidently a practical man, with no
eye to the speculative. It was not until 1814 that he
added a few lines bearing on the Cave's "economic"
history:

"This cavern sometimes serves as a temporary abode
for those wanting shelter, in case of shipwreck, or other
accident, which happen on the river near it. Families
have been known to reside here tolerably comfortable
from the northern blasts of winter. The mouth of this
cave was formerly sheltered, and nearly hid by some
trees growing in front of it, but the rude axe has leveled
them to the earth and the cavern is exposed to the open
view of the passenger. Emigrants from the states,
twenty-seven years ago used to land here and wagon
their goods across the Illinois country, it not being more
than one hundred and twenty miles from this place to
Kaskaskia on the Mississippi."

The Cave, of course, had more than criminal uses.
How on one occasion it served as a "temporary abode
for those wanting shelter" is recorded in *The American
Pioneer,* published in 1842. In this magazine Dr.
Samuel P. Hildreth, under the title of "History of a

Voyage from Marietta to New Orleans in 1805," gives an interesting account of the schooner Nonpareil and her voyage south, based on data furnished him by members of her crew. The boat was built at Marietta and started down the river April 21, 1805. She was a seagoing vessel intended to run on the lakes near New Orleans. The captain doubtless steered his course by a copy of *The Navigator*. We quote from Hildreth's account of what the crew found in 1805 at the well-known lair of outlaws:

"As the Nonpareil approached near the mouth of this dreaded cave, a little after twilight, they were startled at seeing the bright blaze of a fire at its entrance. Knowing of its former fame as the den of a band of robbers, they could not entirely suppress the suspicion it awoke in their minds of its being again occupied for the same purpose. Nevertheless, as they had previously determined not to pass this noted spot without making it a visit, they anchored the schooner a little distance from the shore and landed in the skiff. Being well armed with pistols they marched boldly up to the cavern where, instead of being greeted with the rough language and scowling visages of a band of robbers, they found the cave occupied by smiling females and sportive children. A part of the women were busily occupied with their spinning wheels, while others prepared the evening meal. Their suspicions were not, however, fully removed by all these appearances of domestic peace, still thinking that the men must be secreted in some hidden corner of the cave ready to fall on them unawares. On a little further conversation they found the present occupants of the dreaded cave consisted of four young emigrant families from Kentucky going to settle in Illinois. The females were yet in the bloom of life. Their husbands had bought or taken up lands a few miles back from the river, and after moving their families and household goods to this spot had returned to their former residences to bring out their cattle, in the meantime leaving their wives and children in the occupancy of the cave till their return.

"Having brought, with their spinning wheels and looms, an abundance of flax, the women spent the weary days of their husbands' absence in the useful employment of spinning. A large fire in the mouth of the cave gave cheerfulness to the gloomy spot and enabled them, at night, to proceed with their labors, while its bright rays were reflected upon the looms, beds, and household utensils which lay piled up along the side of the cave. By day the sun afforded them light, the mouth of the cave being capacious and elevated, while the roof sheltered them from the rain. They were in daily expectation of the arrival of their husbands, when they would move out on to their farms in company.

"A little conversation soon dissipated all suspicions of harm from the minds of their visitors . . . and, borrowing from them a torch, they explored the hidden recesses of the cave. At this time no vestige of its former occupants remained but a few scattered barrel staves, and the traces of their fires against the blackened sides of the rock. The walls, even at that early day, were thickly scored with the names of former visitors, to which they hastily added their own, and thousands have no doubt been added since. Bidding a warm farewell to this singular and solitary community, they entered their boat, greatly wondering at the courage and confidence of these lonely females. Their surprise, however, in a manner subsided when they reflected that they were the daughters of Kentucky and from the land of Daniel Boone."

The Nonpareil experienced no trouble with river pirates, but was wrecked during a storm on the Mississippi and never reached her proposed destination. So, in one form or another, every flatboat and other early river craft suffered more or less trouble. History records many robberies and other misfortunes, but its pages also show that, notwithstanding the numerous trials and tribulations, early river life, rough as it was, was more of a romance than a tragedy. Going down the Ohio and Mississippi proved, in many instances, "easy sailing" compared to the flatboatman's overland trip north over the Natchez Trace and other wilderness roads infested with highwaymen.

The usual plan of the river robbers was to station one or two of their men and women at some prominent place on shore to hail a passing boat. These decoys pleaded to be taken aboard, claiming they were alone in the wilderness and wished to go to some settlement further down the river, or that they desired to purchase certain necessities which they lacked. If the boat was thus enticed ashore, the crew saw their cargo unloaded, and plundered, or beheld their craft continue its course down the river in the hands of the enemy, themselves held as hostages or murdered.

Boat wreckers were another common source of great danger. Under one pretext or another they managed to get aboard the boat and scuttle it near a place where their confederates were prepared to make an attack. Or, like Colonel Fluger, they waited until they found a boat tied along the bank and then bored holes in the bottom or dug out the caulking. When the ill-fated boat began to sink, the fellow-wreckers rushed to the rescue and appropriated the goods for their own use, killing part or all the crew if necessary.

Then, as now, a number of dangerous channels existed in the Ohio and Mississippi. They were designated as such in *The Navigator*. Near the head of some of them lived reliable settlers who made it a business to pilot boats through for pay. Pirates frequently succeeded in passing themselves off as trustworthy local pilots. Boats turned over to such men for safe steering were usually grounded and immediately thereafter delivered into the hands of outlaws in waiting.

One of the dangerous channels, against which voyageurs were warned by *The Navigator,* ran from the head of Walker's Bar (a bar beginning about two miles below Cave-in-Rock) down to Tower Rock, and from there extended to the foot of Hurricane Island, a total distance of about eight miles. The author of the river guide, after devoting considerable space to directions for navigating this channel and avoiding the Hurricane Bars, adds a suggestion: "Just below the Cave, on the right bank, there is a person who is sometimes employed to pilot boats through this serpentine channel, and it is better for a stranger to pay a dollar or two for this purpose, than run the risk of grounding on either one or the other of these bars in low water. When the water is high there is no occasion for a director."

The outlaws at Cave-in-Rock turned to their advantage the suggestion published in *The Navigator*. About ten miles above the Cave, near Battery Rock, or on what has long since been called the Jonathan Brown Old Place, the robbers stationed a man who offered to pilot, for a small sum, single boats or small fleets through this "serpentine channel." He explained that the person referred to by *The Navigator* as living "just below the Cave" was out on a visit and would not return for a week or more. In the event the first man failed, another, standing ready a few miles further down at Ford's Ferry, offered his services. The pilot who succeeded in being employed grounded the boat in front of the Cave if, by the time he reached the place, he judged the cargo was worth the risk and the crew could be overpowered. If more time was required, he guided the boat to the head of Hurricane Island. There it was either wrecked or taken safely through the channel, the procedure depending on whether or not he judged a profitable robbery possible. Boatmen who declined to take a pilot aboard at Battery Rock or Ford's Ferry were likely, if the water was comparatively low, to inquire for a director "just below the Cave." The man procured there, whether a member of the Cave band or not, invariably guided the boat safely through. Thus by helping to maintain one reputable and reliable place near the Cave for procuring the services of a pilot, the robbers experienced little trouble in trapping the boats they selected for that purpose.

Although most of the prospective victims were given little consideration until after they had come within ten or twenty miles of the Cave, in a number of instances the river pirates began setting a trap for a boat long before it arrived at Shawneetown.

The fact that the victims were piloted to the Cave by certain members of a band, or enticed into the place by some other means for the sole purpose of robbery, is recorded by many early writers; none of them, however, gives any details. All authors who touch on the Cave's history publish statements based on what other men and women heard other people had experienced while in the hands of the outlaws. Only one instance has been found in which the victim himself (Dr. Charles H. Webb) recited to an author the details of how he was decoyed to the Cave and how he escaped from the men then occupying the place. The old flatboat robbers and flatboat wreckers left no first-hand accounts of the methods they employed.

The year 1788 roughly marks the beginning of the big inflow of settlers into the region west of the Alleghenies, also the beginning of counterfeiting and other outlawry at Cave-in-Rock. Many travelers and homeseekers followed the trails and went into the interior afoot, on horseback, or in wagons; others took the river to some river point and either settled there, or proceeded overland to an inland section. Thus, by "long lines of wagons" and "great fleets of boats" the middle West became settled. In the meantime many a small party traveled alone over the trails or drifted down the river in a single boat or in a small fleet, into the new and sparsely populated country, and became easy prey for highway robbers or river pirates who were likely to appear at any time and in any disguise.[3]

The earliest connection of the Cave with the name of any outlaw who became famous was in 1797, when Samuel Mason, of Revolutionary fame and hideous fate, seems to have occupied it as a main trap for his carefully worked out scheme of river piracy on a large

---

[3] Conflict with pirates, cut-throats, and counterfeiters was only one of the perils to which the boatmen were exposed on their long and trying trips into the western wilds. Floating ice, heavy winds and rains, treacherous currents, hidden bars, and large snags were among the natural dangers that constantly engaged the attention of the steersman. Many boats, managed by careless or inexperienced men, were overturned, the craft and cargo damaged or lost, and, as was frequently the case, some or all on board drowned. Poorly constructed boats were put out of commission after meeting with only a few minor obstacles.

scale. He erected a great rude sign on the river bank near the mouth of the Cave, proclaiming to every passerby that his "Liquor Vault and House for Entertainment" was open to the public. Many captains and their crews and many flatboat passengers were lured to it. After Mason and his family left for the South, most of the succeeding bands, during their necessarily short stay, operated a gambling and drinking place on the same principle.

It was a common practice among outlaws frequently to change not only their headquarters but their names. While at Cave-in-Rock Mason was also known as "Wilson." Thomas Ashe, who wrote about it, probably did not know that the Wilson he described was Samuel Mason. Among the various men who appeared after the departure of Samuel Mason, alias "Wilson," was one Jim Wilson. Whether Jim Wilson was his real name is not known. However, between Samuel Mason as "Wilson" and a later man known as "Jim Wilson" there has been more or less confusion for almost a century, especially in tradition. In 1897 William Courtney Watts wrote a historical romance, *Chronicles of a Kentucky Settlement,* in which he presents James Ford, of Ford's Ferry notoriety, as "James Wilson." James Ford was in no way connected with Mason or with Wilson, but his presentation under the fictitious name of "James Wilson" had added to the already existing confusion.

After James Ford's death, which occurred in 1833 – and many years before Watts applied the name of "James Wilson" to him – a writer published a sketch of the career of one Jim Wilson at the Cave. This sketch is here recapitulated, not as a story that can be verified in all its details by history, but as a semi-historical tale which may convey a better idea of the methods, life, and fate of the Cave's outlaws than formal history. Only one who will make a study of the Cave's past – from the available authenticated records down to some of its absurd traditions – will recognize this story as a picture in which facts fairly divide the scene with fiction, and painted in colors that bring joy to the hearts of readers of dime novels. When and by whom it was written or first published has not been ascertained. It apparently was not written before 1836, for the author, in his introduction, attempts a description of the Cave as it appeared that year. The writer evidently had read Thomas Ashe's account published in 1808, and was also familiar with some of the Cave's printed history and oral traditions. The story was probably first published in an old magazine or newspaper. In 1893 it appeared, anonymously and without credit, in the *Crittenden Press,* of Marion, Kentucky. From that weekly it was copied by many newspapers in the lower Ohio Valley, and is now preserved, under various titles, in many a scrap book.

This old story is interesting because it was written when stories of the Cave were still fresh. Inaccuracies and confusions of names and dates may have crept in, but it remains the first concise and inherently reasonable account of how the Cave was first occupied as a den by river criminals. In the presentation of the usual method of the Cave's renegades, it matters very little whether the first of those desperate captains of crime bore the name of Wilson, Mason, or Harpe. In this case it seems clearly the story of Samuel Mason about 1797. The names they assumed might vary with every flatboat or raft that passed. An alias is ever the shield of the criminal. The story describes not only a method actually employed by the Cave's outlaws for many years, but also a method by which the career of more than one of these river pirates was, as we shall see later, so tragically terminated. The story runs, as follows:

"About the year 1809, one Jim Wilson, a flatboatman, while passing down the Ohio, was overtaken by a terrific storm. He steered his boat under the shelter of a cliff. On landing he observed the opening of the cave. He was attracted by the commodious rooms with dry ceilings and sanded floors, and resolved that on his return to Pittsburgh he would bring his family hither.

"In the following spring Wilson's boat again landed at the foot of the cliff. This time he was not alone, but with him came his wife, five children, two slaves, and William Hall, the great counterfeiter. His boat was loaded with provisions, stores, liquors, and arms, which he had stolen from the government warehouse at Fort Pitt on the night before his departure. The great cave was soon transformed into a dwelling and tavern large enough to accommodate several travelers.

"Wilson's object for landing and establishing himself in so remote and romantic headquarters will be seen hereafter. A sign was planted at the water's edge bearing these words: 'Wilson's Liquor Vault and House for Entertainment.' This novel sign had a magnetic effect upon the boatmen who were almost daily passing en route to southern markets, with flatboats loaded with produce. The boat crews were generally jovial fellows, fond of rum, rest, and merriment, and hardly a boat passed without stopping. Many were the guests at Wilson's Tavern; thieves and gamblers stopped off here and in a few months the place became infamous for its licentiousness and blasphemy.

"Wilson had been for many years a deep-dyed criminal and only came here that he might vary his crimes, and have a wider field for operation. Out of his guests he soon formed a band of the most noted robbers, murderers, and counterfeiters that, for two years, had no parallel in modern history. Their headquarters were at the Cave, but they had many stations along the Ohio above and below, which were maintained for the purpose of preventing suspicion being cast upon the genial landlord at the Cave. The principal station was at Hurricane Island, where forty-five men were stationed all the time.

"Each boat that landed at the Cave was captured and such of the crew as would not join Wilson's Gang were allowed to drift on to Hurricane Island where they were again captured and the remainder of the crew foully murdered and their bodies cast into the Ohio. With new pilots and crews the boats and cargoes were taken to New Orleans, and converted into cash which was conveyed to the Cave through the wilderness of Kentucky and Tennessee.

"Many boats loaded with valuable cargoes left port on the upper Ohio and its tributaries, under the guidance of experienced and trustworthy officers. The officers and crews never returned. No returns for sales were ever received. It soon became a mystery that so many honorable men never came back to pay over the proceeds, and to tell the perils of their voyage. It was many months before any serious suspicions were created. After that it was found that the cargoes were disposed of by entirely different crews from those entrusted with them. There was but limited postal or other communication in those days – letters of special importance were carried by messengers who often fell into the hands of Wilson's men. Thereby they kept posted and, by changing the communication to suit their purposes, and forwarding them by different carriers, often thwarted the attempt of justice, and kept their whereabouts enveloped in mystery for many months. 'But it is a long lane that hath no turn.' It was finally ascertained that no tidings could be had of any boat after it had passed certain points on the Ohio near Wilson's Tavern.

"A meeting of the Pittsburgh shippers was called and it was determined to ferret out the mystery. This would be a shrewd piece of detective work which would be attended by many dangers. A large reward was offered for information as to the exact location of the robber band. John Waller, a determined and ambitious man of Maysville, Kentucky, resolved to secure the reward or perish in the attempt. He was furnished with a cargo contributed by various shippers along the Ohio, and with five trusted companions he set out early in the spring of 1810. They floated with the current many days. At last one evening they came in sight of the Cave, and were attracted by the novel sign and also the presence of several females on the bank, who made gestures for them to land. They held a hasty consultation and resolved to land; a few sweeps of the steering oar brought them to the foot of the cliff."

That which follows this clear description of ordinary circumstances is evidently a mixture of fact and fiction that represents the imaginative style of the day. It is quite plain that the author himself had not personally visited the Cave, but had relied upon the fictions of Thomas Ashe or the reflections from Ashe's account that had gained circulation and belief. He accepts the mythical "upper cave" and has the Cave divided off into rooms and a "council chamber," no relics of which have ever been reported by any matter-of-fact observer from that time to this. The leader, "Jim Wilson," he converts into a semi-savage with matted and tangled hair and beard, who is yet a shrewd trader and an orator of no mean power for his day. On the occasion of the initiation of new recruits Jim Wilson delivers a romantic and argumentative speech that is equal to the best fiction of the times.

The story narrates graphically how Waller and his men were overawed and compelled, under fear, to agree to join the robber band; how they were received into it with melodramatic ceremonies and then were oath-bound, but not fully trusted; how they made their escape – the savage and astute robbers being, of course, fooled for the exigencies of the event; how the Waller force combined with its waiting reinforcements, re-turned, captured Jim Wilson and then went to Hurri-cane Island and destroyed that part of the band; and how eventually "Jim Wilson's head was severed, his body buried . . . the head identified and delivered to the proper authorities at Pittsburgh . . . and the captors received the merited reward." This last point is plainly an echo of Mason's fate.

This story of the activities of the early renegades of civilization, and of the river pirates who occupied the Cave bears upon its face the stamp of truth that fits neatly into practically all traditions from about 1795 to about 1820.

Before Mason became famous, however, greater scoundrels than he were to attract public attention, and hold it for some years. The story of the Harpes – "Big" and "Little" Harpe – is one that may freeze the blood as read now in the light of old records and personal accounts that seem to bring the reader into the very presence of these two brutes. In the security of law and order in these days the facts seem remote, but when the sparse settlement of the West in 1799 is realized, and the further fact that wilderness hospitality opened doors to all travelers and admitted these monsters freely with good people, it is possible then to conceive the horror their deeds and presence aroused.

The Harpes - A Terrible Frontier Story

The career of the two Harpes[4] in Tennessee, southern Illinois, and Kentucky, particularly Kentucky, at the close of the eighteenth century has rarely been equalled in the history of crime, either in peace or war. Its beginning was so sudden, its motives wrapped in such mystery, its race so swift, and its circumstances so terrible and unbelievably brutal as to justify Collins, the distinguished historian of Kentucky, in referring to the brothers as "the most brutal monsters of the human race."

At that time, 1798-99, Kentucky had a pioneer population of about two hundred thousand, which was largely centered in the new trading and agricultural towns in the eastern part and in the rich bluegrass country. The remainder of the state, except along the water courses, was well nigh a wilderness. In the southern and western portions buffalo grazed, and bear were plentiful. East Tennessee, where the scourge of crime began, was even more sparsely settled. This pioneer population was vigorous, rude, and accustomed even to Indian atrocities. Among the settlers were many who, as fugitives from justice, had deliberately sought seclusion from the eastern states because of criminal offenses. The Ohio River was infested with inland pirates, and the early rivermen themselves were a rough and violent type. Isolation led well-meaning pioneers to be generous and confiding to those whom they had

---

[4] Prior to about 1824 Harpe was spelled Harp.

tested, but to a great degree might was right, and strangers looked askance at each other and were prepared for the worst.

Yet such a rude and hardy people as these were gripped with horror at the atrocities of the Harpes, at their often unmeaning and unprovoked murders. It is difficult in these days of well ordered government to realize the mysterious terror and excitement that began near Knoxville in 1798 and swept through the wilderness to the borders of the Mississippi, and across the Ohio into Illinois like some sudden, creeping fire that breaks out in underbrush, and grows steadily in intensity and rage until it sweeps forests before it. All this was, in a measure, realized in the breasts of human beings as the hideous crimes of the Harpes increased.

Aside from the wars and the recorded importances of political development, the episode of the Harpes is the most astounding event in the early life of the Middle West. It engaged the memory of men for forty years, and the pens of numerous historians, and writers of memoir have been occupied with it ever since. In the main the story has been well preserved, but in the details there has been the variation that grows with repetition. The most dignified historians have not disdained to seek the minute details attaching to the persons and actions of these two men from the moment they began their criminal career to the thrilling blood-chase in which the older brother was captured and killed, and the younger escaped into exile and to an even more dramatic and terrible death.

To this day the story of "The Harpes" and "Harpe's Head" is told about firesides in the Cave-in-Rock country, in southern and western Kentucky and in eastern

Tennessee. It has been perpetuated in folk ballads and written by scores of pens. [93]

It is the purpose here to bring together the many threads of the tale as they have been verified and corrected by original records sought from Wisconsin to New Orleans, and from Knoxville to Cave-in-Rock and the Mississippi River.

Judge James Hall, while living in Illinois, wrote a brief account of one of the crimes committed by these outlaws, and in April, 1824, published it in *The Port Folio* of Philadelphia. In his introductory remarks he comments: "Neither avarice nor want nor any of the usual inducements to the commission of crime, seemed to govern their conduct. A savage thirst for blood – a deep-rooted enmity against human nature, could alone be discovered in their actions . . . Plunder was not their object; they took only what would have been freely given them, and no more than what was necessary to supply the immediate wants of nature; they destroyed without having suffered injury, and without the prospect of benefit . . . Mounted on fine horses they plunged into the forest, eluded pursuit by frequently changing their course, and appeared unexpectedly to perpetrate new horrors, at points distant from those where they were supposed to lurk."

Judge Hall, up to that time, had done little more than describe one of their last crimes, yet *The Cincinnati Literary Gazette,* May 28, 1825, came out with a statement admitting that there may have been two outlaws by the name of Harpe, but added: "We have no hesitation in asserting that their history, as published in *The Port Folio,* is unworthy of belief . . . The horrible details concerning these men . . . such disgusting

sketches of human depravity and barbarism manifest
either a vitiated taste or a total disregard of the morals
of the community."

As far as is now known, at least two papers published
in the month following came to the defense of Judge
Hall's account. *The Illinois Gazette,* of Shawneetown,
among other things, declared: "The depravity and
bloodshed which marked their existence . . . are circumstances too strongly impressed upon the recollections of our early settlers to be contradicted at this
date."

The Columbian, of Henderson, Kentucky, in a half
column article devoted to the same subject, asserts:
"The account published in *The Port Folio* is correct in
every essential point . . . However it may be regretted
that such monsters as the Harpes ever should have existed to disgrace humanity, yet it is an uncontrovert-
ible fact." [56]

In the August, 1825, issue of *The Port Folio* Judge
Hall published an account of another murder committed by the Harpes – the killing of Thomas Langford, who was among their first victims in Kentucky.
In the same number he devotes a few pages to a verification of the statements he published then and a few
months previous.   And before half had been told about
the Harpes, *The Cincinnati Literary Gazette* was convinced of its error in doubting and disputing the verac-
ity of Judge Hall.   Judge Hall wrote several pages
justifying the publication of the weird and wonderful
facts of the career of the Harpes.   His arguments published in 1825 in his own defense hold good today and
may be equally well applied to the story of the Harpes
here given, which, as far as is known, is the first attempt

to compile a complete history of these notorious outlaws:

"If it is intended to be objected, that these 'horrid details,' even if true, are not proper for publication – I reply, that whatever tends to develop the history or character of a people, is a legitimate subject of public discussion. History to be of any value must be true. It must disclose not only the truth but the whole truth. In vain would the historian seek this in the frail monuments vaguely preserved in the uncertain legend of tradition. He must resort to national records and to the testimony of writers contemporary with the events which he attempts to describe, and if the latter abstain from the narration of 'disgusting sketches of human depravity and barbarism,' history must be curtailed of her most fruitful source of incident, and men and nations stripped of their boldest peculiarity. It is perhaps forgotten that 'depravity and barbarism' constitute almost the sole basis of history, tragedy, and the epic song; that kings and courts are nothing without them; that they revel amid 'the pomp, pride, and circumstance of glorious war;' and stand forth in bold relief in every department of civil subordination. It is to be deplored that such is the fact; but while crime and folly continue to predominate in the affairs of men, they will be found to swell the pages of those who attempt to exhibit correct pictures of human nature.

"In describing the American backwoodsmen, a class of men peculiar to our country, I have thought it proper to introduce among other authentic anecdotes the story of the Harpes. My object was to display as well the extraordinary sufferings to which the earliest emigrants to the western country were exposed, as the

courage with which they met and repelled those hardships."

The Harpes were believed to be brothers. They
were natives of North Carolina. Micajah, known as
Big Harpe, was born about 1768, and Wiley, known as
Little Harpe, was born about 1770. Their father was
said to have been a Tory who fought under the British
flag at King's Mountain and took part in a number of
other battles against the colonists. Before the close of
the Revolution and immediately thereafter many of the
Tories living in the south Atlantic colonies fled toward
the Mississippi. Those who still sympathized with the
King of England and continued to live in the "Old
States" were, in most sections, ostracized by their neighbors. It was to this class that the parents of the Harpes
belonged; and it was, therefore, in an environment of
hatred for and by neighbors that the two sons grew up.

About the year 1840 Colonel G. W. Sevier, son of
Governor John Sevier, in an interview with Lyman C.
Draper, the historian, stated that Big Harpe, when
asked shortly before he was killed why he had committed so many crimes, answered that he had been badly
treated and consequently had become disgusted with all
mankind. [12G] The same statement is made by J. W.
M. Breazeale, another well-known early Tennesseean,
who had lived in Knoxville the greater part of his life
and had investigated the careers of the outlaws.

One writer attributes their acts of fiendish inhumanity to the fact that they believed every man's life,
whether good, indifferent or bad, was predestined and
that the All Wise had foreordained for them a hatred
of humanity and a career of crime. [121] Draper, in his
"Sketch of the Harpes," comments on the fact that
"their tawny appearance and dark curly hair betrayed

a tinge of African blood coursing through their veins."

Criminologists may or may not agree as to the underlying cause of the great thirst for blood possessed by the Harpes, but the fact that they were the most savage and terrible characters in this period of American history cannot be disputed.

About the year 1795 the two men, accompanied by Susan Roberts and Betsey Roberts, left North Carolina for Tennessee. Susan claimed to be the legal wife of Big Harpe, whereas Betsey merely posed as such. Big Harpe, however, claimed both women as his wives. The Harpes cared as little for the laws of matrimony as for any other laws and the legality or illegality of anything they did was a matter of indifference to them.

The two men and their women roamed in central Tennessee about two years. Most of their time was spent with a few stray Creek and Cherokee Indians who at the time were ostracized by their tribes and were committing atrocities against their own people as well as against the whites. The Harpes joined the savages in their outrages, and not only encouraged them in their bloody deeds, but gave them many demonstrations showing to what extent barbarity could be practiced. Asleep or awake they were armed with tomahawks and knives and never took a step from camp without a gun. They were always prepared to shed blood for the satisfaction of shedding it, or to resist arrest should any attempt be made to capture them. They lived like man-eating animals. The women as well as the men wore leather hunting shirts and moccasins made from the untanned skin of animals they killed. They never wore hats except in the coldest weather and then used the kind they "whanged" together with deer skin thongs. [121]

Some time during 1797 the four left middle Tennessee for the new settlement of Knoxville. While wandering toward the eastern part of the state they met a young Methodist preacher named William Lambuth, who was traveling through the wilderness alone. They robbed him and among his belongings found a Bible. In turning the leaves, looking for bank bills, Big Harpe discovered on the front page, written in plain letters the names "William Lambuth" and "George Washington." Pointing to the name of the General, Harpe remarked: "That is a brave and good man, but a mighty rebel against the King." The articles found in Lambuth's possession convinced the Harpes that he was a preacher, whereupon they returned to him not only his Bible but also the gun, the little money, and the horse they had taken. Then abruptly turning from him and shouting, "We are the Harpes," they quickly disappeared. This is probably the only instance in the lives of the Harpes, after the beginning of their murderous career, when they had anyone, old or young, in their power, and showed less than a fiendish barbarity. [121]

Obeying the principle that birds of a feather flock together, the Harpes, it seems, were attracted toward the new settlement of Knoxville. In March, 1798, James Weir, on his way from South Carolina to Kentucky, spent a few days in the town. Writing of his short stay there he says:

"In the infant town of Knox the houses are irregular and interspersed. It was County Court day when I came. The town was confused with a promiscuous throng of every denomination. Some talked, some sang, and mostly all did profanely swear. I stood aghast, my soul shrank back to hear the horrid oaths and dreadful indignities offered to the Supreme Governor of the Universe, who with one frown is able to shake them into non-existence. There was what I never did see before, viz., on Sunday, dancing, singing, and playing of cards, etc. . . . It was said by a gentleman of the neighborhood that 'the Devil is grown so old that it renders him incapable of traveling and that he has taken up in Knoxville and there hopes to spend the remaining part of his days in tranquility, as he believes he is among his friends,' but as it is not a good principle to criticise the conduct of others, I shall decline it with this general reflection, that there are some men of good principles in all places, but often more bad ones to counterbalance them." [109]

The Harpes doubtless felt they could better gratify their thirst for blood in the vicinity of a settlement like Knoxville than in a wide wilderness where subjects for their cruelty were too few. They found a small tract of cleared land on Beaver Creek, about eight miles west of Knoxville. Upon this they built a log cabin for themselves, and a pen for their horses, and, in order to conceal their motives, cultivated a few acres of ground. Under this feint of honest occupation they experienced no difficulty in gaining the confidence of their neighbors. In fact, so easily had they made a favorable impression that within a few weeks after their arrival Little Harpe married Sarah or Sally Rice, a daughter of John Rice, a preacher living about four miles north of the Harpe hut.

In the meantime the two brothers made trips to the seat of justice, for then, as now, the occasion and the desire "to go to town" to see "what's going on" was a common one among the people who lived in the country. Swapping horses was then, and still is to a great extent, one of the features of a day at the small court house towns. So when, on one of their first trips to Knoxville, the Harpes brought with them a fine three-year-old mare and offered to run her in a race, no suspicion was aroused. The horse was apparently superior to any other in town that day and no owner could be induced to venture his quarter nag against her. A Mr. Aycoff, recognizing the mare as an unusually good one, bought her and became so attached to the animal that he kept her almost a quarter of a century. It is interesting to note that twenty years after he purchased her, a gentleman from Georgia, visiting near Knoxville, recognized her as the filly that had been stolen from him many years before. [12G]

The Harpes rapidly increased the number of their trips to town, but it was soon noticed that with each succeeding visit their supply of pork and mutton increased. They sold this meat to John Miller, one of the most respected merchants of Knoxville, through whom the Harpe hams soon became well known. But the reputation of the two brothers for drinking and gambling, and the disturbances they raised in the village were sufficient to arouse suspicion in the community. By this and other evidence John Miller was convinced that the Harpes were hog thieves, and suspected that their dishonesty and meanness had no limit. [12G]

Soon after the arrival of the Harpes in east Tennessee a number of houses and stables near Knoxville were set on fire and many of them burned to the ground. As no motive for such destruction of property could be discovered, the citizens attributed it to downright rascality. So strong had become suspicion against the Harpes that when Edward Tiel, who lived a mile from Knoxville, discovered that several of his best horses had been stolen, he enlisted a number of neighbors and immediately proceeded to the home of the Harpes. The investigators found that the cabin had been deserted recently, but noticed indications that horses had been tied to some near-by trees. Tiel and his men took up the trail and followed it across Clinch River into the Cumberland Mountains. There they captured the two Harpes who were alone at the time. The stolen horses were recovered, but when the captors and their prisoners reached a point about five miles northeast of Knoxville, the horse thieves made their escape. [21]

Tiel and his men tried to effect their recapture but, failing in the attempt, returned to Knoxville. That same night the two Harpes appeared at Hughes' "rowdy groggery," a few miles west of Knoxville, where they had gone to exercise their brutality before leaving Tennessee. Hughes, his wife's two brothers, named Metcalfe, and a man named Johnson, living in Jefferson County, were present when the Harpes, who knew the men, rushed in. Johnson was last seen alive there. A few days later his body was discovered in the Holstein River. It had been ripped open, filled with stones, and thrown into the water. Notwithstanding this excess of caution the stones became loosened and the corpse rose to the surface. When the body was discovered Hughes and the Metcalfes came forth with a declaration that the Harpes had committed the crime. Suspicion fell upon the accusers and as the two Harpes were nowhere to be found, the three men were arrested and put in jail. They were acquitted on trial, due to lack of evidence. The Metcalfes immediately fled the country. A party of "regulators" followed Hughes to his groggery, gave him a whipping, pulled down his house and drove him out of the country. [12G]

The killing of Johnson, as far as is known, seems to have been the first of the murders committed by the Harpes. Up to this time they had apparently confined their operations to stealing hogs and horses, and setting fire to houses. They now began a career of ruthless murder which was so bold that it not only terrified the citizens of Tennessee and Kentucky, but also alarmed settlers in many other sections of the Middle West.

The Harpes evidently had arranged to meet their three women associates at some definite point if they should for any reason find it necessary to separate. Shortly after the killing of Johnson the five met in western Virginia, near Cumberland Gap, and there, in December, 1798, they entered Kentucky – the "dark and bloody ground," to be made even darker by the deeds they were to commit during the next twelve months.

They traveled the Wilderness Road more or less closely, leaving it only when they felt their safety demanded a detour. Their first victim in Kentucky was a peddler named Peyton, whom they entcountered near the Cumberland River in what is now Knox County. They killed him and took his horse and some of his goods, but the details of this deed are not known. [21]

The outlaws continued along this trail toward Crab Orchard and Stanford, in Lincoln County, and overtook two Marylanders named Paca and Bates. Night came on and it was proposed that the party camp on the first suitable spot. This was agreed upon, but the Harpes managed not to find a desirable place until it grew dark. Suddenly, as if by accident, the brothers changed positions, Big Harpe getting behind Bates and Little Harpe behind Paca, the women walking about thirty feet in the rear. The Harpes fired and the two unfortunate Marylanders fell. Bates died instantly. A few minutes later Paca, who was badly crippled and knocked speechless, attempted to rise. Big Harpe rushed up to the struggling man, "splitting open his head with a hatchet or tomahawk he carried in his belt." The Harpes, being in need of some clothing, appropriated only such garments as were immediately useful. They took, however, all the gold and silver and Continental coin found in possession of their victims. [121]

The villains continued along the Wilderness Road and one night in December, 1798, arrived at a public house kept by John Farris in what is now Rockcastle County, not many miles from Crab Orchard. With them came Stephen Langford, of Virginia, who was on his way to Crab Orchard to visit a kinsman and to consider making that locality his home. Langford probably had not met the Harpes until that morning. The story of what took place after they met was related about a quarter of a century later by Judge James Hall, who, in his day, ranked among the best living authors in America, and whose statements were then, and have been ever since, cited as high authority. His story of their encounter with Langford was first published in August, 1825, in *The Port Folio*. After making some slight revisions in his "Story of the Harpes" he republished the sketch in 1828 in his *Letters from the West,* from which book his account of the Langford tragedy is here quoted:

"In the autumn of the year 1799, a young gentleman, named Langford, of a respectable family in Mecklenburgh County, Virginia, set out from this state for Kentucky, with the intention of passing through the Wilderness, as it was then called, by the route generally known as Boone's Trace. On reaching the vicinity of the Wilderness, a mountainous and uninhabited tract, which at that time separated the settled parts of Kentucky from those of Virginia, he stopped to breakfast at a public house near Big Rockcastle River. Travelers of this description – any other indeed than hardy wood men – were unwilling to pass singly through this lonely region; and they generally waited on its confines for others, and traveled through in parties. Mr. Langford, either not dreading danger, or not choosing to delay, determined to proceed alone. While breakfast was preparing, the Harpes and their women came up. Their appearance denoted poverty, with but little regard to cleanliness; two very indifferent horses, with some bags swung across them, and a rifle gun or two, comprised nearly their whole equipage. Squalid and miserable, they seemed objects of pity, rather than of fear, and their ferocious glances were attributed more to hunger than to guilty passion. They were entire strangers in that neighborhood, and, like Mr. Langford, were about to cross the Wilderness. When breakfast was served, the landlord, as was customary at such places in those times, invited all the persons who were assembled in the common, perhaps the only room of his little inn, to sit down; but the Harpes declined, alleging their want of money as the reason. Langford, who was of a lively, generous disposition, on hearing this, invited them to partake of the meal at his expense; they accepted the invitation, and ate voraciously. When they had thus refreshed themselves, and were about to renew their journey, Mr. Langford called for the bill, and in the act of discharging it imprudently displayed a handful of silver. They then set out together.

"A few days after, some men who were conducting a drove of cattle to Virginia, by the same road which had been traveled by Mr. Langford and the Harpes, had arrived within a few miles of Big Rockcastle River, when their cattle took fright, and, quitting the road, rushed down a hill into the woods. In collecting them, the drovers discovered the dead body of a man concealed behind a log, and covered with brush and leaves. It was now evident that the cattle had been alarmed by the smell of blood in the road, and, as the body exhibited marks of violence, it was at once suspected that a murder had been perpetrated but recently. The corpse was taken to the same house where the Harpes had breakfasted, and recognized to be that of Mr. Langford, whose name was marked upon several parts of his dress. Suspicion fell upon the Harpes, who were pursued and apprehended near Crab Orchard. They were taken to Stanford . . ."

The killing of the two Marylanders and the peddler was not known until many weeks thereafter. The report of the murder of Langford spread like wildfire. *The Kentucky Gazette,* January 2, 1799, in a characteristically brief paragraph gave sufficient details of the discovery of the body on December 14 to impress its readers with the seriousness of an act of barbarity that might be repeated by the Harpes at any time. "We also learn," says this paragraph, "that Mr. Ballenger is in pursuit of them, with a determined resolution never to quit the chase until he has secured them."

Captain Joseph Ballenger, the organizer and leader of the pursuing party, was a prominent merchant of Stanford, Lincoln County. He and his men trailed the Harpes and their women to the neighborhood of what was then Carpenter's Station, a settlement near the present town of Hustonville and about eight miles southwest of Stanford. There Ballenger discovered them sitting on a log, evidently confident that no one could detect their whereabouts. [12F] The pursuers rushed on them so suddenly that resistance or escape was impossible.[5]

The five prisoners were taken to Stanford, placed in jail and, about ten days later, tried before the Court of Quarter Sessions.

Hall's story of the frontier tragedy, based on personal accounts that had survived for a quarter of a century, has already been given. It is brief and is correct as far as it goes, but while Hall was hearing it from the lips of men who had it from those concerned with the vengeance of the law, there lay in the custody of the records of the backwoods court of Lincoln County, the grim details of that crime of base ingratitude and cruelty in solitude which so shook the Wilderness. They had lain there forgotten more than a century when they were found and examined in 1918. Yellowed with age, written with the goose-quill pen of that period in a penmanship characteristic of the pioneers, a jumble of half narrative, half legal style, much of which, however, is in use in courts today, these records of a terrible episode in history are eloquent with interest.

---

[5] After killing Langford the Harpes probably continued to travel along the Wilderness Road until they reached Crab Orchard, from which place radiated, besides the Wilderness Road to Cumberland Gap, at least four other routes: the Louisville route, the Frankfort and Cincinnati route, passing Logan's Fort (or Stanford) Danville, and Harrodsburg, the Maysville route, and the Tennessee route. Crab Orchard, being a converging point of roads, many travelers going east waited there until a crowd of a dozen or more was organized, thus assuring each a greater safety in making the trip through the Wilderness. Settlers passing through the Wilderness going west usually left home in a crowd sufficiently large to protect itself. [123] Langford, as is shown later, met the five Harpes in the Wilderness and, notwithstanding their appearance, he doubtless felt that they would at least serve as protection in the event of danger. The Harpes, after killing Langford, probably passed through Crab Orchard and continued northwest via the Frankfort road, toward Stanford and in or near Stanford turned west

The piling up of item on item of court forms, of testimony laboriously written out and signed, of official jail accounts for the handling of the criminals, tells in its own way every detail of a crime committed in fancied obscurity yet which by a series of fortunate circumstances, was to blaze into a notoriety that set all the West on fire with fear and horror. One who holds these long-forgotten records in his hands and curiously searches them could, with patience and without the aid of imagination, build up the story of frontier life and the people who lived it. The story would show that the power of observation exercised by some of the pioneers was equal to any ascribed to a Sherlock Holmes. It would be a story of chance incidents woven into chains of circumstances that were to reveal crime with unerring certainty – a story of the capture of the criminals, of their life in jail, and of the destiny by which each of the three women involved was to have her only child born to her in that frontier jail, the branded fruit of awful parentage. The mute entries in pounds, shillings, and pence for every item, set down on these yellow pages without malice or comment, tell their part of the story as implacably and dispassionately as fate itself.[6]

These records show that all the Harpes gave their name as "Roberts," except Betsey Harpe, the supplementary wife of Big Harpe, whose name is given as

for the purpose of misleading anyone who might pursue them as that course threw them toward both Tennessee and western Kentucky.

[6] In 1799 Stanford was a frontier settlement of less than 200 persons, including slaves. In 1780, when Lincoln County was formed, Logan's Fort or St. Asaph's became the seat of justice. In 1787 (on land presented by Colonel Benjamin Logan, a site about half a mile east of the fort, where the brick court house now stands) the county erected a log court house thirty feet long and twenty feet wide, with a small jury room on each side, the structure forming a T. Near it stood a log jail of two rooms, each twelve feet square. [28] In these log buildings the Harpes were tried and confined.

"Elizabeth Walker." Five witnesses appeared against them, two of whom – John Farris and his daughter-in-law, Jane Farris – lived in the house near Rockcastle River where Thomas Langford, or Lankford, was last seen alive. The fugitives were captured December 25, 1798. On January 4, 1799, they appeared before the three judges of the Lincoln County Court of Quarter Sessions, as it is so recorded, by Willis Green, the clerk, on the twenty-second page of the Record Book marked "September 1798 – March 1802:"

"At a court called and held at Lincoln Courthouse on Friday the 4th day of January 1799 for the examination of Micajah Roberts, Wiley Roberts, Susanna Roberts, Sally Roberts, and Elizabeth Walker for the murder of Thomas Langford.

"Present Hugh Logan, William Montgomery, and Nathan Huston, Esquires, [the three judges who presided].

"The said [naming the five prisoners] were lead to the bar in custody of the Sheriff and charged with feloniously and of their malice aforethought murdering and robbing a certain Thomas Langford on Wednesday the 12th day of December 1798 on the road leading from Kentucky to Virginia through the Wilderness, and denied the fact, sundry evidences were therefore examined and the prisoners heard in their defense."

Five witnesses appeared on behalf of the Commonwealth. The statement of each is written on loose leaves and signed in the presence of Thomas Montgomery, the official notary, and all were therefore in a form to be turned over to a higher court should it become necessary to do so. The affidavit of Captain Ballenger, who lead the pursuing party, is here quoted in full:

"Joseph Ballenger of lawful age, and sworn, deposeth and saith that at about the 19th or 20th day of December 1798 he heard that a murder had been committed in the Wilderness on the body of a certain Thomas Langford, as supposed; that he, at the request of James Blain the Attorney General of this Commonwealth with others (including Thomas Welsh) went in pursuit of some persons suspected of being the murderers who had passed through Lincoln County; that they went to the house of John Blain in Lincoln County where they heard that persons similar to those they were in pursuit of had left Brush Creek, a branch of Green River, and passed over to the Rolling Fork of Salt River; that they pursued them and overtook five persons, the same who this day on their examinations were called Micajah Roberts, Wiley Roberts, Susanna Roberts, Sally Roberts, and Elizabeth Walker; that after taking them into custody they proceeded to search them and found in their possession a pocket book with the name of Thomas Langford, a great coat, a grey coating cloth, a short coat – in the pocket of it were broken pieces of glass – a mixed colored long coat, a pair of breeches, a shaving glass, a whip, a pair of wrappers, and a horse, this day proved to be the property of Thomas Langford said to be the person murdered in the Wilderness, and that they found also a Free Mason's apron and many other things in their possession said to be the property of Thomas Langford. Further saith not."

David Irby, in his sworn statement, explained that: "he and Thomas Langford set out from Pittsylvania County in Virginia for Kentucky, they traveled five days journey together and sometimes one paid their traveling expense and sometimes the other, all of which

Thomas Langford marked down in his pocket book. Before they crossed Inglish's Ferry [Ingle's Ferry in what is now Montgomery Country, Virginia] they got a half bushel of oats which the deponent paid for and also their ferryage at Inglish's Ferry in Wythe County (Virginia) the deponent purchased a cheese which Thomas Langford set down in his pocket book, he says that the pocket book now before the examining court is the said pocket book which Thomas Langford had when they traveled together in Tennessee State. [The trail from Virginia to Cumberland Gap extended into northeastern Tennessee before reaching Kentucky]. The deponent and Thomas Langford separated when they agreed to meet at Frankfort in Kentucky; the deponent heard in Kentucky that the said Thomas Langford was murdered on his way to Kentucky, he set out towards the place where the crime was committed and went to the place where the person who was killed was buried and he, the deponent, and John Farris unburied and raised the decedent and found him to be Thomas Langford."

What Irby saw and heard he further declared convinced him that the murdered man was no other than his recent traveling companion.

John Farris Sr. swore that on Tuesday night, December 12, 1798: "a man came to his house on the Wilderness Road who called himself Thomas Langford and who, after he had told him his name, he recollected to have been acquainted with in Pittsylvania County, Virginia, in the youth of Thomas Langford."

He said his guest remained all night and started the next morning for the settlements. In the meantime, Farris had: "an opportunity of viewing his clothing and actually did very curiously examine the outward clothing of the said Thomas Langford." A few days later he heard that "a man was killed on the Wilderness Road, and on inquiring into the circumstances he was induced to believe that the person murdered was Thomas Langford . . . but not being fully satisfied that the person found dead was Thomas Langford, he went to the coroner of Lincoln County, obtained from him an order – the said coroner having before that time held an inquest on the body – and in pursuance of the said order, in company with David Irby and Abraham Anthony who buried the said Thomas Langford as he supposed, raised him and inspected him . . . and that the whole visage of the person, by him and others raised, answered his idea of Thomas Langford, but he knew him more particularly by the loss of a tooth in the front part of his jaw."

His daughter-in-law, Jane Farris, wife of William Farris, also identified various things found in the possession of the outlaws as the property of the murdered man. She evidently observed the actions of the travelers closely, for she states: "Thomas Langford had on leggins at her house and as part of the list of one of them was torn Susan Roberts sewed it to the leggin with white thread." She adds that the five prisoners and their victim came to the house together and "All appeared very cheerful with each other, Langford seemed to be somewhat intoxicated, he had a small glass bottle which was filled with whiskey at their house which Micajah Roberts and Wiley Roberts paid for." The six left the Farris house together, but shortly before leaving "there was some misunderstanding between Thomas Langford and Micajah and Wiley Roberts . . . and Mr. Langford said to Mrs. Farris, in the presence of all, that he would not offend her for all in his saddle bags which was worth five hundred pounds."

The statement made by Thomas Welsh, who was in the pursuing party, is practically the same as Captain Ballenger's. He, however, adds "there was none of the alteration in the great coat at the time of the finding . . . and must have been made by the criminals since they were taken into custody, they having, for several days after they were taken in custody, the possession of the great coat."

There is nothing in the records to indicate what was said by the prisoners when they were heard in their defense. The decision of the court was that the five prisoners "ought to be tried for the murder of the said Thomas Langford before the Judges of the District Court holden for the Danville District at the next April Term, and it is ordered that they be remanded to jail."

Thomas Todd, the prosecuting attorney, in the requirement of the law, "acknowledged himself indebted" to the Governor of the Commonwealth "in the sum of ten thousand pounds current money" should he fail to appear before the judges on the first day of the April term of the Danville District Court then and there to prosecute the prisoners. The witnesses "acknowledged themselves severally indebted . . . to the sum of five hundred pounds current money" should they fail to appear and give evidence on behalf of the Commonwealth.[7]

---

[7] A perusal of the accounts kept by Joseph Welsh, the sheriff of Lincoln County, reveals many interesting facts. John Gower against the Commonwealth of Kentucky runs: "For making a pair of handcuffs for Wiley Roberts 9s. And putting on and taking off when committed and before trial 2s. 6d. To putting on and taking off the handcuffs after trial and before removal to the District jail 2s 6d," making a total of 14s. For this same service on

On January 5 the five prisoners were taken by the sheriff and a guard of seven men to Danville, there to await trial before the District Court in April. The distance from Stanford to Danville is about ten miles. Neither history nor tradition tells how this cavalcade made the trip over the trail, whether afoot, on horses, or in wagons, or by a combination of these means. The condition then reached by the women may have necessitated the use of a conveyance for them. This party of thirteen doubtless attracted much attention along the road, for five prisoners, of whom three were women, was a sight not often seen. The ten mile trip to Danville made by the guards with the captured Harpes along this historic highway, winding through an almost unbroken forest, readily lends itself to anyone's fancy.[8]

Evidently John Biegler, "Jailer of the District of Danville," to whom the prisoners were delivered and who had them in his custody several months, felt there was some likelihood of his charges escaping. His account against the state shows that on January 20, 1799,

Micajah Roberts, Gower received, respectively 2s. 6d.; 1s. 3d., and 1s. 3d., a total of only 5s.

The sheriff received the following sums: "For summoning a court for the examination" of the five prisoners, £1. 5s. "For summoning twelve witnesses vs. Micajah Roberts and others, at 1s. 3d. each, 15s." "For imprisoning, 2s. 6d., keeping in jail 10 days at 1s. a day, 10s., Removing to District jail, 7s. 6d., total 20s.," making a total of £5.

Another bill presented by the sheriff was for eight men guarding the five prisoners in the Lincoln County jail for fourteen days at 4s. 6d. each per day, making a total of £25. 4s. The last bill shows he paid seven of the guards "for one day and traveling twenty miles in removing the above prisoners to the District jail and returning at 2d. per mile, 6s. 4d. [sic]" making a total of £2. 4s. 4d.

The total of all these accounts is a little more than £35. or what would today be about $175.00.

[8] Danville, in 1799, with a population of a little over 200, was one of the most important towns in Kentucky. In 1784 the court authorized the building of "a log house large enough for a court room in one end, and two jury rooms in the other end on the same floor . . . and a prison of hewed or

he bought "Two horse locks to chain the men's feet to the ground, 12s. and 1 bolt, 3s." It seems to have become necessary to fasten the front door more firmly, for, on February 13, he purchased "one lock for front jail door, 18s." Two weeks later he bought three pounds of nails for 6s. "for the use of the jail." The expense items further show that four men, two at a time, were employed to guard the prisoners.

But with all these precautions, the two Harpes escaped on March 16, leaving their three women and two new-born infants behind. There is nothing in the court records indicating how they escaped. The jailer's expense account merely shows an item dated March 19: "Mending the wall in jail where the prisoners escaped, 12s." Breazeale, forty years later, wrote – but cites no authority for his statement: "the jailer, soon after their escape, resigned his office, left the jail, bought a farm and settled himself in the country where he very shortly became wealthy – no one ever knew with certainty by what means, but the general suspicion was that he had acquired his wealth by receiving a large bribe from the Harpes to permit them to escape."

How they escaped was doubtless a subject of much conjecture and discussion. Colonel Daniel Trabue in his *Autobiography* says that the two men "took two guns from the guard at Danville." Whether or not the guard or guards were present and resisted the prisoners when they took the two guns is not stated. Judge James Hall, continuing his brief account of the Langford murder, quoted a few pages back, gives no details, but simply ends with the statement: "They were taken to Stanford where they were examined and committed

sawed logs at least nine inches thick." [82] The buildings were still in use when the Harpes were taken there to await trial.

by an enquiring court, sent to Danville for safe keeping, and probably for trial. Previous to the time of trial they made their escape."

Nor do the records contain any hint as to how the two men passed the time of their imprisonment. Lyman C. Draper, in his "Sketch of the Harpes," says that shortly before his escape Big Harpe, contending it would answer the ends of justice as well, proposed to whip at fisticuffs the two best fighters in Kentucky, provided he be set free if he succeeded in whipping the men, and should he fail he would abide by the decision of the court.

The trial of the three women was set for April 15. But during the hundred days they were immured in the log jail there was happening to them the immortal trial that comes to their sex under all conditions. Yoked as they were irregularly, pursuing as they had the lives of the hunted and outcast, they had to bear, in the rigors of winter, in abandonment and in prison charged with murder, the burdens of motherhood – and to such fathers! These items from the jailer's accounts of his expenditures on their behalf tell a story with which imagination is free to work:

"February 8, ¼ lb. Hyson tea, 3s. 9d., 1 lb. sugar, 1s. 6d. for Betsey Walker she being brought to bed by a son the preceding night, 5s. 3d.–February 10, ¼ lb. ginger, 1s. 1d., 1 lb. sugar, 1s. 6d., for ditto, and paid cash to the wife and other assistance 21s. £1. 3s. 7d."–total £1. 8s. 10d.

"March 7, ⅛ lb. tea, 1s. 10d., 1 lb. sugar, 1s. 6d., for the use of Susanna Harpe brought to bed by a daughter the preceding night, 3s. 4d. Paid cash midwife for ditto, 18s."– total £1. 1s. 4d.

"April 9, ¼ lb. tea, 3s. 9d., 1 lb. sugar, 1s. 6d., 1 quart whiskey, 1s. 6d. for the use of Sally Harp brought to bed the preceding night by a daughter."– total 6s. 9d.

It will be noted that when the third child was born – a week before the time set for trial – the second was about a month old and the other two months old.

Such was the state of affairs when, on Monday, April 15, 1799, the clerk turned to page 314 of the Danville District Court Order Book and there began his record of the trial of the three women indicted for the murder of Thomas Langford. The court was presided over by Judge James G. Hunter and by Judge Samuel McDowell, who served in the absence of Judge Stephen Ormsby. "Susanna Roberts, spinster of Lincoln County was set to the bar in custody of the jailer," so runs the record, and pleaded "not guilty;" but "for reasons appearing to the court" her trial was postponed until the third day of the term. "Elizabeth Walker" and "Sally Roberts" were not called on to appear personally that day before the judges, but their cases were postponed until the 18th.

On the 17th "Susanna Roberts" again appeared in court. A jury of twelve men was sworn, which, after hearing the same evidence given in Stanford, presented in the form of written affidavits, declared her "guilty."

On the 18th another jury was sworn and "Elizabeth Walker, spinster of Lincoln County," was tried on the same evidence presented against "Susanna Roberts," but found "not guilty." The court proceedings of that afternoon show that the judge "saith he will not further prosecute the said Sally Roberts (spinster of Lincoln County) . . . and therefore it is considered by the court that she be acquitted."

Thus, with the same evidence against each woman, one was found "guilty," and one "not guilty" and one was "acquitted."

On the 19th Susanna, who had been found guilty, appealed for a new trial and it was granted. The Attorney General, however, concluded not to prosecute her, and, at his suggestion, the clerk was ordered to record "certain of the reasons which moved him to enter into *nolle prosequi* in this case . . . to-wit: Upon considering the circumstances attending the case of Susanna Roberts and although she has been found guilty of the charge in the indictment contained by a verdict of her peers, yet as Eliza Walker has been tried on the same indictment, on which trial the said Eliza was found not guilty and the same proof produced against her as was produced against the said Susanna, and in consequence also of the Court having granted a new trial and from the probability [of the evidence] which would be produced on the trial of the said Susanna at the next term by the two other women, in the same indictment contained, who are acquitted and discharged, operating in favor of the prisoner, and also by the advice of the prosecutor and of the Court, and also to save to the Commonwealth the expenses which attend her long detention and further prosecution, I have been induced to direct the Clerk to enter a *nolle prosequi* as to the said Susanna Roberts." [9]

---

[9] The account of the Danville jailer shows that the two men had been confined 71 days, Sally and Betsey 102 days, and Susanna 103 days, for which a charge of 1s. per day for each was made; 449 days £22. 9s. In the same record is a memorandum to the effect that the three infants had been in jail 69, 43, and 9 days, or a total of 121 days. The jailer evidently intended to make a charge for this item, but there are no figures to indicate the contemplated amount. Four men for guarding the jail 103 days received a total of £6. 6s. An item shows: "April 12, 21¾ cords wood from the 5th of

January until this day for the use of guards, court, and prisoners @ 6 [sic] cutting the wood for the above, 2s. 6d., £2. 14s. 4d." The total of the three items is £31. 9s. 4d. The seven Danville items previously noted amount to £5. 7s. 11d. This makes the Danville expense a grand total of £36. 17s. 3d., or what would today be about $185.00. This, with the $175.00 Stanford account makes a grand total of the now known expense items a sum that would today be about $360.00.

The Harpes - Renewal of the Terror

What had happened to the Harpes and their women was a natural outcome of the frontier outlook upon life. The three mothers had gained the sympathy of the court and the community in their apparent distress and helplessness. It was believed that they had obtained a happy release from their barbarous masters. It is probable that many of the persons who now helped in the hunt for the escaped Harpes did so not because they were highway murderers and should therefore be shot or hanged, but because they deserved particular punishment for their brutal conduct toward the young women. At any rate the settlements were united in the pursuit of the two men, who had so curiously escaped.

The acquitted women declared that, above all things, they desired to return to Knoxville and there start life over again. A collection of clothes and money was made among the citizens of Danville and an old mare was given to help them on their way to Tennessee. The three women, each with a bundle over her shoulder and a child under her arm, and the old mare loaded down with clothes and bedding, left the jail one morning on what was considered no easy journey even when undertaken with good horses and the best of equipment. They walked down the street in Indian file, led by the jailer, who accompanied them to the edge of town to point out the road that led through Crab Orchard to Tennessee. These forlorn and dejected travelers, however, had covered less than thirty miles when they changed

their course and went down along the banks of Green
River. A few days later they traded their horse for a
canoe and then went down the stream and were soon
lost sight of by the spies who attempted to watch them.
[12F]

The brutal killing of Langford had stirred the country for almost two months, and now that the murderers
had escaped and the gnawed bones of the two Marylanders were found, with all evidence pointing to the
Harpes as the perpetrators of this terrible murder, the
citizens became even more enraged. They were aroused
to the realization that the villains must be captured and
disposed of at once. The case required prompt action
and any and all methods that might bring about the extermination of the Harpes were endorsed.

On March 28, 1799, *The Kentucky Gazette* published the following paragraph: "The criminals in the
Danville district jail for the murder of Mr. Langford,
(as mentioned in our paper of the 2nd of January last)
have made their escape. By an order from W. E.
Strong, Esq., a justice of the peace for Mercer County,
all sheriffs and constables are commanded to take and
re-commit them."

An entry in the Danville District Court Order Book,
page 370, under date of April 22, 1799, reads: "It is
ordered that the Commonwealth's writ of capias issue
from the clerk's office of this Court to the Sheriff of
Lincoln County commanding him to take Micajah Roberts and Wiley Roberts who have lately broken the
jail of this District and are now running at large and
them, the said Micajah Roberts and Wiley Roberts,
safely to keep so that he have their bodies before the
Judges of the District Court holden for the Danville
District on the first day of their August Term, to answer

for the felony and murder of a certain Thomas Langford whereof they stand indicted."

Lynching parties had been organized since the middle of March and in the meantime a committee was sent to James Garrard, Governor of Kentucky, presenting to him the necessity of capturing the outlaws. A memorandum on this subject in the Executive Journal, entered in the month of April, states that "the governor authorized Josh Ballenger to pursue them into the state of Tennessee and other states, and to apply to the executive authorities of such states to deliver them up."

Ballenger and his men began their chase before they received official notice of the governor's action, and were soon on the trail. Near the headwaters of Rolling Fork, a branch of Salt River, they suddenly found themselves face to face with the Harpes, who, although surprised, were prepared to shoot. The pursuers retreated in confusion and the Harpes, taking advantage of the situation, made their escape. Henry Scaggs, one of the party, suggested that the crowd go to his farm and, with the aid of his dogs, continue the chase. Scaggs was one of the "Long Hunters" who came to Kentucky in 1770 with Colonel James Knox and a pioneer who had ever since been looked upon as "a valiant man in battle and a great hunter." Urged by him they resumed the pursuit and continued it until late that night, when most of the men, becoming discouraged, left the party because the trail of the Harpes led them through very thick and almost impenetrable cane.

A few men, led by Ballenger, continued the search, but in a section where the heavy cane was no impediment. Scaggs, believing the canebrake should be penetrated, went to a "log rolling" a few miles north of the home of Colonel Daniel Trabue, and there, with the aid of Major James Blain, tried to organize another party. But the men declared that the cane was too thick and the chances of capture too slight to justify the risk, and the "log rolling" went on. Scaggs then – on or about April 10 – rode to the farm of Colonel Daniel Trabue, a Revolutionary soldier and one of the most prominent and altruistic of Kentucky pioneers, who lived about three miles west of what is now Columbia, Adair County.

While Scaggs was discussing his plans with Colonel Trabue, the Colonel was patiently awaiting the return of his son, John Trabue, a lad of thirteen, who had been sent to one of the neighbors to borrow some flour and seed beans. The boy was accompanied by a small dog, and, in the midst of the discussion, the dog walked into the yard badly wounded. [12E] An investigation was immediately made. The neighbor reported that the boy had left the house a few hours before with the flour and beans. All efforts made that night to find him were futile. They began to suspect that he might have been kidnapped by the Harpes. The search continued for many days, but all in vain. Evidence of the Harpes was discovered by George Spears and five other men about fifteen miles southwest of the Trabue farm, near the East Fork of Barren River, where the outlaws had killed a calf and made moccasins out of the skin, leaving their old moccasins behind. The footprints indicated the presence of two men, but there were no signs to show that a boy was with them. [63]

Little did the pursuers realize what had actually happened. The innocent lad, walking home over an old buffalo trace, had met the Harpes as they were crossing it. There they killed the little fellow, cut his body to pieces, and threw it into a sinkhole near the path, where it remained hidden about two weeks and was then discovered by accident. The murderers had taken the flour but not the seed beans.

Colonel Trabue, in his autobiography or journal, written some twenty-five years after this tragedy, deplores the fact that the log rollers did not continue the pursuit: "It is a pity they did not go, for then John Trabue might not have been killed." He adds that these men ever after "reflected very much on themselves for their negligence, and said this ought to be a warning to others hereafter to always do their duty."

In pioneer times the execution of the law by officials was in many instances an unavoidably slow process, and it therefore frequently became necessary for the law abiding citizens to organize themselves into bands and, by any method the emergency might demand, establish order and safety. No matter how achieved, preserving peace and fighting danger was looked upon by good citizens as the imperative duty of all. Had the then slow-acting laws been relied upon, the sly and quick-traveling Harpes probably would not have been captured for years, and their victims might have been numbered by the hundreds. On the other hand, as suggested by Colonel Trabue, it is possible that had the men who were called upon by Scaggs done what was in those days considered a duty, Langford might have been the last victim of the Harpes and their career ended.

A report that mad dogs were running through the country and were likely to spring from behind any bush or tree at any time could not have alarmed the people more than did the realization that the Harpes had escaped from jail and were killing all who chanced to be in their path. On April 22, the Governor of Kentucky was again appealed to for help, and he immediately signed a proclamation which was published in the Frankfort *Palladium* on May 2 and May 9, 1799:

"BY THE GOVERNOR, A PROCLAMATION.

"Whereas it has been represented to me that MICAJAH HARP, alias ROBERTS, and WILEY HARP alias ROBERTS, who were confined in the jail of the Danville district under a charge of murder, did on the 16th day of March last, break out of the said jail; – and whereas the ordinary methods of pursuit have been found ineffectual for apprehending and restoring to confinement the said fugitives, I have judged it necessary to the safety and welfare of the community and to the maintenance of justice, to issue this my proclamation and do hereby offer and promise a reward of THREE HUNDRED DOLLARS to any person who shall apprehend and deliver into the custody of the jailer of the Danville district the said MICAJAH HARP alias ROBERTS and a like reward of THREE HUNDRED DOLLARS for apprehending and delivering as aforesaid the said WILEY HARP alias ROBERTS, to be paid out of the public treasury agreeably to law.

"In testimony whereof I have hereunto set my hand and have caused the seal of the Commonwealth to be affixed.

"Done at Frankfort on the 22nd day of April in the year of our Lord 1799, and of the Commonwealth the seventh.

"(L. S.)

"By the Governor   JAMES GARRARD

"Harry Toulmin, Secretary.

"MICAJAH HARP alias ROBERTS is about six feet high –

of a robust make, and is about 30 or 32 years of age. He has an ill-looking, downcast countenance, and his hair is black and short, but comes very much down his forehead. He is built very straight and is full fleshed in the face. When he went away he had on a striped nankeen coat, dark blue woolen stockings,– leggins of drab cloth and trousers of the same as the coat.

"WILEY HARP alias ROBERTS is very meagre in his face, has short black hair but not quite so curly as his brother's; he looks older, though really younger, and has likewise a downcast countenance. He had on a coat of the same stuff as his brother's, and had a drab surtout coat over the close-bodied one. His stockings were dark blue woolen ones, and his leggins of drab cloth."

Before this proclamation by the Governor had time to circulate throughout the state, report reached the people that the Harpes had killed a man named Dooley, near what is now Edmonton, Metcalfe County, [28] and had butchered another named Stump, who lived on Barren River about eight miles below Bowling Green. [12D]

Stump was fishing, and seeing smoke rising on the opposite side of the river, a little distance from the bank, presumed some new arrivals were preparing to settle. He stepped into his cabin and got his violin, and then crossed the stream to greet the newcomers. He was clad in his shirt and trousers, without hat or shoes, but he probably felt that what he lacked in wearing apparel would be more than counterbalanced by the hearty welcome to the Wilderness he was prepared to give his new neighbors. So, in this scant attire, and with a turkey over his shoulder, a string of fish in one hand and his fiddle under his arm, he entered their camp. He probably never realized that his good intentions had led him into the hands of the Harpes. They stabbed him, cut open his body, filled it with stones and threw it into the river. [12F] Some of Stump's neighbors, says *The Kentucky Gazette,* were suspected of having committed the murder and were taken into custody, but an investigation proved their innocence and also proved beyond all doubt that the Harpes were the perpetrators of the crime.

The criminals continued their raid down Barren River into the lower Green River country to a point near Henderson, Kentucky, and then, either by land or water, rapidly worked their way to Diamond Island in the Ohio and to Cave-in-Rock, in or near any of which places they evidently had arranged to meet their women.

How many men, women, and children these two brothers killed and what course they followed while rushing through the lower Green River country and the Ohio Valley between Henderson and Cave-in-Rock will never be known. Shortly before reaching the Cave, they committed a murder in Illinois at the mouth of Saline River, about twelve miles above Cave-in-Rock. Twenty-six years later this incident was briefly summed up in the *Illinois Gazette,* published at Shawneetown: "There are persons living in this country whom we have heard recount the story of the Harpes with great minuteness, and the place is still pointed out, on the plantation of Mr. Potts, near the mouth of the Saline River, where they shot two or three persons in cold blood by the fire where they had encamped." [56]

The many reports – some false and others only too true – of the inhuman acts committed by the Harpes had, in the meantime, put every community on its guard. Captain Ballenger, after pursuing the outlaws a few weeks, found that, owing to the many conflicting rumors, he had been thrown off the trail and was moving in a direction opposite the one taken by the Harpes and, therefore, he gave up the chase.

Captain Young, of Mercer County, in the meantime organized a company with the determination to exterminate the Harpes and all other outlaws, or at least drive them out of the country. Commenting on Captain Young's expedition, Edmund L. Starling, author of *A History of Henderson County, Kentucky,* writes: "Captain Young and his men recognized the perils of their undertaking; they understood the wily machinations of the enemy, and, with blood for blood emblazoned upon their banner, started upon their mission of capture or death, utterly regardless of their own personal comforts or the hardships attending a campaign in such a wild and comparatively unmarked country."

Having met with success in Mercer, Captain Young and his men continued their pursuit and finally reached Henderson County. There they were joined by a number of citizens. The combined forces swept over the entire country, including Diamond Island, driving the outlaws out of that part of Kentucky across the Ohio River into Illinois. A number of the criminals fled to Cave-in-Rock. The character of the men who usually centered at the Cave was well known to the refugees, for many of them had helped to make the place notorious.

Captain Young and his outlaw exterminators having covered the territory they set out to relieve, left Henderson County and returned to Mercer County – a distance of more than one hundred and fifty miles – and were there given a grand ovation. [124]

Governor Garrard, however, must have felt somewhat apprehensive regarding the return of the Harpes, for the Executive Journal shows that on June 7 he "deputed Alexander McFarland and brothers" to take charge of "these inveterate enemies of human happiness" should they be found "in any adjacent state."

It seems quite likely that while in the Danville jail the Harpe women, by some means, sent a message to, or received one from, "old man Roberts," the father-in-law of Big Harpe, who then lived in Russell County, Kentucky. At any rate, as already stated, they started down Green River shortly after leaving Danville. They paddled their way down that river until they reached its mouth, a distance of more than two hundred miles. After stopping in the neighborhood of Henderson, they continued down the Ohio about ninety miles to Cave-in-Rock. It was in this section of the Ohio Valley that they expected, sooner or later, to meet the Harpes. Tradition has it that shortly after the three women arrived at Cave-in-Rock two of them proceeded up the river, one to Diamond Island and the other to a neighborhood south of Henderson, while the third remained at the Cave; and in this manner they watchfully awaited the arrival of the Harpes. The two women who had been loitering near Henderson and Diamond Island, posing under assumed names as widows, either had left their watching places voluntarily or were forced to flee from them with their husbands. At any rate, they finally arrived at Cave-in-Rock and there, in a very short time, the two Harpes and their three women and three children were once more united.

As a result of Captain Young's raid through Henderson County, Cave-in-Rock became somewhat crowded with outlaws. Realizing that their number was too great to maneuver with any secrecy and safety, many left the place voluntarily, some continuing down the river, others working their way inland, and a few remaining "to pursue their nefarious avocation." [124]

The Harpes, however, were driven from the Cave. This aggregation of outlaws was doubtless a depraved conglomeration of evil doers, but in the Harpes they found two human brutes beyond even their toleration.

There is a tradition to the effect that the Harpes had been at the Cave only a few days when they brazenly related the performance of an act which, to their surprise, was not cheered by their companions. A flatboat had come down the river and its passengers, not realizing they were near the famous rendezvous of outlaws, landed about a quarter of a mile above the Cave at the foot of a small bluff, later known as Cedar Point. Among the travelers on board were a young man and his sweetheart who, while their companions were making some repairs to the boat, strolled to the top of the cliff and there sat down upon a rock. The view from that point is still beautiful and was probably even more so in primeval days. While the two lovers were sitting on the edge of the cliff with their backs to the wild woods behind them, leisurely considering the landscape, or the life before them, the two Harpes quietly approached from the forest and, without a word of warning, pushed the lovers off the cliff. They fell on a sandy beach forty feet below and, to the surprise of all, escaped unhurt. The Harpes returned to the Cave, and, as already stated, boasted, but without the expected effect, of the prank they had played.

Shortly after this, two families, carrying a supply of tools and provisions, were floating down the Ohio in a flatboat, intending to settle in Smithland, but when they came near Cave-in-Rock they were captured and robbed by the outlaws. The two or three passengers who were not killed in the battle preceding the robbery, were brought ashore. The Harpes, seeing an opportunity to give their fellow criminals an exhibition of brutality, stripped one of the captives, tied him to a blindfolded horse and led the animal to the top of the bluff over the Cave. By wild shouts and other means the horse was frightened and at the same time forced to run toward the edge of the cliff, and before long the blindfolded animal with the naked man tied on its back ran off the bluff and fell a distance of more than one hundred feet to the rough and rocky shore below. Then the Harpes pointed to the mangled remains of man and horse as evidence of another triumph over law and order. Their fellow cave dwellers probably had never seen such a sight before and evidently did not care to witness one again. It is likely that only sympathy for their women and babies saved the Harpes from death at the hands of the other outlaws. All the Harpes left the Cave at once.

It is probable that their hasty departure took place some time in May, 1799. Neither history nor tradition tells in what direction they fled. The people of Kentucky doubtless concluded that since they had driven these outlaws across the Ohio into Illinois, they would continue their flight north or proceed by flatboat to some section along the lower Mississippi.

About the middle of July east Tennessee was shocked to hear of the cruel murder of a farmer named Bradbury, who was killed along the road in Roane County, about twenty-five miles west of Knoxville on what has since been known as Bradbury's Ridge. [21] The Harpes were not suspected of the crime, for the impression prevailed that they had fled permanently and, although their whereabouts was unknown, it not only seemed quite improbable but almost impossible that they had returned in so short a time. It soon developed, however, that they actually had made their appearance again, for a few days later – July 22, 1799 – they murdered a young son of Chesley Coffey, on Black Oak Ridge, about eight miles northwest of Knoxville. One version has it that the boy was hunting strayed cows and while in the woods was slain by the Harpes, who took his gun and the shoes he wore, and left his body lying under a tree. [12G] Another account is that "Young Coffey was riding along the road one evening to get a fiddle. These terrible men smeared a tree with his brains, making out that his horse had run against the tree." [63]

Two days later they killed a man named William Ballard, who lived within a few miles of Knoxville. "They cut him open and, putting stones in his body, sank it in the river." [63] It was believed by the neighbors that the Harpes mistook Ballard for Hugh Dunlap, who had been active in endeavoring to arrest them the year before. [21]

The Harpes continued their course northward. They crossed Emery River, near what is now Harriman Junction, and, while their women were resting for a few days in some secluded spot, the two men skirmished alone in Morgan County. On July 29, on the spur of a mountain since known as Brassel's Knob, they met James and Robert Brassel. James Brassel was afoot and carried a gun; Robert was on horseback and unarmed. The Harpes, who were riding good horses, pretended to be in a hurry, but seeming to have a desire to comply with the custom of civilized travelers, slowed up and saluted the men with the question: "What's the news?" The Brassels related in detail an account of the murder of William Ballard and young Coffey. The Harpes replied that they had not only heard of these tragedies, but that they were now in pursuit of the men who had committed the crimes. They further asserted that they were going to wait for the rest of the pursuing party which was coming on behind, and requested the Brassels to join them when the reinforcements arrived. To this the two innocent brothers willingly agreed. They had no more than done so when Big Harpe, accusing them of being the Harpe brothers, seized James Brassel's gun, threw it on the ground and immediately began tying his hands and feet. Robert, suspecting that he and his brother had fallen into the hands of the dreaded Harpes themselves, jumped from his horse and attempted to obtain his brother's gun in an effort to rescue him. In this he failed and, realizing that his only hope of escape was flight, he ran into the woods, leaving his horse behind. He was pursued by Little Harpe, whom he succeeded in outrunning, and, although shot at, he was unhurt.

Robert continued his flight about ten miles when he met a Mr. Dale, who, with two or three other men and Mrs. Dale, was traveling toward Knoxville. He persuaded them to return with him to the place where he had left his brother. The men had only one gun among them for their protection; nevertheless they tried to help the bewildered man. When they reached the spot in the woods a short distance from the road where Robert had left his brother, they were horrified to find that James was not only dead, but that his body had been "much beaten and his throat cut." His gun was broken to pieces. The tracks indicated that the two Harpes had gone toward Knoxville, from which direction they were coming when they overtook the Brassel brothers. After the pursuers had followed the tracks a few miles, they were much surprised to find themselves running upon the Harpes coming back. At the time the two Brassels were attacked by the Harpes the outlaws were alone and had with them nothing but their guns. But now, on their return, they were accompanied by their women and children, heavily loaded with clothing and provisions, apparently prepared for a long journey and for battle and siege.

When this fierce procession of men and women on horseback came in sight, one of Dale's men suggested that if the approaching cavalcade showed no signs of fight, no effort to arrest them should be made. This immediately met with the approval of the majority. No attempt to fight was made. The murderers, in the words of Colonel Trabue, "looked very awful at them" and then passed on. The pursuers, too, continued their journey for a while in silence, lest any words they should utter might be overheard and mistaken by the Harpes as a threat. Robert Brassel complained bitterly of the lack of courage displayed by the men he had relied upon to help capture or kill the murderers of his brother. [63]

Thus, uninterrupted, the two Harpes and their wives, with their stolen horses and other plunder, and with an ever-increasing desire to shed blood, continued their expedition to Kentucky. Somewhere near the Tennessee-Kentucky line, either in what is now Pickett County, Tennessee, or Clinton County, Kentucky, they killed John Tully, who lived in that section of Cumberland County which in 1835 became a part of Clinton County.

In the meantime citizens of east Tennessee were alarmed. They now fully realized that the Harpes had actually returned and were likely to appear any day in any neighborhood. Every man carried his gun, his dirk, or carving knife, and made every preparation to slay the monsters.

Robert Brassel resumed his pursuit of the Harpes and was soon joined by William Wood and others. When they arrived near the farm of John Tully they met Nathaniel Stockton and a number of neighbors looking for Tully, who they supposed was lost in the woods. The search continued and "near the road they found Mr. Tully, killed, and hidden under a log." [63] The company buried him and some of the men agreed they would pursue the murderers.[10]

Immediately after it was discovered that Tully had been murdered, William Wood and Nathaniel Stockton started afoot to Colonel Daniel Trabue's farm, a distance of forty miles. They suspected that because Colonel Trabue had been active in the pursuit of the Harpes after his son had been murdered, the monsters

[10] A special act of the Kentucky legislature was passed and approved December 18, 1800, for the relief of the widow of John Tully, extending the statutory time of payment for lands taken up by him on the south side of Green River under a settlement act and exempting her in the interval from paying interest. The extension was given until December 1, 1810. The preamble of the act recites its enactment because "Tully . . . having obtained a certificate for a settlement of two hundred acres of land . . . having settled on said land, was assassinated by the murderers called Harpes, and consequently left his wife, Christiana Tully, a desolate widow with eight small children." This is a notable instance of pioneer liberality and sympathy for a widow in distress, particularly in spite of the fact that, according to Colonel Trabue, Tully not only knew the Harpes, but also, less than a year before they murdered him, had carried messages to them from the Harpe women when the outlaws were making for Cave-in-Rock.

were on their way to his home and store and might be captured there. They related to the Colonel the details of the crimes the Harpes had recently committed and he, before they had finished, decided to forward the news to the governor of Kentucky. In order to impress the governor with the fact that the report was not another wild rumor, Colonel Trabue, who was a justice of the peace in Green County, prepared a written statement, giving a brief account of the recent acts of the Harpes, as related to him by Nathaniel Stockton and William Wood, and forwarded it to him in the form of an affidavit. [63]

This sworn statement, consisting of about five hundred words, was published in the *Kentucky Gazette* on August 15, 1799. From it some of the details of the three crimes just related were taken. It begins with the declaration: "About the middle of July there was a man killed by the name of Hardin, about three miles below Knoxville: he was ripped open and stones put in his belly, and he was thrown into Holston River." After briefly noting the circumstances and the exact date of the killing of Coffey, James Brassel, and John Tully, it calls attention to the fact that the night after the Harpes murdered Tully "they passed by old Mr. Stockton's going toward their father's-in-law, old Mr. Roberts." A point of great human interest is the concise and vivid description of the two Harpes given in the affidavit prepared by Colonel Trabue: "The big man is pale, dark, swarthy, bushy hair, had a reddish gun stock – the little man had a blackish gunstock, with a silver star with four straight points – they had short sailor's coats, very dirty, and grey greatcoats."

Colonel Trabue, in his *Autobiography,* does not give a copy of his affidavit, but relative to it, he writes: "I sent out that night for some neighbors and made arrangements. We sent one man off the next morning by sunrise to Frankfort to the Governor, that he might have it published in the newspapers. Mr. Wood's and Mr. Stockton's statement I wrote down and had them swear to it, what they knew of their own knowledge and what Robert Brassel had told them. I sent another man down to Yellow Banks [should read Red Banks] to General Samuel Hopkins with the news and the statement. I directed the men to go as fast as they could, and spread the news as they went; it was also immediately put in the newspapers. The man I sent to General Hopkins was John Ellis. As he went on he spread the news. He happened to go the same route the Harpes had taken. When they heard of him they pursued and tried to overtake him. Ellis had a good horse and went sixty or seventy miles a day. The whole state got in a great uproar, because it was uncertain which route the murderers would take."

The two messengers sent by Colonel Trabue rode over trails that wound through a sparsely populated wilderness where danger in one form or another was likely to be encountered at any moment. One rider dashed in a northerly direction about ninety miles, while the other rushed westward twice that distance. Each "spread the news" along his route, and from every settlement he passed, the report – "The Harpes are here" – was hurriedly sent out. The warning, in comparatively little time, reached practically every family in Kentucky and many in Tennessee. The press verified the reports and soon the people saw for themselves in "black and white," which was then considered the garb of "gospel truth," that the Harpes had returned to Kentucky and were guilty of crimes even more brutal than any heretofore perpetrated.

The Frankfort *Palladium,* on August 15, 1799, published the names of four men and on what day in July each was killed by the Harpes, and concludes its paragraph with the statement that "we are happy to hear they are closely pursued and sincerely hope they will ere long meet the punishment which the atrocity of their crimes demands." *The Western Spy and Hamilton Gazette,* of Cincinnati, on September 3 published a Frankfort news item giving practically the same facts and expressing the same hope.

Such widespread terror and fear as was aroused by the raid of the Harpes found expression, no doubt, not only in the *Kentucky Gazette* and the *Palladium,* but in all the papers published in Kentucky and Tennessee. Stewart's *Kentucky Herald,* of Lexington, the *Mirror,* of Washington, Mason County, Kentucky, and the *Gazette* and the *Impartial Observer,* both of Knoxville, Tennessee, were in existence at the time. Careful research in these four papers has failed to reveal any allusion to the Harpes, for the copies available are of other dates than those likely to mention these outlaws in their presentation of current events. It is possible that a number of current newspapers in the east and south printed more or less about the Harpes and thus warned the people of the possibility of their sudden appearance. As we shall see later, the *Carolina Gazette,* of Charleston, South Carolina, in its issue of October 24, 1799, devoted twenty-five lines to the Harpes. This story, in all probability, was not its first and only paragraph relative to them.

Although the alarm was being spread by the people

and the press, and many a man had prepared to slay the outlaws, the report of the latest butchery was soon followed by another. The day after Colonel Trabue sent the messengers to Frankfort and Henderson, the Harpes traveled up Marrowbone Creek and, about twenty-five miles south of Colonel Trabue's home, stopped at an out-of-the-way place on which John Graves and his thirteen-year-old son were cultivating a crop and making preparations for the rest of the family to join them. [63]

The Harpes arrived at their cabin late in the evening and got permission to spend the night. "Early in the morning, probably before the Graveses awoke, they, with Graves' own axe, split the heads of both open and threw the bodies of both in to the brush fence that surrounded the house." "There they lay," writes Draper, in one of his note books, "until some one, seeing so many buzzards around, made an investigation and discovered what had taken place." [12E] This tragedy was announced in the *Palladium* of August 22, in a paragraph quoted from the *Guardian of Freedom,* Frankfort, Kentucky. The statement then published is another verification of the notes made by Draper many years later.

From the Graves cabin they traveled north twenty miles or more into Russell County to the home of old man Roberts, the reputed father of the two women Big Harpe claimed as wives. The only reference to this "old Mr. Roberts" is in Colonel Trabue's affidavit sent to the Governor of Kentucky in August, 1799. Local tradition has nothing to say about Roberts – when he came or left, or where his cabin stood. Evidently he was still living in Russell County in 1802, for in November of that year Reverend Jacob Young, a Methodist preacher, met "a brother-in-law of the infamous Micajah Harpe," who, although his name is not stated in the preacher's autobiography, must have been a son of the "old Mr. Roberts" in order to qualify for the connection. At any rate, two of the Harpe women were doubtless invited by their father to remain with him. If, however, such an invitation was not extended, the women would have appealed to him for help had they been inclined to reform, and he, as many other fathers would have done, might have consented to make an effort to lead them from the vile associations into which they had fallen. What these two daughters might and should have done they failed to do. They clung to their companions in crime and with them fled westward south of Green River toward Mammoth Cave and Russellville.

While on the way the Harpes killed a little girl and a negro boy. Writers do not agree as to just where and when these two murders took place. It is likely they were enacted while the Harpes were going to Logan County and that they led up to a third child-murder even more inhuman. The first of these tragedies, as briefly related by Breazeale, is that "they met with a negro boy going to mill, dashed the boy's brains out against a tree, but left the horse and bag of grain untouched." The other recorded by Collins is equally brief: "One of their victims was a little girl found at some distance from her home, whose tender age and helplessness would have been protection against any but incarnate fiends."

They soon reached Logan County. There, according to T. Marshall Smith, they discovered, about eight miles from Drumgool's station, now Adairville, the two Trisword brothers, who with their wives, several children, and a few black servants, were camping for the night. The next morning before sunrise, while the emigrants were still asleep, the Harpes and two Cherokee Indians made a wild attack on the tent occupied by the travelers and killed the entire party except one of the men, who ran for help. When the rescuing party arrived upon the scene it found the ground covered with the bodies of the dead, some of them badly mangled. While several of the men were occupied burying the dead, others were looking for evidence of the direction the outlaws had taken.

This account, because it lacks verification, is not here presented as one true in its details. It is known, however, that as a result of this tragedy or because of some other atrocity committed about this time by the Harpes, William Stewart, sheriff of Logan County, organized a party of about a dozen men to search for the highwaymen. This pursuing party, having reason to believe that the outlaws were traveling south, rushed toward the Tennessee line. In the meantime, however, the cunning Harpes were working their way northward. They stopped a few hours about three miles northeast of Russellville, on the Samuel Wilson Old Place, about half a mile up Mud River from what is now Duncan's bridge over Mud River on the Russellville and Morgantown road. There the Harpes watered their horses at the same spring that quenched the thirst of the hundreds of people who a few weeks before attended the Great Revival conducted by the Reverends John and William McGee and James M'Gready. Samuel Wilson, an eye witness, in his description of this religious meeting, says: "Fires were built, cooking begun, and by dark candles lighted and fixed on a hundred trees around and interspersing the ground surrounded by tents, showing forth the first, and as I believe still, one of the most beautiful camp meetings the world has ever seen." This was one of the first of the Great Revival meetings that so spontaneously stirred what was then called the West. The Harpes doubtless knew or inferred from the condition of the place that it had been used recently for religious purposes. [121]

The Harpe men had no patience with their children and often reprimanded the three women, declaring that the crying infants would some day be the means of pursuers detecting their presence. They frequently threatened to kill them. To protect their babies, the mothers many a night went apart, carrying their children sufficiently far away to prevent their cries being heard by the unnatural fathers. But the long-feared threat was at last carried out. [12F]

It is a strange sequence of events that on this same camp ground and almost immediately after the Great Revival, one of the Harpes killed his own child in the presence of its mother. A large maple tree still marks the spot near which this deed was enacted.

The details of this murder as given today by tradition are practically the same as those published by T. Marshall Smith: "Big Harpe snatched it – Susan's infant, about nine months old – from its mother's arms, slung it by the heels against a large tree by the path-side, and literally bursting its head into a dozen pieces, threw it from him as far as his great strength enabled him, into the woods." This terrible tragedy is briefly referred to by Hall and Breazeale, both of whom state that Big Harpe, just before his death, declared he regretted none of the many murders he had committed except "the killing of his own child."

The traditions of today and the three early writers

just referred to are probably wrong as to the kinship that existed between the murdered child and its murderer. Draper, in his sketch of the Harpes, gives a more flexible statement: "Tradition says they killed one of their own children." They had only three children and all of them were born in the Danville jail. Big Harpe's boy, born to Betsey, and his girl, born to Susan, lived many years, as is shown later. The child that was so cruelly murdered by Big Harpe could have been no other than the daughter of Sally, who had married Little Harpe. So, in all probability, if Big Harpe committed the crime, his brother's child was the victim.

The Harpes - Big Harpe's Ride to Death

Rumor had it that the Harpes had left the neighborhood of Russellville, going south, and were probably making their way to west Tennessee. In the meantime, however, two small families had wandered into Henderson County, Kentucky, and were living in a rented cabin on a small farm on Canoe Creek, some eight miles south of Red Banks or Henderson. About twenty miles southwest of this point, near the headwaters of Highland Creek, were Robertson's Lick and, west of it, Highland Lick. A few miles east of these, near the present town of Sebree, was Knob Lick.

The Highland Lick road and a few trails led to these salt licks, and, because of these roads and the salt wells with their "salt works," many pioneers considered the section a very desirable one in which to live. Settlers were constantly coming for a bushel or two of salt and then returning home. The coming and going of people therefore attracted less attention along the Highland Lick road and its by-paths than in most other sections. And since only a few months before about fifteen outlaws had been killed in Henderson County, and all the others had been driven out [124] there was little likelihood of undesirable persons appearing on the scene. Principally for this reason, the two small families of recent arrivals on Canoe Creek attracted no particular attention, and least of all were they suspected of being notorious criminals. A good description of the Harpes was in wide circulation, and through General Hopkins they became especially well known in the lower Green River country. The return of the Harpes seemed as improbable as a second bolt of lightning in the same spot.

John Slover lived about a mile from the cabin rented by the new arrivals, but had seen them only once or twice and then from a distance. Slover's career as an Indian fighter in eastern Kentucky was well known to his friends and acquaintances and was often the subject of discussion at fireside talks. In fact, his escape from Indian captivity was so singular and romantic that John A. McClung devoted a whole chapter to it when, in 1832, he published his *Sketches of Western Adventure.*

One day Slover was hunting near Robertson's Lick, writes Draper in his "Sketch of the Harpes," and, after killing a bear in the woods, returned to a path leading homeward. While leisurely riding along he heard the snap of a gun that failed to fire. Quickly turning in the direction of the sound he recognized his two new neighbors, well-armed and wilder looking than Indians in battle. Comprehending the great danger of an encounter with two fierce men apparently prepared for murder, the experienced Indian fighter put spurs to his horse and escaped. Slover reported this experience to some of his friends and ventured the opinion that the two men were the Harpes. None doubted that an unsuccessful attempt had been made to shoot him but, on the other hand, none agreed with him that the Harpes had returned and were loitering around the licks.

A day or two later a man named Trowbridge left Robertson's Lick to carry some salt to a farm on the Ohio near the mouth of Highland Creek. Trowbridge never returned, and his disappearance remained a mystery until a few months later when one of the Harpe women made known the facts. Trowbridge was killed by the Harpes about eight miles above the mouth of Highland Creek and his body sunk in the stream.

When General Hopkins received a report of Slover's narrow escape, although doubting the presence of the Harpes, he detailed a number of men to watch the place on Canoe Creek. While loitering around their cabin the Harpes evidently not only wore clothes different from those in which they were seen by Slover, but also managed to change their general appearance to such an extent that Slover, inspecting them from a distance, did not recognize the two men as the same who had attempted to shoot him. The women were nowhere seen by the spies, for, as learned later, they were waiting for the Harpes to meet them at some designated place and time. The guards, after watching the house about a week without results, quietly returned to their homes, not realizing that the two suspected men were aware of their movements.

The next day the Harpes started toward the hiding place of their women and children. They traveled south about fifteen miles to the home of James Tompkins on Deer Creek, not far from what was then known as Steuben's Lick, near which place, according to one tradition, General Steuben of Revolutionary fame was wounded, some fifteen years before, by an Indian. They rode good horses. Both were fairly well dressed and, upon meeting Tompkins, represented themselves as Methodist preachers. Their equipment aroused no suspicion, for the country was almost an unbroken wilderness and preachers as well as most other pioneers, were often seen traveling well armed. Tompkins invited them to supper, and Big Harpe, to ward off suspicion, said a long grace at table. In the course of their conversation one of the Harpes asked their host about his supply of venison. Tompkins, convinced that he was dealing with men from whom he had nothing to fear, admitted to shooting no deer lately for the simple reason that his powder was exhausted and had been for some time. Big Harpe, with affected generosity, poured a teacupful from his powder horn and presented it to Tompkins. That same powder, as we shall see, later performed a most singular service. [28] Bidding their host a farewell, ministerial in its pretense, the two desperadoes, pretending to have an engagement some miles south, took the trail in that direction.

That same evening, however, they made their appearance on the farm of Squire Silas McBee, one-half mile northwest of Tompkins' place. Squire McBee was a justice of the peace and had been active in fighting outlaws. The murderers were, therefore, very much disposed to butcher him. It was early in the evening and the moon was shining brightly when they approached his house. The Squire kept a half dozen dogs for bear and deer hunting and, hearing an uproar among them, the McBees went to the door to investigate the cause. They saw the pack fiercely attacking two men, but, suspecting that the intruders might be of an unwelcome character, made no effort to restrain the hounds. After a fierce fight with the dogs, the Harpes withdrew.

Foiled in their attempt at Squire McBee's, they proceeded about four miles northwest and late that night reached the house of Moses Stegall – about five miles east of what later became the town of Dixon. Stegall (also spelled Steigal, and various other ways) was absent, but his wife and their only child, a boy of four months, were at home and had, only a few hours before, admitted Major William Love, a surveyor, who had come to see Stegall on business. Mrs. Stegall, expressing an opinion that her husband would return that night, invited him to remain. He climbed to the loft above on a ladder on the outside of the house and was in bed when the new arrivals entered the cabin. [57] Stegall at one time lived in Knox County, Tennessee, [21] and evidently was acquainted with the Harpes, for Mrs. Stegall knew them but had received instructions from the Harpes never to address them by their real names in the presence of a third person. [12E] Major Love came down and met the two men, little suspecting who they were. In the conversation that followed the murderers themselves inquired about the Harpes and, among other things, stated that, according to rumor, the two outlaws were then prowling around in the neighborhood. [27]

Mrs. Stegall, having only the one spare bed in the loft, was obliged to assign it to the three men. After Major Love had fallen asleep one of the Harpes took an axe which he always carried in his belt and, with a single blow, dashed out the brains of the sleeping man. The two villains then went down to Mrs. Stegall's room. She, knowing nothing to the contrary, presumed Major Love was still asleep. While reprimanding her for assigning them a bed with a man whose snoring kept them awake, they proceeded to murder her and her baby. After gathering some bedding and clothing, among which was Major Love's hat, and leaving the three bodies in the house, they set it afire. [27] It was soon a smoking ruin.[11]

[11] Tradition says Major William Love's charred corpse was buried near the site of the Stegall house. His widow survived him many years and is buried at Piney Fork Camp Ground, about six miles east of Marion, Kentucky. On the marble slab at the head of her grave is the inscription: "My

Such, briefly, is the account of the killing of Mrs. Stegall as given by all writers who describe this tragedy and as still told in western Kentucky by those who are familiar with local traditions. Breazeale, however, published some details which are very characteristic of the inhumanity of the Harpes, but which are not woven into any of the other versions. They are probably omitted more for the reason that the accounts are sufficiently gruesome without them than because of the possibility that such brutality might be questioned.

This version has it that on the morning the two Harpes burnt Stegall's house, they arose and asked Mrs. Stegall to prepare breakfast for them. She consented to do so, explaining that since her child was not well and she had no one to nurse it the meal would necessarily be somewhat long in preparation. The men then suggested that she place the baby in the cradle and let them rock it. This she did. "After Mrs. Stegall had prepared their breakfast and the ruthless and savage murderers had partaken of her hospitality, she went to the cradle to see if the child was asleep, expressing some astonishment (as Micajah Harpe acknowledged when he was afterward taken) that her child should remain quiet for so great a length of time . . . She beheld her tender, harmless, and helpless infant lying breathless, with its throat cut from ear to ear . . . But the relentless monsters stayed not their bloody hands for the tears and heart-broken wailings of a bereaved mother. They instantly dispatched her, with the same instrument (a butcher knife) with which they

name was Esther Love, daughter of Wm. & Nancy Calhoun of Abbeville, South Carolina, born Sept. 30, 1765. died Mar. 2, 1844. My husband Wm. Love was killed by the Harpes Aug. 1799. Blessed are the dead which die in the Lord."

had cut the throat of the child; then set fire to the house and fled." [21]

Before leaving the Stegall farm they stole Major Love's horse and one belonging to Stegall. They concealed themselves along the road that ran between Stegall's and McBee's, reasoning that if the Squire saw the light of the burning house, he would hasten there in the morning over this road and thus easily become their victim. While lying in wait for McBee, the outlaws halted two men named Hudgens and Gilmore, who were returning from Robertson's Lick with packs of salt. The Harpes accused them of murdering the Stegall family and burning the house. The charge was denied, but when the two prisoners were told they must appear before Squire McBee to prove their innocence, they willingly submitted to arrest. While marching them along, Big Harpe purposely dropped behind and shot Gilmore through the head, killing him instantly. Hudgens, seeing this, ran away, hoping to escape, but was overtaken by Little Harpe, who snatched from him his gun and with it beat out his brains. [12L]

The murderers then resumed their hiding place, watching for the approach of the expected McBee. In the meantime, John Pyles and four other men from Christian County, returning from Robertson's Lick, found the Stegall house a smouldering ruin, with not a human being in sight. Surroundings indicating that the disaster was still unknown in the neighborhood, they proceeded to McBee to notify him of their discovery. They were unmolested by the Harpes, who doubtless felt confident that the men would later return over the same road with McBee and thus give them the hoped for chance to shoot the justice of the peace from ambush.

McBee knew nothing of the fire until John Pyles reported it. He immediately rode to the home of William Grissom (or Grisson) who lived about a mile north of Stegall's. It so happened that he took a short trail instead of the main road and thus providentially escaped the Harpes. He and Grissom, armed and well mounted, accompanied by Grissom's family, rode to the Stegall home. They not only found the house burned to the ground, as described by John Pyles, but also discovered in the ashes the half-burned remains of Mrs. Stegall and Major Love. They then proceeded to McBee's house, fortunately taking the same short cut over which the Squire had ridden in the morning. They had scarcely dismounted when Moses Stegall rode up. Then, for the first time, Stegall heard of what had happened to his family since he left home. The necessity of organizing a pursuing party had already been agreed upon and Stegall was sent to Robertson's Lick for volunteers. [12M]

That same afternoon or night the Harpes and their women and two children, with all their goods and horses, began their flight. The next morning Stegall returned with John Leiper, Matthew Christian, and Neville Lindsey. These four, with Silas McBee, William Grissom, and James Tompkins, constituted a party of seven daring backwoodsmen, who were prepared to pursue and capture the Harpes, regardless of what danger and hardship the effort might involve.

Then began the chase after the Harpes – a chase made so cold and dramatic by its results, that for more than a century every minute detail of it has been sought by historians and by all who are curious about those full moments when life and death look each other in the eye with the event hanging on the balance of an instant.

Various have been the accounts printed, nearly all agreeing in the main features but differing in those small details, the rendering of which seems to excite as it satisfies the curiosity of the mind. The most accurate account of this chase of death was published in September, 1842, in *The Western Literary and Historical Magazine*. It was prepared by the distinguished historical collector and author, Lyman C. Draper, who rendered invaluable service to western annals by gathering and preserving more data pertaining to the early history of the Middle West than any other man of his generation. His "Sketch of the Harpes" was written, as he is careful to explain, after a long conversation with Squire Silas McBee himself. After its publication the narrative was submitted for correction to Squire McBee, who made but four almost immaterial changes, all of which are noted in the account to follow.

It is well at the outset to point out that Silas McBee was a man of education and wide experience, more competent than any of the others engaged in this whirlwind chase to observe and give an account of all that occurred. He was born in 1765, fought as a youth at King's Mountain, as he had in other Revolutionary battles and Indian wars. He was a brave soldier, an enthusiastic hunter, and an ideal pioneer of public spirit and character. In Alabama he served as a member of its first legislature. After living in western Kentucky, where for many years he did much for the general good, he removed to Mississippi and died there in 1845 at the age of eighty. [41] One of his daughters was the wife of Governor T. M. Tucker, of Mississippi, and another the wife of United States Senator Thomas H. Williams, of the same state.

Here is the McBee narrative of that famous chase:

"Mounted, and equipped, and provisioned for a few days, the little troop started about noon on their expedition against the Harpes, leaving their women and a faithful old negro servant with a few guns, to defend the temporarily fortified domicil at McBee's. The trail of the Harpes was soon struck south of the road leading to the Lick; and after pursuing it a few miles, a spot was reached where the outlaws had evidently dispersed a large drove of buffaloes, with the design, doubtless, of so tramping down and tangling the wild grass and shrubbery as to render it difficult, if not impossible, to discover their course of flight. The pursuing party understood the stratagem, and though a little puzzled at first, they soon regained the trail, which, however, forked off at a little distance – the party dividing, followed each for a mile or two when the elliptical forks again united. After this they had no difficulty in keeping the path. At nightfall they halted and camped on the bottom of the western shore of Pond River, a considerable tributary of Green River. Their simple repast despatched, and horses secured, they retired to rest – the earth their bed, a wallet their pillow, and their only covering the broad canopy of heaven. That night they slept with an eye half open, but nothing occurred, save a smart dash of rain, to require particular notice.

"Early the following morning the pursuit was resumed, fording Pond River with ease, and riding on rapidly till an hour after sun up, when a couple of dead dogs were found in the trail, recognized as having belonged to the unfortunate Hutchins and Gillmore whom the Harpes had so wantonly murdered. From the fact that the bodies were not swollen in such hot August weather, it was inferred that the dogs had not long been killed, and that the fugitives could not be far ahead. They had probably killed the dogs to prevent their barking, and thus the better to enable them to make good their escape. It was now proposed by Squire McBee, in order to advance with the least noise, that four of the most expert footmen should dismount and push on as rapidly as due regard to caution would permit, leaving the horses for the remaining three to lead along more leisurely, yet keeping within hailing distance in case of need. Leiper, Steigal, Christian, and Lindsay, accordingly went ahead on foot, while McBee, Grissom, and Tompkins followed with the horses in charge. The pursuit continued in this manner for a mile or so, when, not finding the outlaws, the footmen again mounted their horses, and all went on together. But a short time elapsed before Squire Mc-Bee discovered the ruffians on a distant hill-side, a strip of low land intervening – both on foot with guns in hand, Big Harpe having a horse by his side, and both holding a parley with a person on horseback [corrected by Draper to *afoot*] whom they had apparently just met. McBee exclaimed 'there they are,' pointing towards them, and at the same time putting spurs to his horse dashed over the low ground and made for the spot. Big Harpe instantly mounted and darted off in one direction, and Little Harpe on foot in another, while the other individual rode [corrected by Draper to *ran*] rapidly towards McBee, and when within sixty or eighty yards suddenly dismounted [Draper eliminated 'dismounted'] and betook himself to a tree. Seeing this bellicose demonstration on the part of an armed man, McBee in the excitement of the moment, drew up his gun, loaded with two balls, and 'blazed away' at that part of the body exposed to view, both bullets taking effect, one passing through the right thigh, and the other the right arm. At this moment Steigal recognised the wounded man as a settler living up Pond River some two or three miles; and perceiving some of the rest of the party in the act of levelling their pieces, Steigal exclaimed 'don't shoot, it's George Smith!' The unfortunate man, who knew Squire Mc-Bee, now calling him by name apologised for his singular conduct by saying, that he was nearly bereft of his senses, expecting every moment that the Harpes would kill him, and when he *treed* he had not recovered from his fright and was totally unfitted to perceive the folly and madness of the act. Little Harpe, he said, had met him with his gun in one hand, and a kettle in the other, going after water; and made enquiries about the settlements, speaking in an elevated tone, evidently that his brother might hear from the camp, not more than eighty rods distant, and come to his aid – such at least was the effect, intentional or not, for Big Harpe rode up and dismounted, and had been there but a few moments when McBee and his party unexpectedly made their appearance. Smith desired Squire McBee to assist him home, which with pleasure he consented to do after the Harpes were secured. He redeemed his promise, and in time Smith recovered both from his fright and his wounds [corrected by Draper to read: 'Smith hobbled home by himself and in due time etc.'].

"After they broke and ran, the outlaws were instantly out of sight. A little search enabled the pursuers to discover the camp, which proved to be a natural room perhaps fifteen feet square, under a shelving rock projecting from the cliff of a ridge facing the south, with a large rock directly in front, leaving but a narrow entrance – affording altogether a very secluded and safe retreat, susceptible of easy defence. The pursuing party were rather cautious in approaching the camp, but Little Harpe's woman alone remained. When questioned about the Harpes, she frankly said that Big Harpe had just been there, mounted each of his women on a good horse, and darted off in great haste. She was asked to point out the direction they had taken, which she readily did – the men, however, in their hurry, overlooked the trail and returned to the camp. Squire McBee, thinking she had purposely deceived them to gain time for Big Harpe and his women, raised his gun and threatened to kill her instantly if she did not give the correct information; upon which she went and pointed it out precisely as she had described it. After perhaps half an hour's delay in finding the camp and parleying with the woman, the pursuers again proceeded with all possible haste, bent on the destruction of Big Harpe, and fully determined that nothing should divert them from their purpose.

"Squire McBee was left to bring on the prisoner, whom he mounted on one of the outlaw's horses, and, though thus encumbered, he kept nearly up with the party. When about two miles from the camp, Big Harpe was again discovered on a ridge a short distance ahead, and some of the party halloed to him to stop, upon which he abandoned his women to their fate, and dashed on alone – Leiper, in the meantime, making an ineffectual shot at the fugitive. Tompkins and Lindsey were left in charge of the two captured women, while Leiper, Christian, Grisson, and Steigal renewed the chase with increased animation. Leiper not being able to draw his ramrod, owing to its swollen condition from the rain of the preceding night, had exchanged guns with Tompkins. The fleeing outlaw was closely pressed, Christian, Steigal, and Grisson each giving him a shot in the pursuit – Christian's alone taking effect, wounding him in the leg. Harpe, discovering that Leiper was considerably in advance of the others, and supposing his gun empty, concluded to take advantage, as he thought, of the circumstance, and get a fair shot at his dangerous adversary. He accordingly stopped his horse, and while renewing his priming, Leiper took unerring aim, and fired – and the same powder which the outlaws had a few days previously given Tompkins, now sped the ball that mortally wounded Big Harpe. Though badly shot through the spine of his back, the wounded ruffian, determined to sell his life as dearly as possible, levelled his gun at Leiper; but even that deserted him in his hour of need – *it snapped!* and he threw it away in disgust. As Leiper and Christian were rapidly advancing upon him, Steigal and Grisson having lagged far behind, Harpe drew a large tomahawk and brandished it furiously to keep off his pursuers, at the same time urging on his jaded horse as well as he could. Leiper and Christian kept close at hand, repeatedly calling upon him to surrender, when he would again brandish his tomahawk in savage defiance. He finally agreed to surrender himself if they would stop their horses; accordingly they all reined up, Leiper and Christian dismounted and made some demonstrations towards loading; perceiving which, Harpe suddenly dashed off. Leiper's horse, which had been standing by his side, though not held by him, now took fright and darted off after Harpe's horse. Seeing the accident, Christian instantly mounted his steed and quickly overtook the runaway horse, returned him to Leiper, and both without loading renewed the pursuit. They easily followed the trail through a small canebrake of thick growth, and just as the fugitive was emerging from it they overhauled him, not more than half a mile distant from where he had taken French leave. His horse was walking quite leisurely, and Harpe's wonted daring and bravery seemed to have forsaken him; and, faint from the loss of blood, he had either lost his tomahawk or thrown it away. They rode up and pulled him from his horse without resistance.

"Just at this moment Squire McBee came up with his prisoner in charge; and Steigal and Grisson soon after joined the party. The dying outlaw, as he lay stretched upon the ground, begged for water, and Leiper took a shoe from one of Harpe's feet, and with it procured some for him near by. McBee now told him that he was already dying, but they should hasten his death; time, however, would be given him for prayer and preparation for another world – to which he made no reply, and appeared quite unconcerned. When asked if he had not money concealed, he replied that he had secreted a pair of saddle-bags full in the woods on an eastern branch of Pond River, some twenty miles from its mouth. From his description of the branch, and their knowledge of the country, they concluded that there was no such water-course, and gave little or no heed to his story; but a report, however, has gained some currency – for the truth of which we cannot vouch, that a considerable sum of specie has been found, within a few years, near the head waters of Pond River.

"Steigal, after reminding Harpe how unfeelingly he had murdered his wife and only child, drew a knife, and exhibiting it to him, said in plain terms that he intended to cut his head off with *that!* 'I am,' said the dying outlaw faintly, 'but a young man, but young as I am I feel the death-damp already upon my brow; and before I die I could wish that old Baldwin might be brought here, as he is the man who instigated me to the commission of all my crimes.' This Baldwin, a very suspicious character, lived at Green Tree Grove, in the then adjoining county of Livingstone, now called Caldwell; and though subsequently tried, he was acquitted, nothing positive being proven against him. When they had somewhat recovered from the fatigue of the chase, after perhaps an hour's delay – during which Harpe lay on the ground upon his right side, unable from weakness to raise himself, and rapidly ebbing his life away – Steigal stepped forward and pointed the muzzle of his gun at the head of the expiring outlaw, who conscious of the intention, and desirous at least of procrastinating it dodged his head to and fro with an agility unexpected to the beholders, manifesting pretty plainly a strong disrelish 'to shuffle off this mortal coil.' Perceiving this, Steigal observed, 'very well, I believe I will not upon reflection shoot him in the head, for I want to preserve *that* as a trophy;' and thereupon shot him in the left side – and Harpe almost instantly expired without a struggle or a groan. Steigal, with the knife he had so menacingly exhibited to Harpe, now cut off the outlaw's head. Squire McBee had with him a wallet in which he had brought his provisions and provender – in one end of this, Steigal placed the severed head, and some articles of corresponding weight in the other, and then slung it behind him across his horse, and all commenced their return. Thus died Big Harpe, long the terror of the west, and his decapitated body was left in the wilds of Muhlenberg county, as unsepulchred as his merited death was unwept and unmourned.

"After the party left the scene of decapitation they

has | LEXINGTON, *Sept.* 10.
eƈ- | The two murderers by the name of
an- | Harps, who killed Mr. Langford laſt
\els, | winter in the wilderneſs, and were ar-
    | reſted and broke the Danville goal,
ck, | killed a family on Pond river, by the
in | name of Staple on the 22d day of
phe | Auguſt, and burnt the houſe ; a party
nce | of men purſued and overtook them
and | and their women ; the Harps parted.
ard. | Micajah Harp, took two of the
\)yal | women off with him ; the men purſued
\iich | him, and in riding about 10 or 12
\iips | miles, caught him, having previouſly
    | ſhot him. He confeſſed the killing of
\)red | Mr. Stump on Big Barren ; he alſo
on | confeſſed of their killing 17 or 18
rth, | beſides ; they killed two men near
\iral | Robertſon's Lick, the day before they
\)yal | burnt Staple's houſe. They had with
gar- | them eight horſes and a conſiderable
ar- | quantity of plunder, ſeven pair of ſad-
oy- | dle bags, &c. They cut off his head.
hu- | The women were taken to the Red
\:hat | banks. The above took place on Pond
\)— | river in the county of Muhlenburg.

FACSIMILE OF NEWS ITEM REGARDING CAPTURE OF
MICAJAH HARPE

Dated Lexington, Kentucky, September 10, 1799, and published in the
Carolina Gazette, Charleston, S. C., October 24, 1799

re-joined Tompkins and Lindsay, who had been left in charge of the two women of Big Harpe, and they all proceeded to the camp of the outlaws, which they gave a careful examination. Nothing of any value was discovered, save a dollar and a half in small change pieces. Ten horses in all were recovered and restored to their several owners. That noble animal which Big Harpe rode, and which had belonged to Major Love, was conveyed to his widow, but did not long survive that terrible ride.

"The head was conveyed to the cross-roads within half a mile of Robertson's Lick, and there placed in the forks of a tree, where for many years it remained a revolting object of horror. To this day the place where that bloody trophy was deposited is known as *Harpe's Head,* and the public road which passes by it from the Deer Creek settlement to the 'Lick,' is still called *Harpe's Head Road.* In subsequent years a superstitious old lady of the neighborhood, some member of whose family was afflicted with fits, having been told that the human skull pulverized, would effect a certain cure, thus appropriated that of the memorable outlaw of the west."

Thus ended the career of "one of the most brutal monsters of the human race." And Little Harpe, having escaped the pursuers, resumed elsewhere, as we shall see later, his life of outlawry. The capture of Big Harpe is briefly described by Breazeale, Collins, Hall, and a few other historians, but none goes into details as does Draper in the sketch quoted. Each of these writers, however, presents some circumstance not mentioned by the others. Some writers say Big Harpe made a confession before he was killed; others are absolutely silent on that feature, neither affirming nor denying it. Local tradition, the current newspapers, and Breazeale are among those who state that Big Harpe made a confession. It is more than probable that he did. *The Kentucky Gazette* of September 5, 1799, prints a statement to the effect that he confessed to killing about twenty people. Colonel G. W. Sevier, about 1840, recalled the number as about thirty-one. [12G] The number of their victims noted in this sketch up to the death of Big Harpe is twenty-eight, exclusive of the Triswords of whom there were probably about ten.

The report that Big Harpe had been captured and beheaded and that Little Harpe had escaped spread rapidly throughout Kentucky and Tennessee, and was soon verified by the state press. Among the newspapers beyond the boundaries of these two states that announced this news was *The Carolina Gazette,* of Charleston, which, in its issue of October 24, 1799, published a paragraph on the subject, dated Lexington, Kentucky, September 10, which is here reproduced in facsimile.

History and local tradition have it that Big Harpe was killed in Muhlenberg County, two miles west of Unity Baptist Church [110] near what has since been known as Harpe's Hill. An oak tree four feet in diameter, which until 1910 stood about a hundred yards from Pond River on the old Slab Road leading from Harpe's Hill to "Free Henry" Ford, was always pointed out as the tree under which Big Harpe was beheaded and his headless corpse lay until it was devoured by wild animals. On the south slope of Harpe's Hill, about a mile and a half east of Pond River and a few steps off the road leading to "Free Henry" Ford, is a large isolated rock known as Harpe's "House." It was at this so-called "rock house" that the Harpes were camping when overtaken by the pursuers. [109]

After Big Harpe had been disposed of and the women held as prisoners, the pursuers began their victorious march to Robertson's Lick, a distance of some thirty-five miles, there to display the head and to warn Little Harpe and all other outlaws what to expect should they attempt any depredations. Draper, as we have already seen, states that before the men started on their return, Stegall placed the severed head in one end of a wallet and some articles of corresponding weight in the other end and then swung it across his horse. The same historian, in one of his note books, wrote: "Big Harpe's wife was made to carry the head by the hair some distance; while slinging it along she kept muttering, 'damn the head!' " [12G] Another account is that the men, knowing they would be obliged to camp out for the night and require more food than still remained, took some roasting ears from a field along the route and having no other means of carrying them, put them unhusked into the bag with Big Harpe's head. Later, when the corn was taken out and prepared for supper, one of the men refused to eat "because it had been put into the bag with Harpe's head." [21]

The head was carried to the neighborhood where the two Harpes had committed their last crime. Authors vary somewhat in the details of just how this gruesome object was displayed as a warning to outlaws, but all agree that it was put up by the side of the highway (about three miles north of what later became the town of Dixon) near the forks of the road running south from Henderson, one branch of which extended to Marion and Eddyville and the other to Madisonville and Russellville, Kentucky. The old road became known as Harpe's Head Road, and its successor, the Henderson and Madisonville Pike, still bears that name.[12]

The captors had traveled about thirty-five miles before they reached the spot decided upon as the most fitting place to display the head. Continuing their jour-

[12] Draper in his "Sketch of the Harpes" places Big Harpe's head "in the forks of a tree," but in a later note [12G] he has it "placed or rather stuck on the sharpened end of the limb of a tree." Breazeale has it "upon the top of a lofty pole, or in the fork of a tree." Collins, in one version, says the men "stuck it upon a pole where the road crosses the creek," and in another, that "a tall young tree, growing by the side of the trail or road, was selected and trimmed of its lateral branches to its top, and then made sharp. On this point the head was fastened. The skull and jaw-bones remained there for many years – after all else had been decomposed and mingled with the dust." In his sketch on Webster County, Kentucky, Collins states that "Big Harpe's head was stuck upon a pole" near an oak tree which was still standing, and that the letters H.H. for Harpe's Head, carved upon it in 1799, were still legible in 1874.

Robert Triplett, in his anonymous autobiography, *Roland Trevor*, publishes an absurd story to the effect that the two Harpes had stolen the daughter of a pioneer living near Henderson. The father pursued Big Harpe, wounded him, and shortly thereafter captured him. This confused and confusing writer says: "Harpe lay near a tree. The father lifted him, and set him up against it, and then went a little way to a branch, from which, in the brim of his hat, he carried Harpe some water, and while he was drinking reloaded his rifle, and shot him. Then with his knife he cut off his head and stuck it on a pole at the fork of the road between Henderson and Madisonville, which place, from that circumstance, was called, and is to this day, 'Harpe's Head.' "

Another absurd story of the Harpes appears in *History of Great American Crimes,* by Frank Triplett who with a few facts and a vivid imagination succeeds in covering some twenty pages on the Harpes. According to his account, Leiper and Stegall organized a pursuing party, and when the wounded outlaw was overtaken one end of a rope was adjusted around Big Harpe's neck and the other thrown over a limb of a large tree under which the wounded man lay. "Appalled by the blasphemies of Harpe, the word was given, and, with a strong pull, his body was run up some six or eight feet from the ground, and whirling round and round in the rapidly gathering twilight, it quivered convulsively for some moments; there was a fierce death struggle and the soul of the most demoniac murderer that ever cursed our continent had gone out into the limitless realms of eternity. When satisfied that Harpe was dead, the corpse was lowered to the ground, the head cut off and fixed in the fork of the tree which had served his executioners as a gallows."

ney some twenty miles further they arrived in Henderson and there placed the three women in "the little log dungeon, then located on the river bank near the present bridge"– the railroad bridge erected in 1885. [124] About a week later they were taken to the court house for trial. The minute book of the Court of Quarter Sessions briefly shows, on pages 4 and 5, what disposition was made of them by that court, an exact copy of which is here given as extracted from the records in the curious courthouse jargon of that day:

"At a Court of Quarter Sessions called and held for the County of Henderson on Wednesday the 4th day of September, 1799, for the examination of Susanna Harpe, Sally Harpe, and Betsey Roberts, committed to the jail of this county for being parties in the murder of Mary Stegall, James Stegall an infant, and William Love at the house of Moses Stegall in this County and in burning his house and robbing and stealing the horses, goods and effects of the said Moses Stegall on the night of the 20th day of August last.

"Present Samuel Hopkins and Abraham Landers Esquires.

"The said prisoners were set to the bar in custody of the Sheriff of this County and being charged with the felony aforesaid denied the fact sundry witnesses were thereupon sworn and examined and the said prisoners heard in their defence by their att'e on consideration whereof it is the opinion of the Court that the said prisoners are guilty of the facts charged against them and that they ought to be tried for the same before the Judges of the District Court holden at Logan Courthouse on the first day of their next October Court, and it is therefore ordered that the said prisoners be remanded to the jail from whence they came there to remain until removed by due course of law.

"John Leiper, Nevil Lindsey, Matthew Christian, and Isham Sellers severally acknowledged themselves indebted to his Excellency James Garrard Esquire, Governor of this Commonwealth in the sum of fifty pounds each to be levied on their lands and tenements goods and chattels respectively and to our said Governor and his successors rendered in case they fail to appear as Witnesses, on behalf of the Commonwealth before the Judges of the District Court holden at Logan Courthouse on the first day of their next October Term, and then and there give evidence against Susannah Harpe, Sally Harpe, and Betsey Roberts charged with felony.

"(Signed) SAM HOPKINS." [13]

A search recently made for details regarding this examining or preliminary trial resulted in the finding of a bundle of papers labeled "1799," in which were discovered four depositions pertaining to the arrest of the Harpe women. They were made September 4, by the four men who on that day were put under bond to appear at the trial in Russellville, to which place the case was ordered for trial. These old documents substantiate the statements made by Squire McBee to Lyman C. Draper who wove them, with other details, into his account of the capture of the Harpes. The depositions show that Moses Stegall arrived at Robertson's

[13] Samuel Hopkins was a Revolutionary general. He was born in Virginia and, in 1797 went to Henderson and there represented Richard Henderson & Co., owners of a large tract of land lying in that section, granted them by the legislature of Virginia. He continued to make Henderson his home until 1819, the time of his death. He served several terms in the Kentucky legislature and from 1813 to 1815 represented his district in Congress. During the war of 1812 he was commissioned a major-general. [124]

Lick on August 22, 1799, to procure volunteers to join in the chase.

Matthew Christian in his testimony recites that immediately after Stegall came to Robertson's Lick with the news of the murder he started for Stegall's farm and became fully convinced that the report with all its terrible details was true. He then proceeded to Grissom's house, which had been designated as a rallying point, preparatory to going to Squire McBee's the following morning. Although it was not known that Grissom's family had left home and gone to McBee's to remain during the proposed pursuit, the men, nevertheless, met at this designated place "where they tarried all night." Christian "found a paper fas'd to the door of Wm. Grayson's [Grissom's] house, signed by Silas Magby and directed to Moses Stegall in the following words: 'Come to my house without delay,' and a jacket hanging up at the said door supposed by the company to belong to Major William Love. That he from there went to Silas Magby's in company with John Leiper, Nevil Lindsey, and Moses Stegall, that on their way to Magby's he heard a gun go off which he supposed was fired by one of the prisoners who had committed the felony." This note was apparently a forgery and shows that the Harpes had planned to kill Stegall; and since it is more than likely that the outlaws had already started on their flight, this attempt to waylay Stegall indicates that the Harpes must have been associated with some accomplice living in the neighborhood, with whom they prearranged this move.

Isom Sellers' statement shows that on August 16, four days before the Stegall fire, the three Harpe women stopped at John Leiper's house and inquired the way to Moses Stegall's and that Sellers "being indebted to Susannah Harpe one dollar gave her an order upon Moses Stegall for the said sum which this deponent saith that Moses Stegall has informed him he has paid agreeable to the aforesaid order." There is nothing to indicate the specific purpose of this statement; however, it is further evidence that Stegall was acquainted with the Harpes and he may have served as a spy or messenger for them.

Nevil Lindsey's deposition gives a detail not mentioned in any printed sketch or oral tradition: "Three case-knives were stuck into the body of Mrs. Stegal, one of them was buried in so deep that the fire which consumed the house would not burn the handle."

John Leiper asserts that when they "had rode about forty-five miles they came up with Sally Harpe standing on the ground and . . . to show them the way they had gone went with them for that purpose, that after riding about a mile and a half they came up with Susanna Harpe, Betsey Roberts, and Micajah Harpe, they rode by the two women and followed Micajah Harpe for about four miles, when this deponent overtook and killed him."

Christian's deposition states that Big Harpe, before he died, "asked for water and that John Leiper went to Pond River and brought him some in a shoe." The depositions of both Leiper and Christian end in practically the same words: "That the said Micajah Harpe a little while before he expired told this deponent that Susannah was his wife and that he wished she could come up and wished her to do better in the future and that the whole of them would do better in the future, escrowed as he was, and that he would acquaint her with one thing that was hid."

Two days after their examining or preliminary trial,

the three women and two infants were sent, by order of Judge Samuel Hopkins, to Russellville, Logan County, there to appear before the judges of the District Court, which court at that time embraced Henderson County. There is no history or tradition as to how the three women were conducted to "Logan Courthouse." They probably were taken on horseback. The minutes of the next term of the court of Quarter Sessions held in Henderson contain a few items that throw some light on the expense of holding and then transferring the prisoners, the total being $281.78.

These entries indicate that the prisoners were accompanied by the sheriff and five guards and that the county attorney and county clerk took part in the second trial. The prisoners and their guard left Henderson September 6, and after traveling the ninety-five miles, the women were turned over to the sheriff to await their trial, September 28.[14]

Major William Stewart was sheriff of Logan County at the time. He more than once had chased the Harpes for many a mile, only to discover that he was going in the wrong direction and to become irritated by his failure. He was, notwithstanding his eccentricities, a just man and one on whom a person in need might depend, and the three women, realizing this, must have

---

[14] The recorded expense items show six men were allowed $7.50 each for guarding the Henderson jail during the ten days the Harpe women were imprisoned. One man was given $4.32 "for victualling Susannah Harp, et al. in the jail for eight days." Andrew Rowan, the sheriff, was allowed $71.25 "for removing prisoners from Henderson to Logan jail, 190 miles" – 95 miles one way – and also $4.54 for cash advanced for diet for said prisoners from Henderson to Logan jail." Five men were allowed $5.70 each for guarding the prisoners en route to Russellville. William B. Blackburn, "attorney for the Commonwealth in this county," received $60.00 and John D. Haussmann, the county clerk, and the sheriff, each $30.00 "for his ex-officio services." These items, with $4.17 paid the sheriff "for summoning and attending the court," make a total of $281.78.

felt encouraged, not only by the prospect of receiving justice, but also of having mercy shown them. Draper, in his notes on information supplied by George Herndon, a Revolutionary soldier, who long lived in Logan County, writes: "The women were, of course, in his charge, and lodged in the old log jail, becoming dirty and lousy, Major Stewart, feeling for their miserable situation, agreed to let them enjoy the liberty, provided they promised not to attempt to escape and thus make him liable, for he did the act on his individual responsibility. They were rejoiced at the offer and he went around the little town and collected some necessary articles of clothing for them, had them and their children cleaned up, placed them in the courthouse and got a couple of spinning wheels and set them to spinning." [12F]

Smith says the murders committed by the Harpes in this section of Kentucky were too fresh in the minds of the people living in and near Russellville and the suspicion that the women had been accomplices in their crimes was too strong to fail to arouse a hatred for the three women. When threats were made to tear down the log jail and lynch the prisoners, the sheriff secretly conveyed them into the country, where they remained until brought back for trial.

This statement probably is not true. It may have originated from the fact that Stegall and some of his friends rode to Russellville for the purpose of killing the women should they be acquitted. Discovering Stegall's motive, Stewart put the Harpe women back in jail, pretending "it would never do to turn such characters loose upon society," but the next night he hid them in a cave about five miles from town and thus shielded them from the revenge-seeking Stegall who, a few days later, returned home. [28]

An examination of the minute book of the old District Court preserved in Russellville, shows that on Monday, October 28, 1799, a grand jury having been empaneled, "made the following presentment: Commonwealth against Susanna Harpe, Sally Harpe, and Betsey Roberts, a true bill." A District Court was presided over by a judge and two associate judges, and Judges Samuel McDowell and John Allen being absent, the women, rather than delay the trial, agreed to be tried before the one who was present, namely, Judge James G. Hunter. Judge Felix Grundy appeared in behalf of the women, and no one, except the prosecuting officer, against them. Each prisoner was tried by a different jury, the three trials taking place on October 29th and 30th. "Susanna Harpe, late of the County of Henderson and parish of Kentucky, spinster, who stands indicted of felony was led to the bar in the custody of the public jailor and pleads not guilty to the Indictment, and for her trial hath put herself upon God and her Country and the Attorney General in behalf of the Commonwealth, likewise whereupon came a jury, to-wit: [twelve men are named] who being tried . . . and having heard the evidence, upon their oaths do say that the Susanna Harpe is not guilty of the murder aforesaid."

Then followed the trials of "Betsey Roberts, spinster," and "Sally Harpe, spinster," both of whom were found "not guilty of the murder aforesaid." No depositions or other records of the proceedings of these three trials can now be found among the various old documents still preserved in the Logan County Court House.

The women were liberated and the act seems to have met the approval of the public.

Major Stewart, in his capacity as sheriff, had many opportunities to talk to his prisoners. Some of the incidents in their lives could not have failed to touch the heart of any man, especially when heard from the lips of the women themselves. Forty years after the Harpe women had been captured, an interview with him on the subject was arranged to procure facts for publication. From this interview we quote:

"Major Stewart said the women seemed grateful to him, and related with apparent candor the story of their lives and their connection with the Harpes. They told him that their husbands had once been put in jail in Knoxville, Tennessee, upon suspicion of crime, when they were innocent; when released, they declared war against all mankind, and determined to murder and rob until they were killed. They said they might have escaped after the murder and robbery at Stegall's, but for the detention at the branch where Smith was shot. Big Harpe, expecting to be pursued, proposed that the three children be killed, that the others might flee without that encumbrance. His two wives and brother consented after some discussion, but the wife of Little Harpe took her child off to the branch where she had seen a projecting, shelving rock, under which she placed it, and lay down at its outer side, determined to remain and die with her child. As her husband came to the branch to let her know they had concluded to put the children to death, he saw Smith, the horse hunter, approaching. He moved toward him, and sounded the shrill whistle on his 'charger'– the understood signal of impending danger. Big Harpe almost in a moment made his appearance at the branch mounted on Love's mare, when the firing commenced. Smith was shot down and the Harpes fled. Big Harpe did not go directly to the camp, but circled around it, fearing the pursuers might already have taken it. These sudden and unexpected events saved the lives of the children by allowing no time for their execution. Little Harpe's wife and child hastily returned to the camp, when the firing took place a little distance below the shelving rock, and were made prisoners with the wives and children of Big Harpe." [28]

The same delay that resulted in the capture and death of Big Harpe brought about a great change in the lives of the Harpe women. But Major Stewart, in the interview given forty years after the women had been in his charge, evidently was somewhat mistaken in some of the details and in the identity of some of the characters he recalled. There never were more than three Harpe children and all of them were born in the Danville jail. We have seen how the child of Little Harpe's wife was killed a few weeks before the women were arrested and taken to Henderson; it is later shown what became of Big Harpe's children, both of whom were with their mothers in the Russellville jail. It is quite likely that when Big Harpe realized the pursuers were close at hand, he proposed that the children be killed and that then Little Harpe's wife took the two infants and "determined to remain and die" with them. A few weeks before, she had seen her own child cruelly murdered by Big Harpe, and probably had, ever since, awaited a chance to escape from the violence and villainy of the lives led by the Harpes. She doubtless concluded it would be far better for her and the two infants to fall into the hands of the pursuers than to kill the infants, even though the killing of them would relieve the five

Harpes of an encumbrance which they considered sufficient to interfere with their escape. At any rate, the desire of Little Harpe's wife to free herself, combined with her effort to save the two infants, exercising itself as it did at this critical moment, delayed the attempt to escape and resulted in the capture and killing of Big Harpe.[15]

[15] Maj. William Stewart was one of the most eccentric characters in early Kentucky history. His life is full of suggestions for romance and song. He was born in South Carolina about 1772, and, at the age of eighteen, "getting into some difficulties, he left his native state." He went to Nashville, says Finley, and from there started for Henderson – possibly with the intention of continuing to Cave-in-Rock. On his way north he joined a man and wife going to the Green River country. To what extent they influenced him is not known. However, when the three travelers reached the place that later became Russellville, they decided to settle there. In 1791 he left Logan County and "after years of toil, hunting, and nobody knows what else, he finally settled in Stanford and, in 1795, became a dry goods clerk for one Ballenger" – the same man who, a few years later, went in pursuit of the Harpes. In 1796 he returned to Logan County and died there in 1852. He was the first sheriff of Logan County. Collins says: "He was one of the celebrities of the place . . . faithful to his friends, and dangerous to his foes."

Smith in a chapter devoted to Stewart calls him William Stout: "Always eccentric in his material and style of dress – often he appeared attired in an entire suit made of various colored 'lists,' taken from the finest broadcloths sewed together, fantastically cut and fitted to his person, while the buttons on his coat and pantaloons were quarter dollars, United States coin, with eyes attached by his own ingenuity (for he was a worker in metals) and his vest buttoned with genuine United States dimes. This dress, however, was rather for high days and holidays . . . On the morning of the day on which he died, he, with but little aid, drew on his curiously constituted, many colored suit of clothes, and in that attire he died and was buried." [121]

The Harpes - Mysteries and Fate of Survivors

Big Harpe was dead, Little Harpe had vanished into the wilderness and the women had again been spared through public sympathy with their apparent helplessness and misfortunes. What was to become of them and of Little Harpe and of the seven determined men who had run down the gigantic monster? How were these men rewarded for their heroism? The records, hunted down with the utmost patience, constitute a new story in which mystery, tragedy, suspicion and pathos all enter to bring about poetic justice. It enables us also to get closer to these terrible personalities.

First as to the seven avengers. On December 16, 1799, the Kentucky Legislature passed "An Act directing the payment of money to John Leiper and others." The preamble stated that "Micajah Harpe, a notorious offender" had committed "the most unheard of murders" and the Governor on April 22, had offered a reward of three hundred dollars "for the apprehension of said Harpe." It recites its enactment because "sundry good citizens . . . were, while in the attempt to apprehend him, reduced to the necessity of slaying him," and further declares by its enactment all doubt as to the right of these men to the reward is removed. The money was ordered paid to "John Leiper, James Tompkins, Silas McBee, Mathew Christian, Moses Stegall, Neville Lindsey, and William Gresham . . . one hundred of which shall be appropriated to the said John Leiper, and the residue to be equally divided among the others."

The second clause shows that "Alexander M'Farling, John M'Farling, Daniel M'Farling, and Robert White, who from motives of public good incurred very considerable expense and toil in the pursuit of the said Harpe and his associates . . . be allowed one hundred and fifty dollars." These four men probably lived near Danville, and, as previously noted, had been appointed by the governor to take charge of the Harpes should they be found "in any adjacent state."

Five of the men who captured and killed Big Harpe fared well. Tompkins and Matthew Christian continued to live in Henderson County, where they died old and highly respected citizens. William Grissom, about 1810, moved to southern Illinois where he continued the life of a well-to-do farmer. Neville Lindsey was identified with the development of west Tennessee. Squire Silas McBee opened up a plantation in Pontotoc County, Mississippi, and ranked among the best and most prominent men in that state. It was there, in 1841, he met the historian Draper, to whom he supplied much data relative to King's Mountain and also the facts used for his "Sketch of the Harpes."

As for Stegall and Leiper, the immediate executioners of Big Harpe, no sooner had they sprung into public notice by reason of their acts, than they were enveloped in a mystery of suspicion almost as deep as that surrounding the Harpes themselves. It has grown deeper with time, though their deaths within eight years after the tragedy of the death chase rendered the suspicion more sinister and seemed to confirm it.

It appears that John Leiper had not only seen the Harpes before he joined the band in the chase, but was strongly suspected of having been secretly involved in some of their crimes committed in central Kentucky.

In April, 1799, when Colonel Trabue's boy was killed by the Harpes, "Leiper then resided in Adair County and knew the Trabue family well." [12E] He probably lived near "old Mr. Roberts," the father-in-law of Big Harpe, who then had a farm in that part of Adair County which, in 1825, became a part of Russell County. Hypocrite that he was, in all likelihood, he joined some of the men who had gone out to hunt the murderer of John Trabue. For some reason he left that section shortly after the Harpes appeared on the scene. He may have feared that the two outlaws had planned to establish themselves near "old man Roberts" and therefore went to Henderson County, where he was least likely to see them again, and so escape any vengeance they might see fit to execute upon him for joining the posse. Thus, not to begin a better life but to escape death, he left Adair County for parts unknown. On July 3, of the same year, the Henderson County grand jury found an indictment against him for "living in adultery with Ann L. Allen, from the 20th day of last May."

When Leiper was asked to join in the Harpe chase it was observed that he hesitated, saying he had no proper horse for such work, but that if Captain Robert Robertson's could be procured, he would go. When such arrangement was made, Leiper boastingly declared that if he got sight of either of the Harpes he "would stick to the chase until he killed them or they killed him." Later, when Leiper and Christian overtook Big Harpe, shortly before he was killed, the outlaw called to Leiper, "I told you to stay back or I'd kill you," and Leiper replied, "My business with you is for one or the other of us to be killed." These and other remarks, as later interpreted by the other pursuers, indicated that more than a casual acquaintance existed between Leiper and the Harpes. Although applauded for taking part in the killing of Big Harpe, and thus ridding the country of a scourge, he was nevertheless condemned for his motive in doing so. He "died suddenly of winter fever some time during the winter of the cold Friday" (Friday, February 6, 1807). Up to the day of his death he was looked upon as a suspicious character by all his neighbors and so, being unworthy of trust and an outcast, lived and died friendless. [12E]

Moses Stegall was at first the hero of heroes in the returning band. He had suffered the loss of his wife, child, and home, and it seems that fate itself had destined him to strike the last deserved blow. He had been regarded as a questionable character, yet no one could trace any particular crime to him. The report of the tragic manner in which he had put an end to Big Harpe kept in the background, for a time, all unfavorable reports heretofore heard. But it soon became apparent that he, too, had a hidden motive in taking so active a part in the pursuit of the outlaws. It was recalled that when he discovered that Big Harpe had been wounded, but was still able to talk, he had stepped forward and deliberately cut off his head. This act was, at the dreadful instant, regarded by the excited spectators as one highly deserved as far as Harpe was concerned, but for Stegall it was soon suspected to have been an act whereby he could silence the tongue of a dangerously wounded man who might still survive sufficiently to reveal some of the lawlessness in which Stegall himself was implicated. That this was his motive is verified by a number of authorities. Draper, after a conversation with General Thomas Love, of Tennessee, who was a cousin of Major William Love, and whose wife was a cousin of Thomas Langford, noted this: "The company, before his arrival, had some confession from Harpe, and Stegall was afraid he would be implicated and wanted him out of the way, for Stegall bore a bad character. Parson Henry says it was suspected that Stegall purposely left his home to give the Harpes an opportunity to kill his victims." [12E]

Forty years after Big Harpe was killed, a preacher traveling from Lexington, Kentucky, by way of the Henderson and Harpe's Head Road to Mammoth Cave, heard the tradition of the capture of Harpe as then told in the neighborhood where Stegall lived. Relative to Stegall's motive, he wrote: "As for Stegall, he never bore a good character and his excessive zeal and forwardness created new suspicions against him as being an accomplice of Harpe whom he might wish effectually to prevent from betraying him by a precipitate death under colour of vengeance." [38]

Governor John Reynolds, in his comments on the notoriety of some of the settlers who, in pioneer days, lived in Illinois near Ford's Ferry and Cave-in-Rock, pictures the last scene in Stegall's life: "In 1806, at the place, ten miles from the Ohio, where Potts resided afterwards, on the road west of the river, a bloody tragedy was acted. A man named Stegall – the same who assisted to kill one of the Harpes in Kentucky – eloped with a young girl and made the above place his residence . . . Two or three brothers of the seduced girl, and her father, followed them from Trade Water, Kentucky, the residence of the father . . . They found Stegall and the others sitting up under a gallery outside of the cabin, with a lamp burning. The assailing party advanced in silence and secrecy, near Stegall, and shot him without doing any of the others any injury whatever . . . and brought back the deluded girl to her home and family." [102]

Thus within about a half dozen years after Stegall and Leiper helped to capture Big Harpe they had passed into the Great Beyond. Tradition insists that but for the persistence of these two men, the other five would have abandoned the hunt for the Harpes – as many others had done elsewhere – and both outlaws, in all probability, would have escaped to add more crimes to their long list.[16]

Such is the story of the Harpes and their principal crimes. No doubt regarding these crimes existed in the various localities. How many similar deeds they actually committed will never be discovered, for in the sparsely settled country isolated settlers could, and often did, disappear without leaving any trace of their fate and in many instances travelers who were killed were missed by no one.

There also hangs somewhat of a veil of personal mystery over these criminals. Who were the Harpes and what sort of men were they in appearance and bearing? Who were the three women that, from choice or because of terror of their mates, lived through such terrible experience with them, bore children to them and so became forever linked with the history of these horrible outlaws?

Whether or not the two Harpes were brothers and the two "wives" of Big Harpe sisters, is, after all, a question that is not definitely settled by any authori-

[16] When, in 1860, the town of Dixon was laid out to be the seat of justice for the newly established county of Webster, one of the principal streets forming the court house square was named after John Lieper and another after Moses Stegall. These pioneers were thus honored, not to show that "the evil men do lives after them," but to reward two men whose names were "linked with one virtue" at least – that of being responsible for the capture and death of Big Harpe.

tative record or direct testimony that has yet been produced. At this date it seems unlikely that any further
proof of their origin, names or relationship will ever
be discovered. When they were active it was necessary
to their safety to assume various false names. They
changed clothing to such an extent as they could, in
order to avoid pursuit and capture, as well as to avoid
suspicion among those they might later approach as
intended victims.

They certainly seem to have been brothers in crime
and brutality; but were they brothers by birth? The
supposed wife and the "supplementary" wife of Big
Harpe were, in the same degree, sisters in their toleration of his crimes, but were they actually sisters
through one sire? Throughout the story the view has
been taken that the two men were brothers and the two
women sisters, for such was the prevailing belief. All
the contemporary and early subsequent accounts so refer to them, except Smith, who, in his *Legends of the
War of Independence,* published in 1855, says the men
were first cousins. He designates Micajah or "Big"
Harpe as "William Harpe," a son of John Harpe, and
Wiley or "Little" Harpe as "Joshua Harpe," a son of
William Harpe, who was a brother of John Harpe.
Smith also represents Susan, the wife of Big Harpe,
as a daughter of Captain John Wood, and Betsey, Big
Harpe's supplementary wife, as Maria Davidson, a
daughter of Captain John Davidson. Their fathers,
he says, were North Carolinians, both captains in the
Revolutionary army, but in no wise related by blood.
Concerning the two women, he says that they were ab-
ducted by the Harpes and became their "involuntary
wives." He ignores the fact that the two women seem
to have taken no advantage of any of the chances they

had to escape from these villains, and is likewise apparently ignorant of the fact that the third woman, Sally Rice, the wife of Little Harpe, was associated with the outlaws during their most outrageous actions. This same writer says that "Big Harpe and Joshua Harpe" fought at King's Mountain in October, 1780, and were about twenty years old at that time, whereas all other records show the two men could not then have reached the age of ten.

Smith cites no authority for his various statements, although in the preface to his book he declares that he obtained his materials for his pioneer day sketches by questioning survivors of the times and the events. It is also observed that no other writers of that time present authority for the statements they make as to the origin and relationships of the Harpe band.

Breazeale, himself a resident of Knoxville, had opportunities to gather on the ground early recollections of them. In 1842 he wrote that when the Harpes appeared there in 1797 or 1798, they "professed" to have come from Georgia, "represented" themselves to be brothers, and "said" their name was Harpe. He is careful to add, "whether their real name was Harpe or not, no one knew; nor was it ever ascertained where they had been born and brought up, or who were their relatives." As they soon turned out to be thieves and were driven away from the neighborhood of Knoxville, it is at least possible that the relationship, the name and all else they gave out might have been assumed and false in order to cover their tracks from a former place. After the murder of Langford in Lincoln County in 1799, they were both indicted under the name of Roberts, which they had evidently assumed and under which they pleaded and were held. It may be suggested here that if Roberts was the true name of Big Harpe's two "wives," a shrewd criminal would, it seems, hesitate to assume it as an alias, for the name would help identify him. After their escape from the Danville jail the governor in his proclamation of reward for their capture called them "Harpe alias Roberts," which shows that their actual names were unknown. It is reasonable to assume that they used false names as the necessity arose. When, in Henderson County, they represented themselves as "preachers," they must have used fictitious names for the occasion. The name of Harpe became so full of terror and their description as "big" and "little" brothers was so broadcast, that change of name, appearance and pretended occupation was necessary to their safe movement. It will later appear that Little Harpe, after his escape from Kentucky, assumed various names, none of which he had used before and one of which he signed under oath to an official document.[17]

Having told of some of the deeds the Harpes committed, an effort is now made to picture to the readers

---

[17] Whether or not the Harpes were brothers and Big Harpe's two "wives" were sisters is a question that can never be decided definitely by history, but it is one over which psychologists may long argue. If the two men actually were brothers and the two women actually were sisters, it is an anomaly in nature. The Harpes were not ordinary criminals. They were abnormalities in a type that is itself abnormal. It is well recognized that abnormal products of all kinds in nature are exceptions or variations and are not the rule, and that genius in creation, in destruction, in crime, in art, etc. is very seldom duplicated by the same parentage. Abnormal criminals are extremes of a type opposed to abnormal geniuses of the creative or imaginative type. Brothers or sisters in either class occur seldom, if ever. For these reasons, a parental connection between the two Harpes and between the two women may properly be doubted. It is true that Big Harpe was the heartless leader and that Little Harpe might have been an ordinary weakling, obedient to Big Harpe because he feared him or because he failed to recognize the inhumanity of the crimes he was called upon to commit. No other record is now recalled showing such a horrible partnership between blood brothers.

how the monsters looked who could and did commit these crimes. The career of the Harpes was so swift and so veiled by its criminal nature, that the opportunities to examine in detail their appearance and manner was very brief. "Dead men tell no tales" and since those who saw the Harpes at their work were usually victims, they could leave no record. Those who have left descriptions received them from others who had had them second hand. When the difference in observers and conditions is considered, and when the disguises and changes of attire and situation are allowed for, it is surprising to find that a plausible and convincing portrait is made of Big Harpe.

As already stated, Judge James Hall, in April, 1824, published in *The Port Folio* a brief account of one of the crimes committed by the Harpes, and having been accused of having written a story "unworthy of belief," he published in the same magazine about a year later an account of another of their murders and convinced his critics and other readers that his stories of the Harpe atrocities were true. Judge Hall evidently continued his investigation of the Harpes, and seems to have made a special effort to gather data relative to their personal appearance. He realized that fiction is often a better visualizer of persons and their acts than is formal history. So when, in 1833, he published his romance entitled *Harpe's Head*, and later republished it under the title of *Kentucky, A Tale,* his readers were given a striking picture of the Harpes, and especially of Big Harpe. In his preface to this romance he states that although the tale is the "offspring of invention," nevertheless "two of the characters [the two Harpes] introduced are historical and their deeds are still freshly remembered by many of the early settlers of Kentucky."

Their acts were, he explains "of a character too atrocious for recital in a work of this description . . . and have therefore been merely introduced into a tale wholly fictitious."

Judge Hall's description of Big Harpe is as follows:

"His appearance was too striking not to rivet attention. In size he towered above the ordinary stature, his frame was bony and muscular, his breast broad, his limbs gigantic. His clothing was uncouth and shabby, his exterior weatherbeaten and dirty, indicating continual exposure to the elements, and pointing out this singular person as one who dwelt far from the habitations of men, and who mingled not in the courtesies of civilized life. He was completely armed, with the exception of a rifle, which seemed to have only been laid aside for a moment, for he carried the usual powder horn and pouch of the backwoodsman. A broad leathern belt, drawn closely around his waist, supported a large and a smaller knife and a tomahawk. But that which attracted the gaze of all . . . was his bold and ferocious countenance, and its strongly marked expression of villainy. His face, which was larger than ordinary, exhibited the lines of ungovernable passion, but the complexion announced that the ordinary feelings of the human breast were extinguished, and instead of the healthy hue which indicates the social emotions, there was a livid, unnatural redness, resembling that of a dried and lifeless skin. The eye was fearless and steady, but it was also artful and audacious, glaring upon the beholder with an unpleasant fixedness and brilliancy, like that of a ravenous animal gloating upon its prey and concentrating all its malignity into one fearful glance. He wore no covering on his head, and the natural protection of thick, coarse hair, of a fiery redness, uncombed and matted, gave evidence of long exposure to the rudest visitations of the sunbeam and the tempest. He seemed some desperate outlaw, an unnatural enemy of his species, destitute of the nobler sympathies of human nature, and prepared at all points for assault or defense." [18]

It is a vivid, splendid sketch full-length; a portraiture in full keeping with the idea of a super-criminal and his crimes. In all points except one it is sustained as to its faithfulness by the scattered fragments of description that have come down to us from others speaking independently. The disputed point is the color of his hair. Instead of the "fiery redness" that Hall has set down every other witness makes it black. The fact quite well agreed upon that Little Harpe's hair was red, suggests that in this particular Hall's memory confounded the two. In Governor Garrard's proclamation offering a reward for their capture, Big Harpe is described as being "about six feet high, of robust make," "built very straight," "full fleshed in the face," "ill-looking downcast countenance," "his hair black and short but comes very much down his forehead." Trabue says "the big man is pale, dark, swarthy, has bushy hair." Breazeale says he was a "very large, brawny-limbed, big-boned man" and "of a most vicious, savage and ferocious countenance," while Stewart [12F] reports him as "among the tallest class of men, say six feet two to six feet four inches" and with "sun-

---

[18] Lewis Collins prints this description of Big Harpe in his edition of 1847, and his son and successor, Richard H. Collins, likewise republished it in his *History of Kentucky* in 1874. By both it is credited to Colonel James Davidson. The elder Collins says Colonel Davidson was "personally cognizant of most of the circumstances." Judge Hall's *Harpe's Head* had been published in 1833 and there can be no doubt that Colonel Davidson copied his description of Big Harpe, word for word, from the book, relying upon Judge Hall's opportunities for and good character in accuracy.

ken black eyes, a downcast, sour look; dark hair and high cheek bones." As to the hair being short or long, Draper, as already stated, recorded in one of his unpublished note books the pungent and grim picture of Big Harpe's wife being compelled, after his death, to carry his decapitated head some distance "by the hair." There were evidently times when the hair of both Harpes was, by force of circumstances, long and times when it was short during that terrible year they scoured the wilderness. But Big Harpe's hair was probably black or dark and may have been curly.

Little Harpe seems to have passed comparatively unobserved in the presence of his gigantic elder. Governor Garrard's proclamation does not even mention Little Harpe's height, but says he "is very meager in his face, has short black hair, but not quite so curly as his brother's, he looks older, though really younger." His countenance was also "downcast." Hall says he "was smaller in size, but having the same suspicious exterior, his countenance equally fierce and sinister." Breazeale passes his appearance over, while Stewart, who probably got his account of Little Harpe from the latter's wife while she was in his custody, merely says he was "somewhat under common size, had light hair, blue eyes and a handsome look." It may be thought that the wife formulated that description to lead his pursuers astray. But the Frankfort *Guardian of Freedom,* of February 29, 1804, four years after Big Harpe's death, contained an extract "from a letter from a gentleman in the Mississippi territory," written January 8, 1804, in which is noted the arrest and trial of two outlaws in Greenville, Mississippi, one of whom, although he gave another name, "was proved to be the villain who was known by the name of Little or Red-

headed Harpe and who committed so many acts of
cruelty in Kentucky." Red hair was the particular
mark of Little Harpe.

Curiosity as to the three women must be satisfied with
even a less personal account and description. Hall in
his *Harpe's Head,* merely says of them: "Two of them
were coarse, sunburnt, and wretchedly attired and the
other somewhat more delicate and better dressed."
Major Stewart, who had them in personal charge for
some time and saved them from being lynched, says
that Susan, Big Harpe's first wife, was "rather tall,
rawboned, dark hair and eyes, and rather ugly," and
was about twenty-five years old. Betsey, the "supplementary" wife, he described as "rather handsome, light
hair and blue eyes and a perfect contrast with her sister." Sally, the wife of Little Harpe, he records was
"really pretty and delicate," about twenty years old, but
he gives no word of description. It is to be assumed
that when Major Stewart saw them they had been restored to cleanliness and decent attire. [12F]

One is tempted to pause and reflect upon these three
women, all young and once innocent as other girls, who
had so swiftly ridden the "hurricane of all horrors"
with two such men, had borne them children as nomads
do traveling the desert. One had had her child
snatched from her arm by Big Harpe and seen its brains
dashed out against a tree. Yet apparently not one of
the three attempted to escape her fate, although frequently separated and having opportunity to do so.
The normal man accustomed to normal women wonders
what they looked like and in what respect the horrors
of their experience had affected them. In the absence
of all description that curiosity cannot be gratified.

The two wives of Big Harpe, if they were really

sisters, and daughters of "old Mr. Roberts" mentioned but once in the pitiable record, had a brother of whom the Reverend Jacob Young, in his *Autobiography of a Pioneer*, has drawn a portrait scarcely less vivid than that which Hall drew of his ferocious brother-in-law, Big Harpe. It is a curious sensation to gaze even upon this brother of two such women. The wandering preacher tells how, in 1802, he entered a cabin in Russell County, Kentucky, where he had an appointment to conduct religious services. While singing to a small audience that came barefooted and bareheaded, a man of remarkable size, who was even more poorly clad than the others, walked into the room. Then follow the preacher's words:

"Had I not been used to seeing rough men on the frontier of Kentucky I should have been frightened. I looked him fully in the eyes and scanned him closely. His hair appeared as though it had never been combed, and made me think of old Nebuchadnezzar and his head 'like eagles' feathers.' He wore no hat; his collar was open and his breast bare; there was neither shoe nor moccasin on his feet. I finished my hymn, kneeled down and prayed and took my text to preach. The man looked for no seat, but stood erect gazing on the preacher. Before I was half through I saw the tears roll down his rough cheeks. I closed and told them that on that day four weeks I would be there again. I rode away, but could not forget the big man. I was sure he had distinguished himself some way, which made me anxious to find out his history. I soon found out that he was brother-in-law to the infamous robber Micajah Harpe, a character so well known in the history of Kentucky. No doubt they had been together in many a bloody affray. On my next round he joined the church, and soon afterward became a Christian. He could neither read nor write. I procured him a spelling book. His wife taught him to read, and he soon learned to write. On my fourth round I appointed him class leader. He trimmed off his hair, bought a new hat, clothed himself pretty well, and became a respectable man. I heard of him several years afterward, and he was still holding on his heavenly way." [19]

But what was the ultimate fate of the Harpe women, whether hard, commonplace or tinged with compensatory romance? Draper in one of his note books gives these last glimpses of them:

"Betsey Roberts [the supplementary wife] was married to John Hufstetter. They lived on Colonel Anthony Butler's plantation [near Russellville] as a tenant, and Mrs. Hufstetter became 'chicken raiser' to Mrs. Butler. Many years ago they moved to Red River, in Tennessee, and thence elsewhere, probably Duck River. . . Her child grew up and was known as Joe Roberts, and the last known of him he was enlisted in the army.

"Susan Harpe, as she was called, also lived in a cabin on Colonel Butler's plantation, six miles south of Russellville, and being industrious made a living chiefly by weaving. Her daughter, 'Lovey,' grew up to woman-

---

[19] It is probable that in the early days many an outlaw was "said to be" a kinsman of the Harpes. The case of Mrs. George Heatherly, referred to in the *History of Caldwell and Livingston Counties, Missouri,* 1886, is one instance discovered. The Heatherly Gang, according to this account, operated in the Upper Grand River country of northern Missouri in 1836 and a few years preceding. They robbed many white settlers and often stole horses from the Indians. "Old George Heatherly was regarded as a thief in Kentucky and Mrs. Heatherly (his wife) was a sister of the notorious Kentucky murderers and freebooters, Big and Little Harpe . . . Old Mrs. Heatherly is said to have been the leading spirit of the gang, prompting and planning many a dark deed, and often assisting in its execution." There is no proof advanced, however, that this woman was a sister of the Harpes.

hood – very pretty, common size, round features, hand-some form, black hair, rather dark skin and a dark and sometimes bad, devilish eye. Her temper was bad at school – always pouting and angry – no one associating with her. Yet it is thought had Lovey Harpe, with her beautiful form and naturally pretty appearance, been properly brought up, under the circumstances she would not only have been a belle, but really a fine woman. But, soured from neglect and obloquy, it is no wonder she threw herself away. And both herself and her mother were finally driven from the neighborhood for their bad character – went to Christian County on the waters of Pond River, where Colonel Butler had a mill – there old Susan died, and poor Lovey, destitute and forsaken, went down the Mississippi to Pearl, where, by this time, Colonel Butler had removed – and with his family went to Texas. . ."[20]

"When Sally Harpe was tried, her father, Parson Rice, was present, a man of fine, irreproachable char-acter, and took his prodigal daughter home near Knox-ville. It was said, and doubtless truly, that Sally was thought a fine girl until she married Wiley Harpe. In 1820 Major Stewart was at Ford's Ferry on the Ohio (a few miles above Cave-in-Rock) and saw Parson Rice,

---

[20] It is interesting to note that Susan Harpe, wife of Big Harpe, many years after his death tried to convey the impression that Little Harpe, not Big Harpe, was the greater villain. Draper, recording some statements made to him by George Herndon who lived near Russellville, says that Big Harpe's wife told Mrs. Herndon that "Big Harpe said to Little Harpe that he thought they had better quit killing people and go to some backwoods country, for if they did not, he feared they would be detected and killed. Whereupon, Little Harpe flew into a passion, cursed his brother for a coward, and said if he ever talked that way again he would shoot him." In order to defend him further, she declared that "Some days before Big Harpe's death he fancied the ground continually trembling beneath his feet." In this way she tried to show that Big Harpe actually did suffer great fear and remorse of con-science and insinuated that Little Harpe was beyond the reach of such feelings. [12F]

his family, Sally and her [second] husband moving to
Illinois. He did not recognize them, but thought he
knew them, particularly Sally, who eyed him closely
and, after a little, went to one side, sat down and with
her face in her hands, had a weeping spell, doubtlessly
recounting her Harpe adventures, prompted by the
presence of one of the few persons who had treated her
with civility and kindness in her wayward career. After
he left them, Major Stewart recollected hearing the old
gentleman called Rice and the identity flashed upon his
mind. Sally Harpe's daughter had then grown to
womanhood and was a fine looking young lady." [12F]
The girl referred to by Stewart as Sally Harpe's daughter was, in all probability, not a daughter of Harpe.

And so vanished from the scene, swallowed up in the
events of the rapidly developing country, all the prin-
cipals in this terrible epic of pioneer days.

But Little Harpe's career was not finished. He continued the life of an outlaw and after a few years, as we
shall see, received his deserts at the hands of frontier
justice.

Mason - Soldier, Pirate, Highwayman

In the pioneer history of the Ohio and Mississippi valley, Samuel Mason stands as one of the shrewdest and most resourceful of outlaws. The Harpes were more widely known and were more terrible characters; their notoriety was due to their great brutality. Mason robbed along the roads and rivers solely for the purpose of getting money; the Harpes killed men, women, and children simply to gratify a lust for cruelty. The two Harpes were the worst and most abnormal of their kind, while Mason was one of the shrewdest and therefore one of the most "successful" of bandits.

These three offer the criminologist a field for study of one of the phases of pioneer life – a life that has long been of interest from a historical standpoint. Samuel Mason will be cited in history and criminology as a striking example of a lawless man receiving his just reward. In the meantime, genealogists will probably continue to exclude this "black sheep" from his family. An attempt was made long ago to tear his "branch" from the family tree so that his name and those of his children would not mar the beauty of a stem honored with the names of famous men and women. It was without doubt the frontier life that Samuel Mason entered, and not the family from which he sprang that made him what he was.

Mason was a most striking and interesting figure. He had excellent birth; he had been a fighting soldier on the western frontier in the American Revolution, acquitting himself with courage. It is not clear how such a man in time of peace developed into a highwayman and after years of outlawry came to such a terrible death. A portion of his history is missing and probably will always remain a mystery, but his criminal exploits will lack the proper contrast unless his origin and his early services as a patriot are presented.

He was born in Virginia about the year 1750. Thirty-five years after his death Draper recorded in one of his note books that "Mason was connected by ties of consanguinity with the distinguished Mason family of Virginia, and grew up bad from his boyhood." [12H] This has been assumed in some quarters to connect him closely with George Mason, one of the signers of the Declaration of Independence, but there is no proof of it. He was a captain in the American Revolution. Two of his brothers, Thomas and Joseph, were among the useful, honest pioneers in the West. They started with George Rogers Clark on his expedition to Vincennes, but "when Clark reached Louisville he scattered some of his men among the neighboring stations of Beargrass [near Louisville]. . . Of this party were . . . Thomas and Joseph Mason, brothers of Captain Samuel Mason." [12C] Another brother, Isaac Mason, married Catherine Harrison, sister of Benjamin and William Harrison, and as early as 1770 moved from Virginia to Pennsylvania where he became one of the wealthiest and most influential citizens of Fayette County. [76] These three Mason brothers, like Samuel Mason himself, were, each in a different way, products of their environment and their times. Pioneer times, like most other periods, produced a variety of characters and Samuel Mason rapidly developed into a product quite distinct from most men of his day.

It is not often that the lineage of a highwayman can be traced back to a position so honorably distinguished as that of an officer in the American Revolution, yet such was Samuel Mason. After fighting for the freedom of his country he drifted down the Ohio to western Kentucky and the Cave-in-Rock country and there began a wild and free career unrestrained by either human or divine law.

Before taking up Mason's military history it may be well to recall a few facts pertaining to the American Revolution: The first battle in that war was fought at Lexington, Massachusetts, April 19, 1775; the surrender of Cornwallis took place at Yorktown, Virginia, October 19, 1781. While these and other battles between were being fought in the colonies along the Atlantic coast, the frontiersmen west of the Alleghenies were engaged in the same war with the British and their Indian allies. On June 24, 1778, George Rogers Clark left Louisville with about one hundred and fifty men and floated down the Ohio, passing Cave-in-Rock, and at Fort Massac, near the mouth of the Cumberland, began his march through Illinois; he captured Vincennes August 1 and thus saved the west for the American colonies. Between Vincennes and the Old Settlements lay a vast country held, after many hard fights, by the settlers who occupied it.

It was in this frontier defense of the upper Ohio River region that Samuel Mason took part. A complete history of his career as a Revolutionary soldier cannot, at this late day, be compiled; but, from the few statements regarding him that appear in printed history and from a few old documents still extant, sufficient evidence can be gathered to show that Mason was

not only a soldier, but that he took a very active part in
the struggle.

When and where he enlisted is not known. He probably did so in Ohio County, Virginia (now West Virginia). In the *List of the Revolutionary Soldiers of
Virginia,* issued in 1912 by the Virginia State Library,
his name appears as a captain of the Ohio County
Militia. The earliest record of his military life is one
showing that in May, 1777, he pursued some Indians
who had robbed and killed a family about fifty miles
below Pittsburgh. Mason started from one of the forts
above Fort Henry, now Wheeling, West Virginia, and
"at the head of ten militia gallantly followed the murderers." Although he killed only one Indian he
frightened and scattered the others so badly that the
expedition was regarded a success. "This brave young
man," says the report written a few days later, "will no
doubt meet a reward adequate to his merit." [131]

About two months later we find him at Grave Creek
Fort, twelve miles below Fort Henry. He started on
another Indian pursuit July 15. On the 17th he wrote
an account of this chase and forwarded it from Fort
Henry to General Edward Hand, whose headquarters
were at Pittsburgh. The original letter is in the Draper
Collection. More than a dozen documents signed by
Mason are preserved in the Draper Collection; all are
signed Samuel Mason, except one letter, dated August
12, 1777, which is signed Samuel Meason.[21] The letter
of July 17, 1777, like other documents just referred to,
shows that Samuel Mason was at least sufficiently
familiar with the "three Rs" to attempt to report in his
own handwriting some of the operations of the militia

---

[21] Family names were spelled indifferently in colonial and republican
times. In the fashion of English speech Meason was pronounced Mason.

under him. In it he describes how a number of men, led first by Lieutenant Samuel Tomlinson and then by himself, had gone in pursuit of Indians and returned after two futile scouting expeditions. The suggestion made in this letter that he and his company be transferred to Fort Henry was carried out. [12J]

Fort Henry was a comparatively old place when this letter was written. The three Zane brothers and a small party of emigrants had settled there in 1769. The fort was built in 1774 and was at first called Fincastle. In 1776 the name was changed to Fort Henry in honor of Patrick Henry, Governor of Virginia. Up to the latter part of August, 1777, it was not garrisoned by regular soldiery, but its defense, like that of some of the other frontier forts, was left to those who might seek shelter within its walls. By 1777 it had become a flourishing settlement with about thirty houses around it. Scouts were employed to watch for Indians and a warning from the men on guard made it possible for all the inhabitants of the place to retire to the fort on a moment's notice.

General Hand, expecting an Indian attack on the fort, ordered Captain Mason and his men to proceed there immediately and help defend it. Captain Mason arrived August 12, and sent a report the same day to General Hand that he would "urge and push" the work and expected to be fully prepared in a few days to resist the enemy. [12J] By the middle of the month there were less than one hundred militia stationed at the fort. After all preparations had been completed the men became impatient, for there was nothing to indicate the approach of Indians.

On the night of August 31 Captain Joseph Ogle, who with twelve other men had been watching the path

leading to Fort Henry, came in and reported that no
signs of the enemy had been discovered. That same
night, however, four hundred Indians, led by a few
whites, succeeded in placing themselves in ambush near
the fort. They lay in two lines concealed by a corn
field. Between these lines, along a road leading through
the corn field, were stationed six Indians who could be
seen by any one entering the road from the fort, and
who were placed in that position for the purpose of
decoying some of the whites within the line. The next
morning – September 1 – two men going out after some
horses walked along the road and passed some of the
concealed Indians, unaware of their presence. They
had proceeded but a few steps when, to their great surprise, they discovered the six Indians standing not far
ahead. The two men turned and ran for the fort. One
of them was shot, but the other was permitted to escape
that he might give the alarm.

Mason, hearing there were only six Indians near the
fort, proceeded with fourteen men to attack them. He
soon discovered that he had been trapped by several
hundred and that retreat was impossible. All of his
men were massacred. Captain Ogle and twelve scouts,
ignorant of the strength of the enemy, rushed from the
fort expecting to rescue their comrades, but most of
them were killed in the attempt. Of the twenty-eight
soldiers who took part in this bloody battle only five
escaped, among them Captains Mason and Ogle.
Mason, after being severely wounded, concealed himself behind a fallen tree until the Indians withdrew.
[140]

Mason's venture from the fort, it seems, was a daring
deed performed without consideration of its various
possible consequences. Dr. Joseph Doddridge, in **one**

of his manuscripts written about 1820, says that the garrison was too hasty in concluding that the warning sent by General Hand was a false alarm, and further comments that Mason's act was another instance of the "folly and rashness of our militia of early times." [130]

In the light of a knowledge of Mason's later life, this act of bravery, foolish though it may have been, suggests that he then may have had in him the daring necessary for an outlaw, whose self-assurance of success was too great to give the possibility of failure serious consideration.

Captain Mason remained at Fort Henry until the autumn of 1779. His presence there is shown by a score of receipts now in the Draper Collection, one of which reads: "Fort Henry 27th April 1778 Received fourteen Flints of Zephaniah Blackford for the Use of my Company Given my hand. Samuel Mason Capt." [12N] He was on Brodhead's Allegheny campaign in August and September, 1779. [130] After this expedition he retired from active service at Fort Henry and was succeeded by Captain Benjamin Briggs. Mason was, however, militia captain in Ohio County, Virginia, as late as May, 1781, as his attendance at the Courts Martial proves. [76]

Such is, in brief, a glimpse of Mason's military career as gleaned from scattered records. In 1845 Draper filed among his manuscripts a letter which states that "Capt. Mason resided where Daniel Steenrod's house now is, two miles east of Wheeling, and kept a tavern there in 1780." [12M] Another of his notes is to the effect that Mason lived on Wheeling Creek at the Narrows, and that in the spring of 1782 Indians stole some of his negroes. He and a man named Peter Stalnaker went in pursuit. The Indians, seeing the two men coming, concealed themselves behind a large rock a little above the Narrows and from that position they shot and killed Stalnaker. Mason fled and escaped unhurt. [12A]

Captain Samuel Murphy, whom Draper interviewed in 1846, gave the historian a number of facts pertaining to the siege of Wheeling and in his comments on Mason said: "Mason, many years before [i.e. before he was wounded at Wheeling] had stolen horses from Colonel Hite [in Frederick County, Virginia] was pursued and overtaken, and Mason wounded and the horses recovered. Mason's brother, Colonel Isaac Mason, was a very respectable man. When Mason subsequently turned robber, he would give the up-country people a sufficient sum of money to take them home." [12B] In *The Casket Magazine* of July, 1834, William Darby writes: "Well would it have been for Captain Samuel Mason if he had fallen with his gallant companions on the field at Wheeling." Mason evidently did not remain around Wheeling longer than a year or two after the close of the Revolution. Why or when he drifted to east Tennessee is not known.

What character of man Mason was when he reached the prime of life can be gathered from an unpublished paragraph written by Draper about 1840, after an interview with Colonel G. W. Sevier: "He first took possession, without leave or license, of some unoccupied cabins belonging to General John Sevier in Washington County, east Tennessee, with several worthless louts around him; one was named Barrow. Mason and his party were not known to work and were soon charged with stealing from negro cabins on Sabbath days when their occupants were attending church; and articles thus stolen were found in their possession. General

Sevier gave notice to Mason, who had by sufferance remained on his place, that he and his party must leave the country within a specified time. Knowing the character of General Sevier, that he was a man not to be trifled with, Mason and his friends wisely took themselves off." [12H]

We next hear of him in western Kentucky. It is likely that one of his purposes in going to that section of the country was to take up the land granted to him for services rendered as a Virginia soldier in the Revolution. When he moved west is not known. Finley says he settled on Red River, south of Russellville, in 1781. His youngest son, as we shall see later, was born in western Kentucky about 1787, showing that the Masons had arrived some time during or before that year. In 1790 a petition was circulated by the settlers in Lincoln County, Kentucky, who were living on the Virginia military grants between Green and Cumberland Rivers, asking the General Assembly of Virginia to establish a county south of Green River. As a result, two years later, all western Kentucky was formed into a new county called Logan. This petition was signed by one hundred and fifteen men, among them Samuel Mason and one named Thomas Mason, who may have been the eldest son of, or one of the brothers of, Captain Samuel Mason. Inasmuch as its signers, as far as is known, were "respectable citizens," it is likely that Mason was considered such when he signed, either because he tried to be one or because he succeeded in passing as such.

The petition recites: "That your Petitioners find themselves sensibly aggrieved by their distance from Courts of Justice, it being near two hundred miles from this settlement to Lincoln Court House, by which, when

business renders our attendance indispensably necessary, we are frequently exposed to much danger in
traveling through an uninhabited country, being subject
to fines and other inconveniences, when from high waters, enemies near our frontiers, or other causes, it is
impossible to attend." [106] Mason possibly did not
then dream that in the near future he himself would
become one of the worst "enemies near our frontiers"
and be regarded as one of the great dangers to which
men were exposed "in traveling through an uninhabited
country."

Mason's domestic life in the wilderness of the lower
Ohio evidently was, in the beginning, up to the standard
of the average early settler. But in the wild woods, far
away from companionship and influence of law-abiding
citizens, the best of men were subject to deterioration.
Men of education, illiterates, and all other pioneers
were alike exposed to this strong influence of frontier
life. Many men who, by their inborn nature or by their
own choice disregarded law and order, necessarily became, by one route or another, outcasts. Mason fell and
fell fast, and became not only an outcast, but a notorious
outlaw. The only argument that can be presented in
his defense is that he was, to some extent, a peculiar
product of his times – only more "highly developed"
than contemporaneous outlaws who were products of
the same influences and environment. It should be
added in justice to Mason that, unlike the Harpes, he
was out for booty and that he personally never shed
blood unless it became absolutely necessary for his own
safety.

To what extent Mason had fallen by 1794 can be
gathered from an entry quoted from Benjamin Van
Cleve's diary, made in July of that year on his return

to Cincinnati from Fort Massac. Van Cleve, with
Major Thomas Doyle and a number of other men, left
Fort Washington, now Cincinnati, on March 16, 1794,
with ten boats to repair Fort Massac and to supply the
place with provisions. They arrived at the fort June
12, and three weeks later some of the men, including
Van Cleve, started on their return up the river. On
July 8 they landed at Red Banks, now Henderson.
Here are the entries taken from *The American Pioneer,*
published in 1843:

"July 8. [1794] Came to Red Banks.

"July 9. The weather unpleasant, and the company
of soldiers disagreeable. We [four men] determined
to quit the boat and travel the residue of the way by
land. Made preparations to set off in the morning.
This place is a refuge, not for the oppressed, but for all
the horse thieves, rogues, and outlaws that have been
able to effect their escape from justice in the neighboring states. Neither law nor gospel has been able to
reach here as yet. A commission of the peace had been
sent by Kentucky to one Mason; and an effort had been
made by the south-west territory (Tennessee) to introduce law as it was unknown as yet to which it belonged;
but the inhabitants drove the persons away and insisted
on doing without. I inquired how they managed to
marry, and was told that the parties agreed to take each
other for husband and wife before their friends. I was
shown two cabins, with about the width of a street between them, where two men a short time ago had exchanged wives. An infair was given today by Mason
to a fellow named Kuykendall who had run away from
Carolina on account of crimes, and had run off with
Mason's daughter to Diamond Island station, a few
weeks ago. The father had forbid him the house and

threatened to take his life, but had become reconciled, and had sent for them to come home. The parents and friends were highly diverted at the recital of the young couple's ingenuity in the courtship, and laughed heartily when the woman told it. She said she had come down stairs after all the family had retired, having her petticoat around her shoulders, and returned with him through her parents' room, with the petticoat around both; and in the morning she brought him down in the same manner before daylight. This Kuykendall, I was told, always carried in his waistcoat pockets 'devil's claws,' instruments, or rather weapons, that he could slip his fingers in, and with which he could take off the whole side of a man's face at one claw. We left them holding their frolic.

"I afterwards heard that Kuykendall was killed by some of the party at the close of the ball.

"July 10. Left Red Banks."

Ministers and certain others, in pioneer days as at present were licensed to solemnize marriages according to the laws established by the state. But a compliance with the church law was, in the eyes of the Masons, a useless form. They disregarded all laws, as it suited them. In that section of Kentucky the execution of the laws was in the hands of Captain John Dunn, a Revolutionary soldier who was one of the first settlers at Henderson and who, in 1792, was appointed its first constable. Starling in his *History of Henderson County, Kentucky,* says that Captain Dunn was "the only recognized officer of the law in all this territory" up to September, 1796, when he was authorized to "raise three men to act as patrol at the Red Banks." This increase in patrol became necessary not only because the number of settlers was gradually growing larger, but also because the wild conduct of such men as Mason made it imperative.

That the presence or absence of the patrol was a matter of equal indifference to the Masons is shown by some notes Draper received from Mrs. William Anthony, daughter of Captain John Dunn. [12K] In her letter she writes that Mason and his family were among the original settlers of Henderson County and that with Samuel Mason were "a brother-in-law named Duff, and perhaps a son-in-law." Whether or not this Duff to whom she so briefly refers was the counterfeiter Duff is not known. She states that about 1795 Samuel Mason requested Captain Dunn to sign "some instruments of writing." Captain Dunn declined to sign the paper, saying he would have nothing to do with any such "rascal" as he was. This refusal aroused Mason and a few days later he and four of his men "fell upon Captain Dunn in Henderson, drew their concealed weapons and beat him entirely senseless and until they thought he was certainly dead, and then threw his body over a fence close by. But Captain Dunn unexpectedly recovered." Their hatred of Dunn then grew greater than ever.

Shortly after Captain Dunn experienced this narrow escape from death Hugh Knox, afterwards Judge Knox, of Henderson, "incurring the displeasure of the Masons, was badly beaten by them. Others fared no better." One day the Masons stole a negro woman and her two children belonging to Knox and took them to "their then quarters at the mouth of Highland Creek." Knox raised a party, including Captain Dunn, and managed to regain the three negroes. Dunn's participation in this rescue aroused the Masons against him to an even greater degree. One day Thomas Mason, the oldest son of Samuel Mason, came to Red Banks with his rifle and threatened to kill Dunn. Mrs. Dunn, hearing of the threat, begged Thomas Durbin, Dunn's cousin, who had just arrived with a flatboat going down the river, to try to pacify young Mason and take the gun from him. Durbin being a stranger, it was thought he would succeed. But Durbin had little more than begun talking to Thomas Mason and made known the object of his interview, when Mason, without any comment, shot him dead, and fled.

Mrs. Anthony in the same letter to Draper writes: "Late in December, 1797, early on a cold morning, Captain Dunn, accompanied by Thomas Smith, started on horseback for Knob Lick, carrying out corn meal and intending to bring back salt. As they were coming near the ford on Canoe Creek, three miles below Henderson, Captain Dunn remarked that many a time, in former years, he dreaded the crossing of that creek on account of the Masons, as it was so well fitted to waylay the unwary, but now that the Masons had gone so far below [to Cave-in-Rock] he no longer apprehended danger from them. The words were scarcely uttered – they were about midway the small stream – when the crack of a rifle told too plainly that villainy yet lurked there. Captain Dunn fell from his horse into the partly frozen stream. Thomas Smith got but a glimpse of the person who did the deed; he could not, in the confusion of the moment, define his features. The wretch darted off and Smith conveyed Dunn home, where he died in a few hours. When asked if he knew the person who shot him he answered that 'it was that bad man.' This allusion was probably to Henry Havard, a young man who was a friend and supposed accomplice of the Masons." Thus ended the life of the first constable of Red Banks, and with this killing the work of the Masons in Henderson County ended. And with his departure from there, Mason's life went from bad to worse.[22]

About the time Mason and his gang left Henderson County there appeared in Red Banks and on Diamond Island a man named May. Mrs. Anthony calls him Isaac May, some refer to the same man as Samuel May, but he is best known as James May. He later played a very important part in Mason's history. Writing of this outlaw's early career, Mrs. Anthony says: "May loitered about Henderson and had a lame sister with him – at least she passed as such and thereby excited some remarks. At length May stole some horses and he and his sister made off and were pursued and overtaken at Vincennes. May was brought back to Henderson, and the very first night after they got him there he managed to break away and make his escape, which he effected by making an extraordinary leap. He joined Mason's gang . . ." He joined Mason in the South and there performed another extraordinary act of which, as is shown later, Mrs. Anthony has more or less to say.

---

[22] In her account to Draper Mrs. Anthony states that in addition to Henry Havard, Samuel Mason had, besides his own family, at least two other accomplices while living near Henderson: Nicholas Welsh and a man named Hewitt. Henry Havard, after the assassination of Captain John Dunn, fled to his father's home on Red River, Tennessee. The regulators there, upon hearing that he had been employed by Mason to kill Dunn, "raised and went to old Havard's, found Henry hid between two feather beds and shot through the beds. They made the old man pull out the body of his son and when they found his brains were oozing out they knew he was quite dead." Hewitt was captured on the Kentucky shore opposite Diamond Island, by regulators who were "strongly inclined to kill him, but finally refrained, but made him break his gun." Nicholas Welsh, who ran the tavern in which Mason and his men made their headquarters when in Red Banks, disappeared immediately after Captain John Dunn was shot, and was never again heard of.

During the greater part of 1797 the Masons were
established at Cave-in-Rock. Their headquarters while
in and near Henderson seems to have been changed
from time to time. For a while they had a camp at the
mouth of Highland Creek, as stated by Mrs. Anthony,
but most of their time previous to 1797 was spent not
far from what now is the town of Hitesville, in Union
County, Kentucky. A small stream, tributary to Highland Creek, on or near which the Masons lived, still
bears the name of Mason's Creek. About twenty miles
south of this old camp is "Harpe's Head," where two
years later the head of Big Harpe was placed on the
end of a pole. About ten miles northeast of the Mason
Creek country is Diamond Island, where many early
pioneers going down the Ohio in flatboats became the
victims of the Masons.

Fortesque Cuming stopped at Diamond Island May
16, 1808, about ten years after Mason had left it. Commenting on the place, Cuming says, in his *Tour to the
Western Country*: "Nothing can be more beautifully
situated than this fine island . . . It is owned by a Mr.
Alvis, a Scotchman, of great property in South Carolina, who bought it about two years ago [1806] of one
Wells, the original locator. Alvis has a negro quarter,
and near one hundred and fifty acres of land cleared on
the Kentucky shore opposite the Island. This used to
be the principal haunt of banditti, from twenty to thirty
in number, amongst which the names of Harper [sic]
five Masons, and Corkendale [Kuykendall] were most
conspicuous. They attacked and plundered the passing
boats, and frequently murdered the crews and passengers. At length the government of Kentucky sent a
detachment of militia against them. They were surprised, and Harper, one of the Masons, and three or

four more were shot, one in the arms of his wife, who escaped unhurt though her husband received eleven balls. The rest dispersed and again recruiting, became, under Mason, the father, the terror of the road through the wilderness between Nashville in Tennessee and the Mississippi Territory."

Cuming's account is fairly accurate, but if by "Harper" he refers to Big Harpe or Little Harpe, he is mistaken. The "detachment of militia" that ran out this band of Diamond Island outlaws could more properly be called a "regiment" of local regulators, for there is nothing on record to show that any state militia was ever sent to the island. In pioneer days regulators, as a rule, relied upon their own "military strength" and exercised it without formal orders from "official headquarters."

Diamond Island is about fourteen miles below Henderson. It is some three miles long and a half-mile wide, and more or less diamond shaped. In Mason's day it was covered with gigantic trees and luxurious vines and presented so wonderful a scene that it attracted early travelers who passed it. In pioneer days it was, according to comments written by many travelers, the most beautiful island in the Ohio. Zadok Cramer in *The Navigator,* published in 1806, says it is a "large and noble looking island." J. Addison Richards in his *Romance of American Landscape* refers to it as "the crown-jewel in this cluster of the Ohio brilliants." Thomas Ashe, whose trip down the Ohio was "performed in 1806," goes so far as to say it is "by far the finest in the river, and perhaps the most beautiful in the world!" About a generation after Mason and other outlaws abandoned it as a trap for victims, Edmund Flagg visited the Island and found that "it is said to be haunted." In 1917 it was, according to one man's idea,

"sure ha'nted." This once luxuriant forest island is
now a cornfield, celebrated for its wonderfully fertile
soil and for its "Diamond Island Canned Corn." All
that is left of its former splendor is its size. Its heavy
fringe of cottonwood and willow still attracts attention
and helps repicture the Island as it was in the olden
days. The gnarled roots along the bank and the drift-
wood piled here and there on the beach seem to hold
dumb the secrets of Mason and his men and the tragedies enacted there more than a century ago.

Robbery and its booty were uppermost in Mason's
mind and were the object of his every act. Nevertheless, in selecting Cave-in-Rock, seventy miles down the
Ohio River, as his next headquarters he chanced to
choose a place, judging from the present appearance of
the landscape, that was far more picturesque than Diamond Island. All the primeval beauty of the Island
has long ago disappeared, and some of the wild charm
of Cave-in-Rock and its surroundings has vanished
with the original forest. Flatboat pirates have come and
gone; the Ohio still flows on as majestically and as mys-
teriously as ever, but all its flood of waters will never
wash away the legends of tragedies connected with the
two places.

Mason made Cave-in-Rock his headquarters during
the greater part of 1797. River pirates were numerous
in the old flatboat days – especially before 1811 when
the first steamboat was run from Pittsburgh to New
Orleans. Travelers were warned by those who had
made trips down the river and knew the usual methods
followed by river pirates; but with all their intended
precautions and in spite of all the instructions received
many of the inexperienced became easy prey for the
robbers. The Cave had often been used by travelers as

a temporary stopping place and had become a well known shelter. But the fact that it had also served as a temporary abode for outlaws seems not to have been widely circulated before this time. Mason recognized in it a hiding place that offered him the shelter of a good house and also one that was very convenient and reasonably safe. Besides, it was peculiarly fitted for his purpose, for its partially concealed entrance commanded a wide view both up and down the river.

He also recognized the necessity of enticing his intended victims into the Cave in an innocent manner or by some unusual method. Mason's reputation as an outlaw was beginning to spread. He overcame the obstacle of publicity by changing his name to "Wilson." In order to lull any suspicion he concluded to convert the Cave into an inn and he and his family therefore fitted it up for the purpose of accommodating guests. On the river bank where it could be seen by those going down the stream he raised a large sign: "Wilson's Liquor Vault and House for Entertainment." And thus it came about that Cave-in-the-Rock was transformed into Cave-Inn-Rock and finally to Cave-in-Rock.

Daniel Blowe, in 1820, briefly recorded that "Mason's gang of robbers made Cave-in-Rock their principal rendezvous in 1797, where they frequently plundered or murdered the crews of boats descending the Ohio." Most historians who touched on the subject after Blowe's time publish, with equal brevity, the same statement. Henry Howe, in his *Historical Collections of the Great West,* published in 1852, says: "Sometimes Mason plundered the descending boats but more frequently preferred to wait and plunder the owners of their money as they returned." Compara-

tively few men returned north by river and it is therefore likely that not many single boats or small flotillas
going south floated by unmolested. In this connection
Judge James Hall comments that the boats that were
permitted to pass the Cave and Hurricane Island, six
miles below, were pointed out by Mason, who on such
occasions would jokingly remark: "These people are
taking produce to market for me." [61]

Mason discovered that many of his men who went
south with captured boats never returned to report, and
he realized that sooner or later an attempt would be
made to capture him if he continued his work at the
Cave. He therefore decided to go south. For these
and probably other reasons he, as stated by Monette,
"deserted the Cave in the Rock on the Ohio and began
to infest the great Natchez Trace where the rich proceeds of the river trade were the tempting prize."

By what means and under what circumstances Mason
and his family moved south is not known. After leaving Henderson County he remained longer at Cave-in-
Rock than at any other one place. His name is insepar-
ably associated with Cave-in-Rock, both in history and
tradition, but neither history nor tradition has preserved
an account giving the details of any definite robbery
committed by him while there. It is likely that he left
the Cave in ample time to avoid being driven out by
a body of men who had been organized by the merchants of Pittsburgh for the purpose of trying to exterminate him and all other river pirates. No record
of Mason's whereabouts during 1798 and 1799 can now
be found. During these two years many robberies occurred along the Mississippi River and along various
trails on the American side of the river from Kentucky
to New Orleans, but the guilty men were seldom cap-

tured. A number of these robberies, on both river and land, were doubtless perpetrated by Mason under one or more assumed names.

According to Audubon, the ornithologist, the Masons made their headquarters for a while on Wolf Island, in the Mississippi, twenty-five miles below the mouth of the Ohio. About 1815, or a number of years after Mason's career was closed, Audubon gathered the following about the famous outlaw's stay on this island:

"The name of Mason is still familiar to many of the navigators of the Lower Ohio and Mississippi. By dint of industry in bad deeds, he became a notorious horse-stealer, formed a line of worthless associates from the eastern part of Virginia (a state greatly celebrated for its fine breed of horses) to New Orleans, and had a settlement on Wolf Island, not far from the confluence of the Ohio and Mississippi, from which he issued to stop the flatboats, and rifle them of such provisions and other articles as he and his party needed. His depredations became the talk of the whole western country; and to pass Wolf Island was not less to be dreaded than to anchor under the walls of Algiers. The horses, the negroes, and the cargoes, his gang carried off and sold."

In March, 1800, Mason appeared in New Madrid, Missouri, then Spanish territory, and applied for a passport. This was issued to him, as appears later, on the recommendation of a man whom he had met casually at Red Banks (Henderson, Kentucky) and who was unaware of the real character of the person he introduced. The passport not only permitted Mason to settle on Spanish territory with the privilege of purchasing land, but it also served as a document designating him as a desirable citizen. When he applied for this permit, he may have resolved to open up a farm

and lead a respectable life. If so, the resolution to reform was of short duration, for he made no attempt to
select a site for a permanent home. In the meantime he
carefully preserved the passport, knowing it might some
day serve, in its way, as a letter of recommendation. It
would also serve as evidence that he had taken an initial
step toward becoming a Spanish subject. Should he
confine his land operations to the American side, and
his river piracy to the waters of the Mississippi, and
make none but American citizens his victims, the
chances were he might some day find a safe and convenient retreat in the Spanish domain west of the river.

During 1800 and the three years that followed, Mason moved over the country with remarkable activity.
A report of a robbery committed by him on the Natchez
Trace, says Monette, was soon followed by an account
of another perpetrated on the Mississippi many miles
away, and vice versa. Men going down the Mississippi,
as those going down the Ohio, encountered many
troubles incidental to the running of boats. They were
always exposed to river pirates of whom Mason was
one. Among other hardships to which they were sub-
jected was the unrestrained authority of the Spanish,
who were then in possession of the land west of the Mississippi and who practically controlled the navigation
of that river.

Mason On the Natchez Trace

Much has been written about the old Natchez Trace, the narrow Indian trail leading from Natchez, Mississippi, to Nashville, Tennessee, at which place travelers took other trails leading to Illinois, Kentucky, and Virginia. In the flatboat days many merchants who had disposed of the goods they brought down the Ohio and Mississippi returned north with the proceeds of their sales by this overland route; others took the ocean route by way of Philadelphia, back to their homes. Many of these pioneer merchants refer to their experience in this wilderness and many early western travelers who rode over this old trail describe it in their books. We shall, however, confine our glimpse of the early days on this historic trace to the facts concerning Mason.

It is more than likely that Mason had committed a number of crimes along the Natchez Trace before he appeared in New Madrid in March, 1800. Many pioneers traveling over this route encountered highwaymen, but none of them succeeded in identifying the men by whom they had been robbed. The first record of a case with which Mason is definitely connected is that of a party of boatmen riding from Natchez to their homes in Kentucky. An account of this incident is told in *Old Times in Tennessee,* by Josephus C. Guild, who received his information from John L. Swaney. Swaney told Guild that more than fifty years before, while carrying the mail over the old Natchez Trace, he frequently met Samuel Mason and talked with him.

Swaney began carrying the mail over this old Indian trail about 1796 and was familiar with the route before Mason appeared on the scene. The distance from Nashville to Natchez he estimates at about five hundred and fifty miles. It was, in his mail-carrying days, a mere bridle path winding through an almost endless wilderness. He rode it for eight years, making a round trip every three weeks. Traveling at the rate of about fifty-five miles a day permitted him a day's rest at either end of his route. He frequently met Indians along the Trace. At Colbert's Ferry, on the Tennessee River, he always found the Indian ferrymen "contrary," for they would not cross the river for him if he got to the landing after bed time. At the Chickasaw Agency, about half-way between the two places, he changed horses. The only white men he saw were the few settlers, scattered forty or more miles apart, the occasional traveler returning north and, now and then, Samuel Mason and some of his band. Swaney rode a good horse and carried with him, besides the mail (consisting of a few letters, newspapers, and government dispatches) a bushel of corn for his horse, provisions and a blanket for himself, a pistol, a tin trumpet, and a piece of flint and steel.

Merchants and boatmen brought their provisions and other necessities on pack-horses or pack-mules. It was from these that Mason captured much of the food and most of the clothing he and his people required. These travelers, as a rule, sewed their money in rawhides and threw the hides in the packs with supplies. At night, before making a fire, they hid their valuables in the bushes some distance from the camp in the event of a surprise at night by robbers. It was in this wilderness that Mason looked for and found many of his victims. He and his band were the terror of all who traveled through the Indian nation, except Swaney.

Mason frequently sought interviews with Swaney, with whom he had many friendly chats. The outlaw often asked what was said about him by the public. He told Swaney that no mail-carrier need fear being molested by him and his men, for mail was of no value to them, and that he "did not desire to kill any man, for money was all he was after and if he could not get it without taking life, he certainly would shed no blood."

"Among Mason's first robberies," continues the historian who interviewed the mail-carrier, "was that of a party of Kentucky boatmen returning home from Natchez. They had camped at what was called Gum Springs, in the Choctaw Nation. They ate supper, and, as a matter of precaution, were putting out pickets before retiring for the night. In going to their positions one of the pickets stepped on one of Mason's men, who were hidden in the grass awaiting an opportunity to pounce upon the boatmen. The robber thus carelessly trod on jumped up, gave a yell, and fired off a gun, calling upon his comrades to shoot and kill every boatman. This was so unexpected to the Kentuckians that they became panic stricken and ran off in the wildest confusion, leaving everything, some even their wearing apparel. Mason and his men went to the camp and carried away everything.

"The next morning, just at daylight, Mr. Swaney came along, and seeing the camp fires burning, rode out, but could find no one. He was going toward Natchez, and having met no party that morning, he instinctively knew that something was wrong, and began to blow his bugle. The boatmen recognized the familiar sound and commenced coming to Mr. Swaney, one and two at a time. He asserted that they were the worst scared, worst looking set of men he ever saw, some of them having but little clothing on, and one big fellow had only a shirt. They immediately held a sort of council of war, and it was unanimously agreed to follow the robbers and recapture their property. It was an easy matter to follow their trail through the cane and grass. Their plan was, as they had no arms, to provide themselves with sticks and knives, and should they overtake Mason and his men, attack them by a vigorous charge, knocking them down right and left with their shillelahs, and if those in front fell at the fire of the robbers, those in the rear were to rush upon, overpower and capture the robbers and recover their property.

"They started in pursuit of the robbers under the lead of the big Kentuckian. They had gone about a mile when they began to find articles of clothing which had been thrown away by the robbers. The big Kentuckian found his pants, in the waistband of which he had sewed four gold doubloons and, to his great joy, the robbers had not found them. After this it was noticed that the big Kentuckian's valor began to fail him, and soon he was found in the rear. The pursuit was kept up about two miles further, when they were suddenly hailed by Mason and his men, who were hid behind trees, with their guns presented, and who ordered them to go back or they would kill the last one of them. This caused a greater stampede than that of the night before, and the big Kentuckian out distanced the whole party in the race back to camp. They abused the big Kentuckian at a round rate for his want of courage, but he only laughed at them, saying he had everything to run for. But, to his credit be it said, he spent his last dollar in procuring supplies for his comrades."

Mason was an active man and this comparatively insignificant robbery was doubtless preceded and followed by others of greater consequence of which, however, no written record or oral tradition now exists. Then occurred the Baker robbery on the old Natchez Trace — a robbery that became widely known through the current newspapers and soon convinced the public that Mason was an outlaw of dangerous character, working over a large territory.

Colonel Joshua Baker, the victim of this famous robbery, was a merchant living in central Kentucky. In his day he made a number of trips south, going down in flatboats and returning by way of the old Natchez Trace. Colonel Baker had the misfortune to come in contact with Mason at least once on land and once on water, and, as is later shown, played an important part in the activities that resulted in ending Mason's career.

In the spring or summer of 1801, Colonel Baker took several flatboats filled with produce and horses to New Orleans. After disposing of his cargo, he set out on his return home, accompanied by four men, each of whom rode a horse. Besides the five riding horses there were five pack-mules in the cavalcade loaded down with provisions, and, among other things, the proceeds of the sales made in New Orleans. Colonel Baker and his men experienced no unusual trouble until they reached the ford across what was then called Twelve Mile Creek, but since known as Baker's Creek. The place is in Hindes County, Mississippi, about twenty miles west of Jackson and near where the Battle of Baker's Creek was fought on January 16, 1863. There, August 14, 1801, the Baker party was surprised by

Samuel Mason and three of his men. A paragraph relative to the robbery that followed was published in *The Kentucky Gazette,* September 14, 1801. It is the earliest printed record so far found of Mason's activities on the Natchez Trace:

"We are informed that on the 14th of August, about sixty miles on this side of the Big Biopiere [Bayou Pierre] River, Colonel Joshua Baker, a Mr. William Baker and a Mr. Rogers of Natchez, were robbed of their horses, traveling utensils, and about two thousand three hundred dollars cash. It seems the company had halted in the morning at a small, clear stream of water in order to wash. As soon as they had dismounted and gone to the water four men appeared, blacked, between them and their horses and demanded the surrender of their money and property, which they were obliged to comply with. Mr. W. Baker was more fortunate than his companions. A pack-horse, on which was a considerable sum of money, being frightened at the appearance of the robbers, ran away, and they being in haste to escape could not pursue. Mr. W. Baker recovered his horse [pack-mule] and money. He, however, lost his riding horse, etc. Colonel Baker and Mr. Rogers came to the first settlement, where they procured assistance and immediately went in pursuit of the villains. It is to be hoped they will be apprehended. One of them who was described by Colonel Baker, formerly resided at Red Banks. A brother of Colonel Baker, our informant, obtained this information from Mr. W. Baker, who lodged at his house [in Lexington, Kentucky] on Thursday night last."

John L. Swaney, the mail-carrier, whose reminiscences have been drawn upon, gives some different details of this incident. The banks at Baker's Creek are high and steep and at this crossing there was then nothing more than a deep-cut bridle path on either bank leading into or out of the stream. The Baker party, after more or less difficulty, rode down to the creek. While their horses and mules were drinking, says Swaney, Mason and his men jumped up from where they had concealed themselves. The victims, realizing they had been trapped and were at the mercy of the outlaws, surrendered. Mason made them drive the pack-mules over to his side of the creek, where two of his men took charge of them but permitted Baker and his companions to keep their riding horses and side arms. Colonel Baker then rode to Grindstone Ford, a distance of about forty miles, and there raised a company to pursue the outlaws.

They followed the trail of the robbers to Pearl River, near Jackson, Mississippi, and there learned that Mason had crossed the stream only a few hours before. In the pursuing party was a man named Brokus, a quadroon Indian. Brokus, according to Swaney, stripped and swam down the river to ascertain, if possible, what route Mason's men had taken. While he was climbing up the bank one of the robbers punched him in the breast with a gun. Brokus thought he was shot and, losing his grip on the sapling to which he was holding, fell back into the river. After considerable swimming and diving he reached the opposite shore. Swaney ends his story of this chase by saying: "Mason then made his appearance and notified Colonel Baker that he would never recover his money. This seemed to be accepted as the final arbitrament, for the pursuit of the robbers was abandoned."

A contributor to *The Natchez Galaxy* in 1829, in a short article entitled "The Robber of the Wilderness,"

gives another account of how Mason made his appearance on the banks of Pearl River and under what circumstances Colonel Baker abandoned the chase. This
Natchez writer has it that when Colonel Baker reached
the river the pursuers took the saddles off their horses
and made preparations to rest for a few hours before
resuming the chase. The tracks made by Mason's
horses showed that his party was much smaller than
theirs. The pursuers therefore anticipated nothing
other than an unconditional surrender. They did not
realize how quickly Mason could turn to his advantage
any condition that presented itself. How the outlaw
mastered the present situation is best told by the contributor to *The Natchez Galaxy*:

"Those preliminaries being disposed of, two of the
party strolled to the bank of the river and, tempted by
the coolness and beauty of the stream, went in to bathe.
In the course of their gambol they crossed to the opposite shore, where they encountered an individual
whose society, under the present circumstances, afforded them very little satisfaction.

"Mason, aware that he was pursued and having ascertained the superior force of his pursuers, determined
to effect by stratagem what he could not hope to do by
open contest. The path into the forest was narrow
here and much beset with undergrowth; and he placed
his men in ambush so that by a sudden onset the party
of Colonel Baker on entering the woods would be
thrown into confusion, and thus be easily despatched or
routed. Chance, however, produced a success more
complete than any he could have anticipated. No
sooner had the two naked and unarmed men reached
the eastern shore of the Pearl, than Mason rushed upon
them before they could collect their thoughts or com-

prehend their danger. He was a hale, athletic figure, and roughly clad in the leather shirt and leggins, common to the Indians and hunters of the frontier.

" 'I am glad to see you, gentlemen,' said he sarcastically, 'and though our meeting did not promise to be quite so friendly, I am just as well satisfied; my arms and ammunition will cost less than I expected.'

"His prisoners were thunderstruck and totally incapable of reply. Having placed a guard over them, Mason walked deliberately down to the shore and hailed the party on the opposite bank, who had witnessed the scene, that has been detailed, in amazement and apprehension. As he approached they instinctively seized their arms.

" 'If you approach one step or raise a rifle,' cried the robber, 'you may bid your friends farewell. There is no hope for them but in your obedience. I want nothing but security against danger to myself and party and this I mean to have. Stack your arms and deposit your ammunition on the beach near the water. I will send for them. Any violence to my messenger or the least hesitation to perform my orders will prove certain and sudden death to your companions. Your compliance will insure their release, and I pledge my honor as a man to take no other advantage of my victory.'

"There was no alternative. The arms and ammunition were deposited as Mason directed. Two of the band were despatched for them, while a rifle was held to the head of each prisoner. No resistance was attempted, however, by Colonel Baker or his party, and the arms were brought across. The banditti were soon in readiness for a march; the prisoners were dismissed with a good humored farewell; and the dreaded Mason, true to his word, was soon lost in the depths of

the wilderness. It is hardly necessary to say that the pursuers, disarmed, discomfitted, and a little chapfallen made the best of their way back to 'the settlement'."
[12L]

Shortly after the Baker robbery John Mason, a son of Samuel Mason, was lodged in the Natchez jail charged with taking part in the affair. It is more than likely that John Mason happened to be in town when he was accused and arrested than that an officer brought him in from the country. At any rate, he was tried, convicted, and punished by whipping. It is possible that he was innocent of the specific crime for which he was punished, for he may not have been present when the Mason band robbed Colonel Baker. About seventy years later George Wiley, who was a mere lad at the time this whipping occurred, wrote a sketch on "Natchez in the Olden Times." In it he says:

"The old jail, too, was the scene of the first public disgrace to the noted Mason, who afterwards, with his robber band, became the terror of travelers from the Ohio River to New Orleans. Mason and his son were brought to Natchez and lodged in jail, charged with the robbery of a man named Baker, at a place now in Hindes County where the road crosses a creek still known as Baker's Creek. They were defended at their trial by a distinguished lawyer named Wallace. He, after the manner so common with lawyers, went to work to get up a public feeling in favor of his clients, and succeeded so well that, although the Masons were convicted, the general sentiment was that they were innocently punished. They were both convicted and sentenced to receive the punishment of thirty-nine lashes and exposure in the pillory. I witnessed the flogging and shall never forget their cries of 'innocent' at every blow of the cowhide which tore the flesh from their quivering limbs, and until the last lash was given they shrieked the same despairing cry of 'innocent,' 'innocent.' After they were released the elder Mason said to the surrounding crowd, 'You have witnessed our punishment for a crime we never committed; some of you may see me punished again but it shall be for something worthy of punishment.' He and his son then shaved their heads, and stripping themselves naked, mounted their horses and yelling like Indians, rode through and out of the town." [26]

This account appears correct in all its details except two. Samuel Mason's son, John, was the only member of the Mason family arrested and whipped. If, as stated by Wiley, two men were punished on this occasion, the other may have been a member of Samuel Mason's gang. The other error is in the statement that the two prisoners were released. It is shown later that after they were whipped they escaped from jail by the aid of some of Mason's men.

William Darby, another citizen of Natchez, in an account published in *The Casket Magazine,* in 1834, tells what occurred shortly after John Mason was whipped: "One of the jury, whose name I omit," writes Darby, "made himself very conspicuous at the trial of John Mason, wishing before the whole court and audience, that 'the rascal might be hung.'" By some means Samuel Mason received a report of the juryman's statement. A few weeks later this same juror, returning to Natchez from one of the settlements, had occasion to ride over a bridle path through a heavy canebreak. He was suddenly confronted by Samuel Mason who stepped out of the cane, armed with a tomahawk and rifle, and, raising the rifle, pointed it at the surprised rider, who immediately threw up his hands. Mason very calmly informed the juror that he had waited for him for two days "to blow your brains out."

The frightened man begged to be spared for the sake of his wife and children. Mason replied that he, too, had children and loved them as much as any other father loved his own, and that this was his first chance to extend to him the same mercy he had shown toward his son John. Then, as if to further prepare the captive for the worst, Mason asked: "Did John Mason ever do you any harm? Did I myself ever do you any injury? Did you ever hear of me committing murder, or suffering murder to be committed?" Mason shrewdly omitted the words, "except when necessary." The juror answered: "Never in my life." "Thank God, I have never shed blood," declared Mason with great earnestness, "but now, come down off your horse, Sir. If you have anything to say to your Maker, I'll give you five minutes to say it."

"The terrified man," continues Darby, "sank off the horse and fell on his knees, uttering a fervent prayer, addressed rather to the man who stood beside him with his gun cocked. At length, his words failed him and he burst into a violent shower of tears. The man himself, who afterward related the whole circumstance, and could scarce ever do so without tears at the remembrance, said he every moment expected death; but Mason, regarding him with a bitter smile, swore his life was not worth taking, wheeled around and in an instant disappeared amongst the cane."

Colonel Baker returned to Kentucky and reports of the daring robbery on the Natchez Trace and of his unsuccessful attempt to capture Samuel Mason were circulated throughout the country. Monette says that

about the time the Baker robbery occurred "the outrages of Mason became more frequent and sanguinary"
and that "the name of Mason and his band was known
and dreaded from the morasses of the southern frontier
to the silent shades of the Tennessee River." Mason's
depredations must have been many, although authenticated records of only a few specific instances are now
found.

It is probable a number of his victims did not survive
to tell the tale, for the wide-awake outlaw realized that
along the trails and on the river, as at Cave-in-Rock, his
greatest safety lay in the fact that "dead men tell no
tales." Those who were permitted to survive had been
treated in such a manner that they would be more likely
to describe Mason as a shrewd robber than a cruel
murderer, and, it seems, most survivors were careful
not to condemn him too severely lest one of his "agents"
silence their tongues with a dagger. Mason usually
kept an intelligent man at Natchez to observe the character of the outfits obtained by those preparing to
travel over the trail. Thus he often received advance
notice of the approach of travelers and information in
regard to their strength. [26] As is shown later, Mason
had at least one agent, Anthony Gass, of Natchez, who
managed to dispose of the stolen goods turned over to
him. The probabilities were, as asserted by a Spanish
official, that this robber had "firm abettors" throughout
the Ohio and Mississippi valleys.

In those days many a traveler was never heard from
after he left home. In some instances it was because he
died a stranger in a strange land, or was murdered but
never missed except by his people far away, who had
no means of learning of his whereabouts or fate. Sooner or later, the impression would prevail among them

that the missing man was actually or probably killed
and robbed. And since Mason was the most widely
known among the outlaws in his day, he was usually
selected as the man at the bottom of the mystery.

An example of such a supposition occurs as an incident in the life of the grandmother of W. L. Harper,
of Jefferson County, Mississippi. She lived along the
old Natchez Trace and frequently accommodated travelers with food and shelter. On one occasion a young
Kentuckian stopped at her house and, becoming ill, was
obliged to remain several weeks. His conduct and
bearing were such that the old lady took a motherly
interest in him. Before he left "she actually quilted
all his six hundred dollars in his coat and vest, partly
to distribute his load, but chiefly to deceive the robbers
then infesting the road. She heard no more of him,
but the supposition was that he was another of Mason's
victims." [81]

A few months after William C. C. Claiborne took
his seat as governor of the Mississippi Territory he
found it necessary to make an investigation of the
robberies on the Mississippi River. On February 10,
1802, he wrote to Manuel de Salcedo, the Spanish Governor General of the Province of Louisiana, residing at
New Orleans, informing him that he had received
notice of "a daring robbery which had lately been
committed upon some citizens of the United States
who were descending the River Mississippi on their
passage to this town" – Natchez – and that it was uncertain whether the persons guilty of this act of piracy
were Spanish subjects or American citizens.

To this the Governor General replied on February
28, saying among other things that "It is truly impossible to determine whether the delinquents are Span-

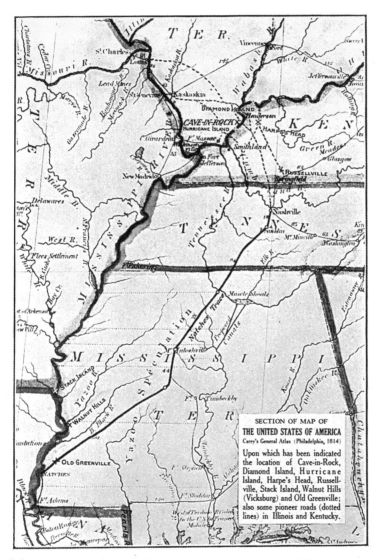

SECTION OF MAP OF
THE UNITED STATES OF AMERICA
Carey's General Atlas (Philadelphia, 1814)

Upon which has been indicated
the location of Cave-in-Rock,
Diamond Island, Hurricane
Island, Harpe's Head, Russellville, Stack Island, Walnut Hills
(Vicksburg) and Old Greenville;
also some pioneer roads (dotted
lines) in Illinois and Kentucky.

MAP SHOWING CAVE-IN-ROCK AND THE NATCHEZ TRACE, 1814

iards or Americans" and that he had given his officers "the most positive orders . . . to take the most efficacious means of discovering and apprehending the criminal or criminals that can be adopted . . . and I assure your Excellency that if the criminals are taken they will be punished in such a manner as to serve as an example to others." He complained that the people of "the States and Western Settlements . . . having the freedom and use of the navigation of the Mississippi" came down into the Spanish territory in great numbers, among whom are "vagabonds . . . who have fled from, or who do not, or can not return to, the United States." [113]

Each governor was willing to arrest highway robbers and river pirates on his own side of the Mississippi, but neither could suggest to the other that if it became necessary for any pursuing party to cross the river into foreign territory, such pursuers might continue the chase without a special permit. Samuel Mason evidently understood and foresaw this condition of international affairs. He had purposely avoided committing crimes on the Spanish side, and now that his notoriety would, in all probability, result in his being hunted along the Natchez Trace, he moved to the Mississippi, there to confine his operations to the river and its American bank, on the very border of a comparatively safe and easily reached land of refuge.

The Baker robbery was in a sense nothing more than another link in Mason's long chain of crimes. Colonel Baker was not daunted by the loss of his money and his failure to capture Mason, for the following spring he started down the river again in a flatboat loaded with merchandise. He supplied himself with guns, not only to protect his boat, but also to better prepare himself for his return home over the dangerous Trace. Some time in April, 1802, when his boat reached a point below Vicksburg, then known as Walnut Hills and Nogales, he came in contact with Mason and some of his men. Colonel Baker wrote a statement giving the details of this attack and forwarded it to Governor Claiborne of Mississippi. Colonel Baker's written statement cannot be found. Its effect, however, is shown by the fact that upon receipt of it Governor Claiborne, who was aware that outlaws had long infested the frontier, more fully realized the necessity for action. The governor sent out three official letters from the capital of Mississippi Territory, each dated, "Town of Washington, April 27, 1802." [113]

The first was written to Colonel Daniel Burnett, at Fort Gibson, who was in command of the militia in Claiborne County. It is here quoted in full from Dunbar Rowland's *Official Letter Books of W. C. C. Claiborne*:

TOWN OF WASHINGTON, APRIL 27, 1802 –
"Sir, – I have received information that a set of pirates and robbers who alternately infest the Mississippi River and the road leading from this district to Tennessee, rendezvous at or near the Walnut Hills, in the County of Claiborne:– a certain Samuel Mason and a man by the name of Harp, are said to be the leaders of this banditti:– they lately attempted in a hostile manner to board the boat of Colo[nel] Joshua Baker, between the mouth of Yazou River, and the Walnut Hills, but were prevented by Colo[nel] Baker's making a shew of arms, and manifesting a great share of firmness. These men must be arrested; the honor of our country, the interest of society, and the feelings of humanity, proclaim that

it is time to stop their career; The crimes of Harp, are many and great, and in point of baseness, Mason is nearly as celebrated: – While these sons of rapine and murder are permitted to rove at large, we may expect daily to hear of *outrages* upon the lives and properties of our fellow citizens.

"The militia of your regiment not being organized, I presume it would not be in your power, to execute (strictly) a military order, I shall therefore only request, that you will immediately endeavor to procure fifteen or twenty men as volunteers, and place yourself, or some confidential character at their head.

"This little force will then proceed to the Walnut Hills, and after making the due examination and enquiry at that place, they will examine the woods in the neighborhood of the Mississippi as high up as Yazou; If you should fall in with Mason and his party you will use all the means in your power to arrest them, or any of them, and I desire, that the person or persons arrested, may immediately be conveyed under a strong guard to Natchez.

"I hope that the honor of taking these lawless men, will be conferred upon the citizens of your neighborhood; should they succeed, I promise them a very generous reward.

"I have written to Lieutenant Rennick upon this subject, and it is probable, he will give you all the aid in his power.

"With great respect & esteem.

"I am sir, your Hble – Servt:
"WILLIAM C. C. CLAIBORNE

"P. S. For your information, I have enclosed you the

statement made by Colo[nel] Baker to me, of the late attempt made to rob him.

"W. C. C. C.

"Colo[nel] Daniel Burnett –"

Another letter was sent to Lieutenant Seymour Rennick, who was in command of a detachment of United States troops at Grindstone Ford on the Natchez Trace. In it the governor referred to the attack made on Colonel Baker's boat and stated that "a certain Samuel Mason and a certain Wiley Harp . . . have been in the habit of committing with impunity murders and robberies . . . I think it is probable they may be found at or near the Walnut Hills; at that place the wife of John Mason resides." He suggested to this officer that the federal government furnish Colonel Burnett with a sergeant and twelve men.

The third letter was addressed "To the Officer commanding the United States Troops near the mouth of Bear Creek on the Tennessee River." In it Governor Claiborne writes that: "I have received information that the road from this territory to Tennessee is infested by a daring set of robbers, among them are a certain Samuel Mason and a certain Wiley Harp . . . I hope, Sir, that if you should receive information of any mischief being done or attempted in the wilderness you will immediately order out a party of men, and make the necessary exertions to arrest the offenders."

The lower Mississippi valley was now aroused. Mason had become a terror in a frontier country that was more or less accustomed to lawlessness and bloodshed. His robberies were current history and the whereabouts of Wiley Harpe was a discussed but unsolved question. A little more than two years before

Governor Claiborne began to move toward the arrest of Mason, the news that Big Harpe had been captured and beheaded in Kentucky near Cave-in-Rock (Mason's one-time headquarters) had rapidly spread throughout the country. With the report also had come the warning that Little, or Wiley Harpe, had escaped and fled south. Up to this time – April, 1802 – there was nothing to point out the actual or probable whereabouts of the missing Harpe. No mention of any murders committed by him appeared in the current newspapers. Indications and hopes were that he had left the country for good or had been killed. Governor Claiborne probably had heard from others besides Colonel Baker that Wiley Harpe was one of Mason's men. Even though he was not convinced of Harpe's presence on the Mississippi, he knew that by linking the names of these two notorious outlaws together, the public would more fully realize the desperate character of Mason and therefore take a more active interest in his capture.

As indicated in his letter to Colonel Burnett, the governor of Mississippi Territory promised "a very generous reward" for the capture of Samuel Mason and Wiley Harpe. Monette says the governor "offered a liberal reward for the robber Mason, dead or alive, and the proclamation was widely distributed." J. F. H. Claiborne, in his *History of Mississippi,* states that the proclamation was issued and a reward of two thousand dollars was offered for the capture of Mason and Harpe. No two historians make precisely the same statements regarding the reward. It is more than likely that a printed proclamation was issued, although an effort to find a copy or reprint has been futile. The proclamation in all probability gave, among other things, the facts embraced in the following statement quoted from a letter written two years later by Governor Claiborne to James Madison, who was then Secretary of State at Washington: "A reward of four hundred dollars for apprehending them was offered by the Secretary of War, and five hundred dollars by myself, in my character as Governor of the Territory."

The extermination of Mason and his band was a matter of serious importance to the law abiding and peace loving citizens of the Territory. And now that a reward of at least nine hundred dollars had been offered and the militia directed to search for the outlaws, the prospects of capture appeared very encouraging. It was known that Mason and Harpe had lived in Kentucky and at Cave-in-Rock, and it was therefore apparently presumed that they were old and constant associates. The two outlaws, however, may never have met in Kentucky nor at the Cave. Whether or not Mason the robber and Harpe the brute were in the same band, both, nevertheless, deserved the severest punishment that could be inflicted by a pioneer people.

A number of highway robbers and river pirates had been arrested during the time Mason was working in Mississippi, but Samuel Mason and Wiley Harpe, the most notorious of them all, had evaded arrest. Where were they likely to be found? As a matter of fact outlaws camped at any place they found convenient and well adapted for their work, but never remained long at any one spot. It was known that Samuel Mason had, at one time, lived about twenty miles northeast of Natchez, near what is now Fayette. [81] Shortly after the Baker highway robbery had taken place it was discovered that at the time of the robbery Mason's headquarters was near Rocky Springs, a stopping place on the old Natchez Trace some forty miles northeast of Natchez and twenty miles south of Vicksburg.[23]

Draper in a brief note [12H] says Mason spent much time at Palmyra and on Stack Island. Palmyra then, as now, was a very small settlement on the Mississippi, about twenty miles below Vicksburg. Stack Island, also known as Crow's Nest or Island No. 94, was washed away shortly after Mason's day, and in time most of its traditions disappeared. It was on Stack Island, near the mouth of Lake Providence, about fifty-five miles below Vicksburg, that we first hear of Mason – after organized bands began to search for him.

Claiborne, the historian, states that: "After the Governor's proclamation had been issued Mason and his gang were closely hunted by the whites and Indians and, having made some narrow escapes, they quit the country and crossed the Mississippi to somewhere about Lake Providence [Louisiana] in the then Spanish ter-

---

[23] One of Mason's daughters-in-law, Mrs. Tom Mason, continued to live for a short time at the Rocky Springs rendezvous after the camp had been abandoned by the others, who rightly suspected that the governor's reward would result in a thorough search along the Trace. It is possible Mrs. Mason's condition made flight impossible, but it is more probable she concluded to remain behind and, in time, find a home in some law-abiding community. Guild, who interviewed Swaney, gives us only one glimpse of this woman:

"After the band had left she started to the Chickasaw Agency where she would be able to communicate with her friends. When Mr. Swaney met her she was on her way, carrying her babe, together with some provisions. Mrs. Mason begged Mr. Swaney to assist her . . . He spent nearly a whole day in assisting the woman, and then made up lost time by riding all night. Mrs. Mason told Mr. Swaney that Mason's band was safe out of reach of their pursuers, and that before leaving they buried their gold in the bottoms near the river and cut the initials 'T.M.' on trees near the spot so they could easily find it in the future."

According to one tradition [114] Mason crossed the Mississippi River and went westward to the highlands northwest of Vicksburg "which are known to this day as Mason Hills" and there hid some booty. "To the present day," continues this chronicle, "many people believe that rich treasures lie buried out in the Mason Hills."

ritory." Whether at Lake Providence (which is on the Spanish side of the Mississippi but practically on the river) or on the nearby Stack Island in the river, Mason was in a position to flee easily into that part of the great Spanish wilderness which today is northern Louisiana and the state of Arkansas. There he could not only conceal himself more effectually, but also live with some confidence that the Spanish authorities would not attempt to capture him.

At Stack Island Mason laid his hand upon fate. The band robbed a traveler and found among his effects a copy of Governor Claiborne's proclamation. [26] Monette says that Mason read it aloud and "indulged in much merriment on the occasion." The statement in the proclamation that Wiley (or Little) Harpe, the Kentucky desperado, was a member of his gang convinced Mason that the authorities were in great fear of the prowess of his band and were driven to arouse the public to terror and activity by conjuring with the dreadful name of Harpe. Mason was feeling good, notwithstanding the hue and cry raised by the promise of rewards for his capture dead or alive. He was perfectly confident of his ability to escape any American militiamen or Mississippi posse. He could afford to laugh at the additional incitement to his capture contained in the declaration that he had joined forces with Harpe.

Nobody can say positively that Little Harpe was at that date a member of the band. It is more than probable that Mason would not knowingly have permitted Harpe to join him. The reputation of the Harpes for brutality was sufficient to condemn them in the estimation of even such outcasts as Mason and his men. Somewhere in that southwest wilderness, however, Little

Harpe was concealing himself from the fate that pursued him. He was hiding under assumed names, not daring to reveal his own even to the most abandoned persons he met for fear of capture. Hunted like a wild animal, it was necessary to lose his identity beyond the most remote chance of discovery.

The question is *was* Harpe with Mason when the latter read his name aloud and made merriment about it? Was the headsman of fate stalking there at Mason's elbow, compelled to keep silence and join in the laughter in that hour of grim jocularity? It was not until April, 1802, that John Setton appears of record as one of Mason's band, was captured with him, tried with him, and escaped with him. It was not until almost two years later, under most dramatic circumstances, that Setton was to be identified as Little Harpe—as the man who brought fate home to Mason and himself and immediately met the pitiless fate he had so long and well deserved. All this will be shown later, but it is one of the mysteries of history whether that day at Stack Island Mason laughed himself out of the fear of Governor Claiborne and committed himself into the hands of fate in the person of Little Harpe. There is a further doubt whether Mason ever did actually discover that John Setton was Little Harpe.[24]

In May, 1802, we find Mason's band at the mouth of White River, about one hundred and fifty miles above

[24] Cramer's *Navigator,* 1818, says: "Stack or Crow's Nest Island has been sunk by the earthquake [of 1811] or swept by the floods . . . Stack not long since was famed for a band of counterfeiters, horse thieves, robbers, murderers, etc. who made this part of the Mississippi a place of manufacture and deposit. From hence they would sally forth, stop boats, buy horses, flour, whiskey, etc. and pay for all in fine, new notes of the *'first water.'* Their villainies (after many severe losses sustained by innocent, good men, unsuspecting the eheat) became notorious, and after several years' search and pursuit of the civil law, and in some cases the *club-law,* against this band of monsters, they have at length disappeared."

Stack Island. *The Palladium* on August 12, 1802, in
a news item dated Cincinnati, North West Territory,
July 31, says:

"A letter dated, Natchez, June 11, from a gentleman who lately descended the river, contains the following interesting intelligence: 'We were attacked by
robbers near the mouth of White River and a breeze
springing up, prevented us from being boarded by two
pirogues, having in each six men well armed. They
hailed us from the shore, telling us they wished to purchase some rifles, and on our refusing to land, they commenced the pursuit. They originally consisted of
three companies, and were commanded by a person
named Mason, who has left the camp at White River,
and scours the road through the wilderness. About
two weeks ago they attacked a merchant boat and took
possession of her, after having killed one of the people
on board.' "

Other robberies in 1802 and in the summer and fall
of 1803 were reported, but by whom they were committed is not stated in the current newspapers. The
one just cited, however, was without doubt some of
Mason's work. It occurred about one hundred and
fifty miles above Stack Island and three hundred miles
above Natchez, and some three hundred miles below
New Madrid, which was then the principal town in
the Spanish territory of upper Louisiana. New Madrid is now the county seat of New Madrid County,
Missouri. The New Madrid country was six hundred
miles from Natchez, out of the Mississippi territory
and in a field where Mason felt he could carry on his
usual activities, unhindered by the men who were pursuing him for the nine hundred dollars reward. Mason
went up the river and had taken steps toward establish-

ing himself a few miles below the town of New Madrid, in a small settlement known as Little Prairie, when in January, 1803, he was trapped and captured. He was arrested, not by the American officials he so much feared, but by the Spanish authorities who suspected that he was guilty of many of the crimes that had been committed on their side of the Mississippi River. The curious story of that frontier pursuit and trial is now to be told from the French records for the first time.

Mason-Trapped and Tried

The official record of the arrest of the Masons at Little Prairie and their trial at New Madrid is still in existence. The whereabouts of this old document has been noted by a few historians who briefly state that "There is in the Mississippi Department of Archives and History a record in French of the trial of Mason for robbery, by the military authorities of New Madrid, dated January, 1803." But no writer has heretofore penetrated into this manuscript to discover what the trial revealed or how it ended. It was found among the papers belonging to J. F. H. Claiborne, the historian, and is now preserved in Jackson.[25]

The document covers one hundred and eighty-two pages. Many of the leaves are badly faded. Although the penmanship is far from good, every word, with few exceptions, can be deciphered. It is filled with interesting facts and equally interesting perjury. From the beginning of legislation down through the pioneer days humanity has ever been the same, and facts and fabrications have been paraded together before officials who are to pass judgment on the evidence presented. The Mason trial is no exception to this old practice in courts, but is rather an exaggerated instance of the tendency, as common in the "good old days" as in our own times.

The manuscript gives a complete history not only of

---

[25] The author is indebted to Dr. Dunbar Rowland, of the Mississippi Department of Archives and History, for the privilege of having a translation made of the record of Mason's trial.

the proceedings during the trial, but also of the arrests that preceded it. It begins with the day New Madrid officials were notified that the Masons were seen at Little Prairie, thirty miles down the river. A clerk then, and every day thereafter, carefully noted what action had been taken by the pursuers and what evidence had been gathered against the suspects, and continued the record through all the other proceedings.

The commandant at New Madrid, by whom the pursuit was ordered and before whom the captives were tried, evidently did not understand English, which was the only language spoken by nearly all the persons who appeared before him. Questions and answers were transmitted through an official interpreter.

There were fifteen witnesses. Eight made declarations regarding their knowledge of Mason and his family; the other seven were the prisoners themselves, who testified in their own behalf. Every witness took "an oath on the cross of his sword" to speak the truth. In a few instances "and by the Holy Scriptures" was added. As a witness was being heard the substance of his statements was recorded in French and after he finished, his testimony was read to him, transposed into English, and he, "maintaining it contained the truth to which nothing could be added or unsaid," signed it as did the presiding officials. Four of these signatures are here reproduced in facsimile.

In the official document many statements and legal phrases are often repeated; they add to its length but

throw no new light on the subject. In the following
more or less paraphrased condensation the number of
words is greatly reduced but the substance of the original is, in the main, retained.

John Mason

The first entry in the old record is dated January 11,
1803. It shows that one Pierre Dapron, a citizen of
New Madrid, appeared in court and made a declara-

Thomas Mason

tion before three officials: the Commandant, Don Henri
Peyroux de la Coudreniere, "Captain of the Army,
Civil and Military Commander of the District of New

John Sutton

Madrid;" Don Pierre Antoine LaForge, "Commissioner of Police and Officer of the Militia," and Don
Joseph Charpentier, "Interpreter for His Majesty in
the English Language." Dapron explained to these
officials that he had returned from Little Prairie and
considered it his duty to declare that Ignace Belan had
informed him that on his way to New Orleans with a
cargo of salt pork he had seen four persons at Little

Prairie whom he suspected of being members of the
Mason band and although they did not attempt to rob
his boat, he felt their presence should be reported.

George Ruddell, a citizen of Little Prairie, appeared
before the court the same day and "told us by means of
the interpreter that a party of eight men and one woman," well armed and mounted, had arrived in town
about two weeks before and had taken possession of an
empty house belonging to an American citizen, Lesieur,
who had not been consulted by them nor had they
shown any passports. In the meantime, they rented a
ten-acre tract from John Ruddell and bought a cow and
sundry provisions. Among other things that aroused
the suspicion of the neighborhood was the careful manner in which the house was guarded by the occupants.
Ruddell expressed the opinion that if this was not the
Mason band, then it was probably a part, explaining
that "since the Governor of Natchez had the militia on
the lookout for these robbers, the original crowd may
have separated into smaller groups." He was inclined
to think that although the man called "father" was not
the exact size of Samuel Mason, whom he had seen
some years before, he nevertheless felt confident that
"father" Mason was among the members of this gang.
He concluded his declaration by stating that he was acting in behalf of the citizens of Little Prairie who suggested that these suspects be arrested and their effects
examined.

The next day, "in view of the above cited declarations," the Commandant ordered four persons, Joseph
Charpentier, LaForge, George Ruddell, and Don Robert McCoy, "Captain of the Militia," to proceed to
Little Prairie – a distance of about thirty miles – and
there meet a division of regulars commanded by Cor-

poral Felipo Canot, who had been ordered to the scene. Upon their arrival at the place further investigation convinced the officers that the new suspects were Samuel Mason and some of his followers, and that about half the number had left the Lesieur house and moved over to a house owned by Francois Langlois. Realizing that the pursuing party would soon be scented by the suspects, it was decided to invade the two houses early in the morning.

At six o'clock in the morning George Ruddell informed Captain McCoy that the Masons had their horses saddled and loaded with baggage and were on the point of leaving for New Madrid, but Samuel Mason, known as "Father Mason," hearing that the interpreter was in town, expressed a desire to see him and explain that he wished to go to New Madrid to "justify himself" and clear himself of the crimes of which he was "falsely accused." Captain McCoy, George Ruddell, and the interpreter walked to the house occupied by Samuel Mason and suggested to him that, in view of his intention to volunteer a justification, he and those of his people with him would do well to go over to the house occupied by his other associates where he would be given a hearing and could make explanations which would be forwarded to the Commandant at New Madrid. To this Mason consented and by eight o'clock his party, consisting of six men, one woman, and three children, was assembled in the Lesieur house which, unsuspected by the Masons, was guarded by concealed militia. Samuel Mason, turning to Captain McCoy, immediately referred to the "unjust imputations" made against him and his people. The Captain expressed the opinion that his explanation and justification had better be made in person to the Commandant. A signal was given by Captain McCoy, and before the Masons realized it, they were "in handcuffs and chains."

Then, in the words of the clerk, "We immediately asked said prisoners their names and the father or oldest gave his as Samuel Mason;" those of his four sons, in order of age, were given as Thomas, John, Samuel Jr. (about eighteen years of age) and Magnus Mason (about sixteen years of age). Another man called himself John Taylor (later in the trial known as John Setton). The woman had three children with her and gave her name as Marguerite Douglas, wife of John Mason. Upon being questioned by McCoy and Charpentier, Samuel Mason answered that they had come from Nogales (Vicksburg) and intended to establish themselves in or near Little Prairie, in accordance with a passport given him. When asked to produce a passport issued "by the authorities of the locality from whence he came," it was discovered he had "none other than the one we ourselves had given, dated New Madrid, March 29th, 1800." This he surrendered to Captain McCoy, who agreed with the other officials present that it was genuine.

The original passport was inserted between two leaves of the record book where it has ever since remained. The following is a translation:

"New Madrid, March 29th, 1800.

"Whereas Samuel Masson, Esqr. has expressed a wish to settle in this district and wishes to arrange his business affairs, We, Don Henri Peyroux de la Coundreniere, Captain of the Armies of His Majesty, Civil and Military Commander of this Post and District of New Madrid, hereby grant permission to said Samuel Masson to proceed to Natchez per boat, and on his

FACSIMILE OF PASSPORT ISSUED TO SAMUEL MASON
Written in French and issued by the Spanish Commandant of the District of New Madrid,
March 29, 1800

return from there, said Samuel Masson may select a suitable place in this District for himself and family. He, Samuel Masson, having by oath attested his loyalty and fidelity to us, we pray that no hindrance be placed to his proposed journey.

"HENRI PEYROUX

"Approved and marked with the flourish of our signature."

"We told them," continues the record, "in order that none of their effects be lost or strayed an inventory of same would be made at once . . . and at two o'clock in the afternoon we proceeded with the above-named inventory." This work required almost two days. Every item was carefully examined and tabulated. There were eight horses, new and old clothes, many yards of silk, muslin and cotton, old and new pistols and guns, "a field stove," a box of salt, three horns of powder, six barrels of flour, English cutlery, various other imported goods and more than a hundred other items, and seven thousand dollars in United States money of various denominations, of which the series number and amount of each was noted.

The following morning, while the inventory was being made, Samuel Mason, on behalf of his people, applied for the return of certain utensils and clothing of which his people had immediate need, and asked for "a pro and con settlement" with the citizens of Little Prairie. These requests were granted. On the 16th, the prisoners, with their property and a military guard, arrived at New Madrid. How they were transported is not stated.

The trial began the morning of the 17th. "The Commandant having learned of the conversation Captain

McCoy and Charpentier had with the prisoners, called on these two officers to make declarations."

Captain McCoy, after taking the oath, declared that his duties as captain of the militia threw him in the presence of Samuel Mason much of the time after the arrest, and that the prisoner frequently spoke to him of the coming trial. Mason, continued the witness, repeatedly asserted that he had never done any wrong on the Spanish side of the Mississippi River, and that if time were given him he could and would, in justice to himself, disclose many criminals. On one occasion Mason asked "if a man became informer, with proofs and evidence of crimes committed in the States, could he obtain pardon for those attributed to him?" McCoy casually answered him that if he could give such information it would, in all probability, clear up matters and greatly help him and his people.

Mason stated to Captain McCoy that although it was widely rumored that he was "the man smeared over with black," who had committed many crimes "along the highway," he could in each instance prove that he was far from the scene when the robberies occurred. He denied that he was implicated in the highway robbery or the boat robbery of a man named Baker, from whom "some three thousand piasters" were taken. But when he, Captain McCoy, remarked that Baker would appear in a few days, "the prisoner seemed disturbed and asked for particulars relative to his coming."

Captain McCoy further declared that while the inventory was being taken he asked Mason how he happened to have so many banknotes and the old man who usually stood as spokesman for his crowd, first seemed startled and then pretended not to understand the question. The question was repeated and the prisoners stared at each other for a moment, when John Taylor (alias John Setton) came to the rescue by saying: "The banknotes were found in a bag hanging in a bush, near the road where we happened to be camping." [26]

Don Joseph Charpentier was next called upon to make a declaration. The record shows that his statements were practically the same as those made by Captain McCoy, but touched on a few additional subjects. He had heard Samuel Mason say that the only thing for which he could be reproached was having served in prison for debt. Mason, he said, asked him and some of the other officers whether or not they thought the money found in his possession was genuine and all answered, in effect, that they presumed Mason knew. To this the prisoner replied that he had made no attempt to pass any of the bills and that if they were counterfeit, he could not be punished for carrying them. He wanted to know by whose authority he was arrested, and whether it was likely he would be turned over to the Americans. He stated he would rather be deprived of all his property and pass the remainder of his days on Spanish soil than be delivered into the hands of the United States officials.

On January 18th Samuel Mason appeared before the Commandant, the Commissioner of Police, the Captain of Militia, and the Interpreter. Answering questions, he stated that he was born in Pennsylvania and had lately come from the District of Natchez for the purpose of residing near New Madrid. As to how he

---

[26] Samuel Mason probably had heard of "money growing on trees." It was a common practice for travelers to hide their money over night in the bushes near the place they camped. It is likely that Mason sometimes "found" the money of highway travelers while they were asleep, or "found" it after he had surprised the campers and driven them off before they could procure their brush-hidden valuables.

made a living he swore he had depended upon his plantation, his "horned cattle," the labor of his sons and the people he sometimes employed. He explained that his plan was to have his four sons then with him, his wife, his son living on the river Monongahela, Mrs. Thompson (a married daughter) and her husband, another son-in-law, and a few other kinsmen join him in the settlement he proposed to establish. He said that he had recently sold his place near Natchez and the only claim he had on land was located on the Monongahela, to which he had fallen heir through a "brother who died young."

When asked why he had not made use of the passport the year it was issued to him, he asserted that he had been kept busy settling his business affairs. He added that he had spent much time in the District of Natchez trying to show that the suspicion held against him of being a robber was groundless, but notwithstanding earnest efforts his attempts were in vain.

His attention was called to the fact that since his passport as a settler's permit had expired, he would be obliged to give new references. He then gave the name of his daughter, Mrs. Thompson, of Cape Girardeau, whose first husband was Mr. Winterington, and General Benjamin Harrison, whose sister married his, Samuel Mason's, brother, the owner of a kiln on the Monongahela. He was requested to cite, if he could, some local people, and he referred to Dr. Richard Jones Waters, saying he was the man on whose recommendation he had received the passport three years before, but admitted that he had known the gentleman only slightly.

Mason's answers show that he knew more or less about the robberies that had been referred to, but in each case he managed to explain how and from whom he received the information. For example, when the Owsley boat robbery, in which he said Phillips was implicated, was under discussion, he stated that in May, 1802, two of his sons were coming up the Mississippi River and were overtaken by two men, Wiguens and John Taylor, in a boat, from whom they heard of the robbery. Later, he met Owsley, the owner of the boat, who requested him to investigate the case. This he did, with some assistance by a Mr. Koiret, and in consequence he knew where the booty had been stored and learned many other details.

He more than once asserted he would throw light on a number of robberies, and not only give the names of the guilty parties, but would produce them, "if the Commandant assured him he would spare his life and exonerate him of all misdeeds which rumor had so unjustly attributed to him." The Commandant replied that "it is customary to spare the lives of such confessors and to show great leniency toward them." After a somewhat pathetic recital before the officials of how his many efforts ended in failure to "justify" himself, and evidently feeling confident he had impressed the Commandant as an innocent man, and to show that he could produce a guilty man, he informed the court that one of his fellow-prisoners, John Taylor, alias John Setton, alias Wells –"and sometimes going by other names he, Mason, could not recall"– was one of the guilty parties. That prisoner, Mason insinuated, could give much information regarding the robbing of Owsley's boat and other robberies, for he knew John Taylor was implicated in them.

John Setton, the man of various aliases, was brought before the Commandant to testify. He admitted that he had changed his name to John Taylor, but explained

that he did so because Samuel Mason demanded it, and
that he suspected Mason had some specific purpose in
insisting upon the name of John Taylor. He also admitted (and probably in a triumphant way) that Samuel Mason was correct in his statement that he, "one
of Mason's fellow prisoners, could give much information regarding robberies." He said that he had been
with the Masons since May 14, 1802 – eight months.

He swore he was an Irishman and had come to
America in 1797, and shortly thereafter enrolled in
Major Geyon's corps but "deserted near the high
coast." Reaching Nogales (Vicksburg) he "worked
for three weeks for His Majesty the King of Spain,"
and then went down the river in the "row-gally Louisiana" to New Orleans where, during the winter, he
found occupation as a carpenter. After this, for a
period of about two years, he shifted around in Spanish
territory, either working with white people or "hunting
with Chaquetaw Indians." One day while in Arkansas
an American officer recognized him as a deserter from
the army and asked for his delivery to a Spanish post.
He was delivered into the hands of the American
authorities and placed in jail. There he met Wiguens,
an American soldier, and a month later both escaped.
They went back to Arkansas and were shortly afterwards arrested by the Commander of the Arkansas
Post, who considered them suspicious characters and
kept them in jail twenty-eight days. They then found
farm employment for a month with a man named Gibson, who obtained for them a passport to go hunting on
White River. They hunted until May, 1802, when they
came down the river some distance in a boat and then
crossed over the country to "Little Prairie of the St.
Francis River," where they sold their skins to one Ful-

som. They continued their trip, for he, Setton, "wished to join his family in Pennsylvania." When "at the crossing of the Chaquetaws below the river Ares," they met, by chance, John and Thomas Mason, Gibson, and Wilson, and he had been with the Masons ever since.

The Commandant asked Setton whether or not he was acquainted with "the man Harpe" and he answered that he had met a man by that name in Cumberland who had since been killed, but had left a brother, whose whereabouts was unknown to him. Setton further stated, upon being questioned, that he did not know whether or not Harpe and any of the Masons ever had any dealings together or had ever met, but he felt confident that Harpe had not been around since he had had the misfortune to fall into Mason's hands.[27]

---

[27] The story of John Setton's life up to this time, as recited by Setton himself, doubtless appeared very plausible to the officials. There was, nevertheless, very little truth in it. This court identified him by the names Setton, Taylor, and Wells. It apparently disregarded Samuel Mason's statement that the prisoner sometimes went by other names which he, Mason, could not recall. These three names were equally unfamiliar; none were connected with the known history of any crime. Mason himself may have been ignorant of the real name and true history of Setton. Be that as it may, Draper in one of his early note books, written about 1840, gives the following facts regarding the man who passed as one John Setton and whose identity, it seems, was then unknown by the historian himself. He states that John Setton was originally from North Carolina and, while traveling along the Natchez Trace, lingering more or less among the Indians, he fell in company with a young man named Bass, who lived in Williamson County, Tennessee. Then, in the words of Draper:

"Bass was not very well and Setton, very friendly, would catch Bass' horse and do him other offices of kindness. When Bass reached his father's residence he invited Setton to sojourn a time, recruit his horse, etc. Setton did so and courted a sister of young Bass and married her. He started with his new wife for North Carolina. When they reached the North Fork of Holston, in Hawkins County, East Tennessee, Setton gave information that his wife's horse ran away and her feet being in the stirrups, had dragged and killed her. This is the story he told negroes. The white persons being absent from home, he had his deceased companion buried hurriedly. He disposed of her clothing and saddle for little or nothing and in a few hours put off with both horses. After he had gone, his conduct led some of the

Setton, continuing his account, swore that John and Thomas Mason took possession of all his belongings, and encouraged him to stay by promising him land on to which he could later move his family and by giving him a contract "to go after Mother Mason," who apparently had some time before refused to live any longer with her outlaw husband and sons. Setton declared that from the very day he met the Masons they had kept him like a prisoner. The promised land had never materialized and the trip for their mother was never attempted, but he was obliged to linger with them because he found no opportunity to escape, and the Masons never allowed him more than two rounds of powder at a time.

He asserted that since he had been with the Masons they had committed no crimes in his presence. They did not demand that he steal horses, but apparently expected him to do so. A number of horses had been brought in and taken away, but he asked no questions and as he heard no comments made regarding them, he had no idea how they came or where they went. He knew, however, that there was an agreement between the Masons and one Burton, of Little Bay Prairie, who bought at twenty dollars all the horses the Masons could supply, provided the animals were such that they could be sold for about sixty dollars.

The Masons occasionally left home "to repair a chimney" and if they remained a few days they invariably

people thereabout to disinter the dead body, and found she had evidently been killed by heavy blows on the head. Setton fled, went first to Louisiana, then down the river, enlisted at Fort Pickering at the Chickasaw Bluffs (Memphis) into Captain Richard Sparks' company. By his conduct he was soon made a sergeant. He was in the habit of going out hunting. One day he borrowed Captain Sparks' elegant rifle, took a canoe and some provisions and started on a several days hunt down the Mississippi. Setton steered up the Arkansas and then joined Mason." [12H] accounted for their prolonged absence by saying they "could not cross the water," "lost their repairing tools," "were hindered by bad weather," or "visited friends," but in no instance had they given the name of the friend they claimed to have seen.

Setton related that when he and the Masons were in Nogales, at the residence of Charles Colin, a Mr. Koiret, an American citizen, chanced to stop in the house. Koiret impressed the Masons as a prospective victim, and he (Setton) being permitted to chat freely with Koiret, soon proved himself "an interesting conversationalist." But when Koiret incidentally remarked that he was simply passing by on his way looking for outlaws who had committed crimes along the Natchez Trace and the Mississippi River, John Mason, on a pretext, lured him (Setton) away from the officer, and, in the meantime, other Masons tactfully managed to "speed the parting guest." Turning a corner of the house, he (Setton) unexpectedly ran into Samuel Mason, who, with drawn dagger, commanded "silence." John Mason seized him and the father and son immediately gagged him, bound his hands and feet, and dragged him into the house where they held him down on the floor for about three hours. Feeling that Koiret had got far beyond hearing distance, they ungagged and untied him, but continued to guard him closely until the next day.

Setton swore that shortly after he had received this brutal treatment Samuel Mason prepared a written statement in which he, under the assumed name of John Taylor, made a declaration that he, Phillips, Fulsom, Gibson, Wiguens, Bassett, and others were implicated in one or more of three robberies – the Baker, the Owsley, and the Campbell and Glass robberies – and in it

further declared that the Masons were in no way connected with any of these depredations.

After the statement had been prepared the Masons
explained to him that they were going to conduct him
to a justice of the peace and they furthermore convinced
him that should he fail to swear to this written confession and declaration of the three robberies, they would
kill him before he had a chance to inform the officers
that the statements were false and not his own. He
related how John and Thomas Mason, armed with
guns, and Samuel Mason, who bore no weapon at all,
forced him to the residence of William Downs, a justice
living below Vicksburg, and that, with seeming calm-
ness, he went through the form required by the law and
the outlaws. He realized that while he and Samuel
Mason were in the house, the two sons were outside in
hiding, prepared to shoot him should the prearranged
signal be given.

The first of the three robberies detailed in the false
affidavit, continued Setton, was the robbery of Baker
on the Natchez Trace, from whom the Masons took
"twenty-five hundred piasters in gold, silver and banknotes." For this John Mason had been imprisoned,
but by the aid of his brother Thomas and others, made
his escape. The object of the confession was to show
that he (as John Taylor) and others were the guilty
men and that Mason was absolutely innocent of the
crime. Notwithstanding his purported statement, he
could prove an alibi, for ten days before the robbery
took place, he had been committed to the Arkansas
prison. He suspected that part of the money found
on the Masons by the officials who arrested them was
a part of the booty obtained in the Baker robbery. The
explanation that the money they had was found "in a

bag hanging on a bush near the road" was suggested by Samuel Mason a few hours before the arrest, saying at the time, "accounting for it in that way won't do any harm."

"The second crime," resumed Setton, "was the one committed on the Mississippi at the crossing of the Chaquetaws below the river Ares," where the Masons robbed a merchant boat belonging to Owsley. The Masons tried to show that he and Phillips took the lead in this affair. He swore he was not connected with the robbery and stated that he understood Phillips had done nothing more than purchase two guns from the boatman and was in no way involved with the men who later bought all the guns that were on the boat, and, with the newly purchased guns attacked the boat and robbed it.

The third robbery Mason wished to throw upon the shoulders of Phillips and others by inserting it in the false affidavit, was the one that occurred on "the road from Kentucky to Natchez," in which Campbell and Glass were deprived of several horses, saddles, and some money. Near the site of this robbery there later was discovered a sign on a tree, reading "Done by Mason of the Woods." The Commandant asked Setton whether or not he thought Mason was guilty of this hold-up and he answered that he did not know but, in his opinion, the stratagem fitted Mason, who, if guilty, could cite it as an instance of the "workings of his enemies" and would be prepared to prove "that he was elsewhere when the robbery occurred." Anthony Glass, the witness thought, was a party to the deception, for he had been a poor man in Nogales until he came in contact with the Masons.

On one occasion Mason proposed to Setton that they

capture a certain store boat, drown the owner, rob the boat, and then sell the goods to Glass, who would pay cash for half its actual value and never betray them. He asserted that he refused to participate in the proposed venture, but he suspected that the program was carried out during one of the "chimney repairing" trips and that some of the booty could be located by Glass.

He also declared that the pistol the Masons showed Downs and claimed to be Setton's had never belonged to him. It was one the Masons had taken during the Baker robbery and had originally belonged to Sheriff William Nicholson, whose initials had been inlaid with silver thread in the handle but had been removed by the Masons, who were not aware that he (Setton) saw them make the change. This very pistol, he said, was now among the goods the officials had taken possession of and was the same one that Samuel Mason carried to Downs, expecting to use it as evidence against him when the case came to trial.

Setton explained that two of the saddle bags now in possession of the Masons were originally tan "and had large tacks fastened at their corners" and that the tacks were broken off by Samuel Mason and the leather dyed black. He also stated that the original color of the trunk they had was red and had been blackened in his presence by Thomas and John Mason.

Setton, in his comments on the Mason family, remarked that every member treated him equally bad, except Thomas, who at times seemed somewhat human. From the conversations of the Masons he inferred that "the father had been a thief and a rascal for more than forty years." On one occasion, Samuel Mason, "after taking three measures," boasted to him that he was "one of the boldest soldiers in the Revolutionary War" and

that "there was no greater robber and no better cap-
turer of negroes and horses than himself."

On another occasion, after he began to feel his liquor,
he pointed with pride to the fact that he had two part-
ners, Barret and Brown, who did some killing as a side
line and always shared the spoils with him in consideration of the advice and powder he furnished them.
Setton also stated that Mason had related to him that
when Mason's eldest daughter was married, he had
arranged with Barret, Brown, and others to steal as
many of the horses of the guests as they could while the
guests were feasting at the bridal celebration, and that
when the discovery of the theft became known, no man
displayed more eagerness to pursue the horse thieves
than Samuel Mason himself. A few days later some
of the men who had taken the horses were captured and
accused Mason of being the promoter of the theft, but
because of the absurdity of the accusation Mason experienced no difficulty in proving his "innocence."

In his comments on John Mason's wife, Setton said
more than once she pretended to be sick and requested
her husband to send for Dr. Wales, whom she knew
well, but it was his opinion that the woman simply
wished "to chat with the physician" and also "to force
the family cooking upon some one else."

Setton cited another instance of Mrs. John Mason's
nature. He related that one day in his presence and
in the presence of two or three of the Masons, Barret,
who had lately shown signs of being dissatisfied with
the treatment he received, declared he would denounce
the whole family. Mrs. Mason, hearing this, immediately jumped up in a rage, knocked Barret's hat off his
head and shouted: "Monster, you are not going to denounce me or any of us!" She was about to plunge a

long knife into Barret's heart, when Thomas interfered, saying: "It is better to part as friends than to part after a fight," and peace was restored.

After Setton's testimony had been heard, the Commandant on the following day, January 20, ordered Samuel Mason to appear again. Mason admitted that he had, in a way, detained Setton, but did so in justice to himself and his sons. The Owsley boat, he swore in his explanation, had been robbed in April, 1802, and immediately thereafter the rumor had become current that the Masons were the guilty men. Mason declared that Owsley did not know by whom he and his five boatmen had been robbed, but in recounting the affair Owsley referred to two incidents which in themselves were sufficient to distinguish this robbery from any other. The first was that after the boat had been plundered, one of the three robbers returned five dollars to one of Owsley's boatmen who had been seriously wounded during the short battle that took place before the boat was captured. The other incident was that after the robbery the outlaws placed a sign on a tree, reading, "Done by Samuel Mason of the Woods." John and Thomas had heard this account a number of times and every version had it that Samuel Mason was accused of the work.

When his two sons first met Setton and Wiguens, who were strangers to them, Setton told them the details of the Owsley robbery, including these two incidents, and a few hours later, after the brothers had made a more favorable impression, Setton confided in them, saying he and Wiguens and also Gibson were among the perpetrators of the robbery. John and Thomas Mason, then recognizing in the two men the outlaws who had committed at least one of the robberies of which their father was being accused, decided to entice Setton and Wiguens to join them and in the meantime seek an opportunity to force them into a public declaration of their guilt and thus vindicate the Mason family. They succeeded in detaining Setton, admitted Samuel Mason, but Wiguens escaped.

Samuel Mason, in his comments on the Baker boat robbery, stated that a few days after the boat had been pillaged, Colonel Baker and a number of other men came to the Mason home near Natchez. The moment Baker saw John he ordered his arrest, saying, "I could pick him out of a thousand." The father proceeded to explain to the Commandant that Baker's mistake could be easily explained, as John Mason and Wiguens resembled each other very much, and added that shortly after Wiguens and Setton first met his two sons, Wiguens told John confidentially that he, Setton, Bassett, Gibson, Fulsom, Phillips, and others were in the Baker robbery.

Going into details, Mason explained that, according to Setton's version, Bassett, Fulsom and Phillips were the men who bought for cash all the guns Baker had on hand and left the boatmen under the impression that these arms were to be used in a search for the Mason gang. Setton then told him confidentially that he and the other members of their band, by prearrangement, appeared shortly thereafter and robbed Baker of all his money and as much of the goods as they could carry. Fulsom, in order to inspire courage in the raiders, assured them they need not fear any pursuing party which Baker might organize, for he (Fulsom) could on very short notice, muster and command five hundred Chacquetaw Indians who would easily annihilate the revenge-seeking Baker. Setton, in concluding his account to the Masons, laughingly remarked that it was strange that two men looking so much alike should be "involved" in the same robbery, and that the guilty man should not be suspected and the innocent one be accused. Shortly after this Wiguens suddenly disappeared, very much to the disappointment of the Masons, who now realized the necessity of guarding Setton more closely.

Samuel Mason (digressing to another Baker robbery) asserted that after Baker had been robbed on the Natchez Trace, Baker and the officers came to arrest John. John submitted immediately, feeling confident that his innocence would be speedily proven. He could have vindicated himself had not some of Bassett's friends refused to declare that they saw John many miles from the scene of the robbery when it occurred. After he had been in prison about two months "he was liberated by men who did not make themselves known to him."

The Baker highway robbery having taken place on the American side and the Owsley robbery on the Spanish side, John, fearing he would be arrested on either side of the river, took his family and hid in the woods for a number of weeks. He hoped that in the meantime his innocence would become established by the guilty parties being brought to justice. But, instead, suspicion against him and against the entire Mason family grew stronger day by day.

Samuel Mason admitted that he had brought John Setton before a magistrate. He further stated that a number of things found in their possession the day of the arrest in Little Prairie were taken by them from Setton and held as evidence of his connection with some of the robberies of which the Masons were accused.

He asserted that after he had urgently requested Setton to declare his (Setton's) crime before a magistrate, and thus, perhaps, receive clemency, "he consented to do so." He and Setton then went "about twelve miles below Nogales" to the office of William Downs, a magistrate. Mason carried with him a pistol Setton told him he had procured as a part of his booty from the raid on the Owsley boat. William Downs "received Setton's confession but was not able to take his oath, as he had no sheriff on guard with him." Mason then, without informing Setton, went in search of Anthony Glass, who, it was rumored, was part owner of the Owsley boat, to have him serve as a witness to the affidavit. Mrs. Glass implored her husband not to act, for she feared his doing so might lead to the exposure of her brother, one Bassett, who had participated in various robberies. Glass, however, pacified his wife by telling her that since Setton was a deserter any sworn statement he might make would necessarily be ignored, and then insisted that he would go to Downs and there denounce Setton as a deserter and have him placed in the hands of the military authorities.

When the two men arrived at the magistrate's house "they discovered that Setton, suspecting some trickery, had left." A few weeks later, Mason swore, Setton again joined the Masons and had been with them ever since. After finishing his testimony Mason suggested that "If Setton told the truth in the testimony he gave in this trial, our statements must agree."

The next morning, January 21, John Mason appeared before the Commandant. The prisoner evidently did not know the contents of his father's and Setton's testimony, but he undoubtedly had some idea of how his father intended to answer many questions should they be asked. Most of his testimony agreed,

in the main, with his father's. He tried to show the
Commandant that he had long attempted to "vindicate"
and "establish" himself and to live "a decent life." He
said he had escaped from prison because he realized
that the defense of his name required his personal attention. He swore that practically all he knew about the
various robberies regarding which he was questioned,
was through reports he had heard from John Setton,
alias John Taylor alias Wells, and from Druck Smith,
alias Smith Gibson. He insisted he had never seen
Phillips, Fulsom, and the other Gibson referred to.

The question of how the Masons came into possession
of the eight horses had not been asked before. John
Mason accounted for each by giving the details of a
purchase or trade. He was asked why "he pursued the
two Frenchmen in a boat until they had reached a safe
harbor." His explanation was that he, Thomas, and
Setton were on the river and followed these men, suspecting them to be robbers involved in some of the
acts of which the Masons were accused. He hoped that
if they were he would succeed in having them verify
Setton's declaration of his own guilt. When the two
men reached Nogales his boat was on the point of over-
taking them. He then discovered that they were French
officials and the pursuit was dropped without giving the
men any reasons for the chase.

He swore that most of the notes and paper money
found in their possession belonged to Setton, who
claimed he had "found it in a bag hanging on a bush
near the road," and who on one occasion remarked
that since then he had more money than he could use.
John Mason added that this statement convinced him
that Setton had stolen the money.

The record of this sworn statement made by John

Mason is abruptly followed by "And the prisoner being asked by the interpreter whether he had anything further to say or anything to unsay, he answered 'No,' but requested, as his father had done before him, that we do not hand him over to the United States Government, and after his declaration was read to him, he persisted that it was true."

Thomas Mason followed his brother John and, like him, gave evidence that agreed, in the main, with his father's. He swore his occupation was "farming and harvesting" and "bringing down flour and whiskey" in boats. He admitted that he had heard of the Baker and Owsley robberies but claimed he knew none of the details except those told to him by Setton, and these he repeated.

When he was asked about Setton's appearance before the magistrate, he answered that he had accompanied him to Downs' but did not force him to make an affidavit. He added that John Mason had received a message from the Governor of Natchez to the effect that if he produced a witness who would turn state's evidence it would "tend to clear him of his guilt;" hence, their anxiety to have Setton make a declaration.

After hearing Thomas Mason's version of the subjects that had been discussed by the preceding witnesses, the Commandant, who evidently had been informed that day that the Masons had also maneuvered further north, asked him whether or not he knew a man named Mosique and the two Duff brothers while in Illinois. He answered he had heard of them and understood that one of the brothers had been killed by Indians. His answers to other questions were to the effect that he knew nothing of the robbing of a negro in St. Louis, of a man named Lecompte, and of a stolen negro woman who had been sold to a priest named Manuel. The officer then asked him whether or not he was aware that the Masons were accused of these crimes, "but the witness continued to profess he had never heard of them."

The fifth prisoner was Marguerite Douglas, wife of John Mason. She swore she had been married eight years. She answered that to her "keen regret" she had heard of the robberies of which her husband and the other Masons were "so falsely accused." Her knowledge of these acts, she swore, was based solely on hearsay. Among other things, she said Setton told her that robbing the Baker boat proved as easy "as robbing some old woman." She also swore she knew nothing about the paper money found in their possession and could not account for the money and goods discovered among her personal belongings other than by suggesting that in packing up so hurriedly she may have placed some of Setton's personal property in her bag.

Samuel Mason Jr., in his testimony stated that he was eighteen years old and that he had lived with his parents all the time until about three months previous. He said his father and brothers had left his mother at Bayou Pierre – between Natchez and Vicksburg – and were away for the purpose of establishing a new home, and that she was now ill and living with her daughter, Mrs. Philip Briscoe. The Commandant remarked to him: "You ought to speak the truth for you have a mother, who, it is reported, is a good and honorable woman, and you ought not to be mixed up in the wickedness of your father and brothers, who, it is said, are guilty of many thefts and robberies." The answers he gave to the few questions asked him agreed with those given by his father.

Magnus Mason, the last of the prisoners, was called

upon January 24. He stated he was about sixteen years old and was born "in Kentucky on the south side of Green River." (The others had claimed Pennsylvania as their native state.) In answer to questions he stated that he had lived "part of his time with his father in Kentucky and part with his mother in Bayou Pierre near Natchez." He declared his father had spent practically all of the past two years away from home trying "to discover men who were committing the robberies." [28]

The next witness was Dr. Richard Jones Waters, the man on whose recommendation the passport had been granted to Samuel Mason. Dr. Waters said he first met Mason in 1791 or 1792 at "Red Banks on the Ohio," (now Henderson, Kentucky) which was after he (Dr. Waters) had settled in New Madrid. He had been traveling in America and on his return, coming to the Ohio River, engaged Charles Lafond, a merchant, and two other men who were on their way tc New Orleans, to take him down as far as New Madrid. When the boat reached the Falls of the Ohio (Louisville) Lafond, hearing that he intended to remain there a few days, asked permission to let the boat proceed to Red Banks, where Lafond expected to dispose of some of the goods on board. The permission was granted on condition that Lafond, without fail, wait for him there. In due time he (Dr. Waters) reached Red Banks and then met Samuel Mason for the first time. Mason claimed that Lafond had gone fishing a few days before and, in the meantime, started his boat south. He (Dr. Waters) did not know whether or not Lafond and his boat ever reached New Orleans, and not until recently, had he suspected foul play.

---

[28] Nothing in the records indicates whether or not the officials recognized the confliction in the testimony given by the Masons and Setton.

A year after this, continued Dr. Waters, he was traveling down the Ohio River, stopped at Red Banks and, to his surprise, met Samuel Mason again. Mason asked him to come to the house to prescribe for Mrs. Mason who was sick in bed. The doctor complied and the result was a trade in which Mason bought seventy dollars worth of medicine and merchandise, paying forty dollars in meat and giving him a demand note for thirty dollars on Felic Concer, of New Madrid. But when he arrived at New Madrid he learned that Concer had left for parts unknown. In 1798, however, Mason paid the note. He then saw nothing more of Mason until March, 1800, when he met him and his son Thomas and a man by the name of Smith who said they had come to New Madrid for drugs. They purchased some medicine from him for Mrs. John Mason and other members of the family and paid for it with merchandise which they claimed they had bought from a store boat. A few days later Samuel Mason called again, not to buy medicine but to ask his assistance in procuring a passport for land on Spanish territory. This he was, at first, unwilling to give, for, although he knew nothing unfavorable concerning the family, he was not assured of their character. After the old man had pleaded with him and declared that although rumor had done all the Masons great injustice he would never regret the endorsement of his character, he procured a passport, giving to the clerk at the time a history of his acquaintance with Mason. A few days afterward Thomas Mason informed him that he was obliged to go to Kentucky to straighten out some business affairs before he settled on the land that would be granted them. He entrusted Thomas Mason with "some valuable papers for delivery at the Falls of the

Ohio." These papers reached their destination but much later than Thomas had promised. No explanation of the delay was offered or demanded.

The record of the proceedings shows that January 26 was devoted by the officials to inspecting the belongings of the Masons and approximating their value. The saddles and pistols referred to by Setton were found as described by him. There was also discovered some "twenty twists of human hair of different shades which do not seem to have been cut off voluntarily by those to whom the hair belonged." These and a number of other evidences were laid aside by the inspectors. The belongings were estimated at about six hundred dollars in value. The silver and paper money amounted to seven thousand dollars, much of which, however, "appears to be counterfeit."

The next day Francois Derousser, a citizen of New Madrid, came forward, stating that he had an important declaration to make concerning the prisoners. He explained that he was a native of Illinois and that in 1791, when he and his family were coming down the Ohio River and had reached a point near Red Banks, where they happened to make a landing, a man – the one he now recognized among the prisoners as Samuel Mason – stepped up to him and, pushing a gun against his stomach, threatened to shoot him if he did not follow. He was led into a hut, where several persons were sitting. Immediately after entering, Samuel Mason shouted: "This is the man who stole my horses and slaves and sold them to the Indians," and, looking around for a rope, Mason seemed to be making preparations to hang him at once. He finally convinced Mason that he could not possibly have been guilty of the thefts.

After keeping him in chains all night, continued Derousser, Mason permitted him to leave, but while he was making some repairs on his boat to resume his trip, Mason came to him and persuaded him to remain two months and work with the Mason boys. Mason promised him a certain quantity of linen, calico, and bed covers for his services and, needing these badly for his family, he accepted the proposition. At the end of the specified time the promised goods were given to him; but three hours after he had received them and while on his way to his boat, Samuel Mason and a Captain Bradley overtook him and robbed him of all the goods. That night he managed to return to his boat and with the aid of Eustache Peltier succeeded in cutting the ice from around it. He started down the river, and after much suffering from cold and hunger he and his family finally landed at New Madrid, where they had lived ever since.

Eustache Peltier appeared before the Commandant, confirmed the declaration made by Derousser, and added that he had heard that a certain Lafond, "an European merchant with an emporium of goods in New Orleans," had stopped at the Mason's house near Red Banks one night about the time he and Derousser made their escape, but neither the merchant nor the boat in which he traveled had been heard from since.

Pierre Billeth, another citizen of New Madrid, declared that he knew some facts bearing on the Masons and felt it his duty to report them. He related to the Commandant that during an excursion in August, 1798, on the Cumberland River, near the mouth, he heard a negro woman belonging to Samuel Mason tell Rees Jones and James Downs that her master had forced her to help dispose of the body of one of his victims. She declared that Mason after stabbing and robbing the man had commanded her to help tie a rope around his neck and drag the body to the Ohio, where they threw it in to the water. This same woman had been stolen by Mason and later sold at public auction by Sheriff James Downs, then of Kaskaskia, to Father Manuel, a priest, who lived near St. Genevieve.

All the witnesses having been examined, and the declarations and proclamations heard, the Commandant January 29, 1803, ordered an itemized account of the cost of the trial, including the expenses incurred in making the arrest at Little Prairie. The account rendered shows that the largest single item was for "the sergeant and nineteen militiamen for seventeen days' guard and sentinel watch of prisoners, at one piaster per day, three hundred and forty piasters." Twenty-two men, besides the officers, were employed in making the arrest and bringing the prisoners to New Madrid, for which they received one hundred and seventy-six piasters. Another item reads, "irons and cuffs made for prisoners, eight piasters." The total expense is given as one thousand fifty-three piasters, or about one thousand dollars.

The last entry is dated January 31, 1803, and, like all the others, is presented in monotonous legal phraseology. It ends with the statement that: "We [the Commandant] hereby direct that the proceedings of this trial, originally set down in writing on ninety-one sheets of paper written on both sides, as well as the pieces of evidence tending to conviction, together with seven thousand piasters in U. S. banknotes, be forwarded to the Honorable Governor General by Don Robert McCoy, Captain of the Militia, whom we have charged to conduct the prisoners, Mason and consorts, to New

Orleans with the view of their trial being continued
and finished, if it so please the Honorable Governor
General."

And here ends the record of the preliminary trial of
the Masons. Captain McCoy, having been appointed
to conduct the prisoners to a higher court, made his
preparations and in due time started for New Orleans.

Mason and Harpe - Double-Cross and Double Death

Out of the mass of perjury and counter-accusations brought out at this examination only one thing was clear – that is that Mason and his gang, as far as testimony and confession went, were not guilty of any crime on the Spanish side of the Mississippi. Whatever crimes they may have committed it was essential to their present safety to locate them on the American or eastern side of the river. The Spanish authorities had no power to punish them for violations of law on American territory, but the Spanish Intendant Salcedo at New Orleans had the power under the comity existing between the Spanish and American governments to deliver them up to the American authorities. The New Madrid court, therefore, ordered the prisoners to be transferred to New Orleans and brought before the intendant.

At that point in the march of events fate took relentless grip on Samuel Mason and Little Harpe, alias Setton, for their crimes. The way of atonement was as swift as its end was to be terrible. It might be quickly summarized, but there is the better way of pursuing the astonishing and dramatic story through the faded records and old scraps of publications of those times, thus getting into actual touch with the persons and with the primitive conditions under which this strange duel of two master criminals was fought out. Each feared the other; Mason, perhaps, not knowing his antagonist.

The grim headsman was silently stalking both. In the language of crime fate was double-crossing both.

From New Madrid to New Orleans was a distance of about nine hundred miles and to travel it by boat in those days required more than two weeks. It was as if it had been decreed that Mason should make a farewell tour through a part of the country in which he had become so execrated. New Orleans was then the capital of the Spanish province of Louisiana, the seat of the highest court, and had been for more than three-quarters of a century the most important town on the Mississippi.

In 1803 New Madrid was a frontier settlement about fourteen years old. It was a military post occupied by a small force of soldiers and a town with a population of about eight hundred who were French, American, Canadian, and Spanish, or an extraction of these peoples. New Madrid remained under Spanish rule until 1804 when, as a part of the province of Louisiana, it became a part of the territory of Louisiana acquired by the United States.[29]

If an official account of what followed Mason's trial at New Madrid was kept it may now exist among the archives in old Madrid in Spain and may contain data relative to the transfer of the prisoners. At any rate, Captain McCoy and his guard evidently started for New Orleans early in February, 1803. It is more

---

[29] Practically all the province of Louisiana, including New Orleans, was transferred from France to Spain in 1769. Spain secretly ceded the same territory to France September 1, 1800, but the French did not take formal possession until November 30, 1803. On April 30, 1803, or about seven months before this formality was performed, Napoleon secretly sold Louisiana to the United States and accordingly, December 20, 1803, at New Orleans, lower Louisiana was formally transferred to the American Republic, and March 9, 1804, at St. Louis, the same ceremony took place for upper Louisiana, which included New Madrid.

likely that, as a matter of economy and convenience, they traveled down the Mississippi in a flatboat. The records show that some of the goods found in the possession of the Masons were carried along as evidence.

There is neither written history nor oral tradition telling of Captain McCoy's departure for New Orleans or how he held his prisoners on board during the trip. At least one very probable scene, however, presents itself, and in it John Setton is the central figure. Samuel Mason was then the most widely known bandit in the Mississippi Valley. But in the eyes of the law Setton now suddenly became the most important character of all the outlaws. He was likely to turn state's evidence, reveal many robberies that were long standing mysteries, and thus convict not only Samuel Mason and his family, but also point out clues that would lead to the extermination of all river pirates.

The boat was necessarily crowded, for even under the most encouraging circumstances room on a flatboat was limited. There were about seventeen persons on board: Captain McCoy, the interpreter, some five men who constituted the guard and crew, the seven prisoners, and the three children. Setton was probably chained in the most conspicuous place where he could be carefully watched. This must have been done not only to prevent his escape, but also to prevent Samuel Mason from trying to persuade him to act in a plot against the crew, or to dictate to him a forthcoming "confession."

One can easily imagine that Captain McCoy and his men frowned at Setton as they would at a chained sheep-killing dog. There was nothing about him to attract them. On the contrary, he was repulsive. Setton's countenance, according to one writer, was always downcast and fierce, his hair red, his face meager and his stature below that of the average man. This combination gave him, as Judge James Hall puts it, "a suspicious exterior." He was about thirty years of age and looked the part of a man who was too much of a villain to smile and thereby try to hide some of his villainy. To his captors he was nothing more than a vicious dog whose life was being spared solely that he might later give Mason a long-deserved, fatal bite.

They not only looked upon him as a thief and murderer, but also as a fool not fit to live. If he were guilty of the crimes Mason laid at his feet, then hanging was too mild a punishment for him. By the same token, if guilty, he was a fool to permit a notorious outlaw to dictate to him just what to confess and whom to implicate. And if he were innocent of the crimes he was even a greater fool for submitting to Mason's demand and declaring in an affidavit that he, not Mason, was the guilty man.

With Captain McCoy and his guards on one side, and Samuel Mason and his family on the other, Setton stood alone between "the devil and the deep blue sea." He and Mason were figuratively and literally in the same boat, but Mason had at least the consolation of knowing that the members of his family on board were also with him in sympathy and ready to obey his command, even though it led to certain death.

Judged by their morals Samuel Mason and John Setton were very much alike, but in their physical aspect they differed greatly. Mason was then about fifty-five years old, possibly sixty. Swaney, the old mail carrier, who saw him often, described him to Guild: "He weighed about two hundred pounds, and was a fine looking man. He was rather modest and unassuming, and had nothing of the raw-head-and-bloody-bones appearance which his character would indicate."

Henry Howe refers to him as "a man of gigantic stature and of more than ordinary talents." William Darby says: "Mason at any time of his life or in any situation, had something extremely ferocious in his look, which arose particularly from a tooth which projected forwards, and could only be covered with his lip by effort."

Regardless of the difference in their physical size and physiognomy, and regardless of the extent of their guilt, both men were held for the same crimes and were now on their way to New Orleans to appear before the Spanish authorities. Less than a dozen towns and forts were then scattered along the river and all were small ones. As the boat slowly floated and sailed down the wide stream between seemingly endless forest and jungle covered shores, Mason had ample time to view the various places where he had committed robberies, and to recall how successfully he had carried out all his attempts. The scenes along the Mississippi have undergone many changes since Mason's day. Nevertheless, many of the views have retained enough of their primitive grandeur to create in the imagination a landscape of continuous virgin forests and a vivid picture of what river life was in pioneer days. But, by searching the old records pertaining to Mason's career, one discovers facts that could never have been foreseen by the wisest prophet nor imagined by the wildest fictionist.

How and when Captain McCoy and his prisoners arrived at New Orleans has not been ascertained, although an effort has been made to find newspaper or other accounts giving details on the subject. There is, however, an unpublished official letter in Spanish, in the Mississippi Department of Archives and History, which shows that upon Captain McCoy's arrival in New Orleans the record of the proceedings of the trial held at New Madrid was submitted to the Governor General of Louisiana and his Secretary of War. These two Spanish officers, after going over the proceedings, concluded that since the evidence taken did not prove that Mason had committed any crime on the Spanish side, the prisoners should be handed over to the Americans. In due time, therefore, they ordered them sent to Natchez.

The official letter referred to is dated New Orleans, March 3, 1803. It was written by Vidal, the Secretary of War, approved by Manuel Salcedo, the last Spanish governor of Louisiana, and forwarded to Governor Claiborne. It briefly reviews the trial and points out to the Governor of the Mississippi Territory that the case falls under American and not Spanish jurisdiction.

Governor Claiborne, in all probability, answered this communication and requested that the Masons be turned over to him, for Captain McCoy and his men, taking the prisoners and some of their stolen property, left New Orleans the latter part of March for Natchez. What occurred when their boat stopped near Point Coupee, Louisiana—some two hundred and forty miles above New Orleans and about one hundred miles below Natchez – is told in the following news item quoted in full from *The Western Spy,* published at Cincinnati, May 4, 1803:

"Extract of a letter from the Reverend John Smith

to a gentleman in this town, dated Point Coupee, March 28, 1803.

"'You no doubt have received the account of old Sam Mason's arrest, with three or four of his sons, some other villains, a woman and three children, about thirty miles below New Madrid, by Captain McCoy, the king's interpreter and a small party. Captain Mc-Coy has since taken them to New Orleans in irons, but as no crime could be charged upon them as being committed in the Spanish Government, the Governor General ordered them to be taken to Natchez and delivered to our Government. The day before yesterday as they were passing this place the mast of their vessel broke, a part of the men were sent on shore to make a new one, and the rest were left to guard the prisoners. In a short time they threw off their irons, seized the guns belonging to the boat and fired upon the guard. Captain McCoy hearing the alarm ran out of the cabin, old Mason instantly shot him through the breast and shoulder; he with the determined bravery of a soldier, though scarcely able to stand, shot him in the head. Mason fell and rose, fell and rose again, and although in a gore of blood, one of his party having shot a Spaniard's arm to pieces, he drove off McCoy's party and kept possession of the boat till evening, when, discovering a superior force they left the boat, the woman and children following with great precipitation. There is a party of Caroles [sic] after them and it is supposed they will succeed in taking them. The commandant at this place has offered one thousand dollars for taking old Mason dead or alive. They will be pursued with the utmost diligence by a set of determined fellows.'"

Mason escaped March 26, 1803. The report of his

flight spread fast. The same facts that were published in *The Western Spy* were sent out from Natchez as a news item, dated April 2, and printed with less detail in various papers, among them *The Tennessee Gazette* of April 27, *The Kentucky Gazette* of May 3, and *The Palladium* of May 5. In the same news item appears a brief statement to the effect that Governor Claiborne had received "official information of the arrival at New Orleans of the French Prefect for the Colony of Louisiana."

Mason hoped, as already stated, that by showing he had committed no crimes on the Spanish side of the Mississippi he would not be punished by the Spanish authorities. He evidently did not foresee the possibility of their turning him over to the Americans. At any rate, the French were taking possession (in form at least) of Louisiana, and since they had never been implicated in any strained relations with the states relative to the free navigation of the Mississippi, Mason was now in equal danger of pursuit on either side. By choice or circumstance he risked the American side. Two months after his thrilling escape from the boat he was seen about fifteen miles northeast of Natchez. This is shown in a report dated Natchez, June 6, 1803, published in *The Palladium* July 14, from which weekly it was copied by various other papers:

"On Tuesday last the notorious Samuel Mason and several of his party, all well armed, were seen on the Choctaw trace near Cole's Creek. Two detachments of the militia of Jefferson County were immediately ordered out by his excellency, the Governor, in pursuit of them. We have not yet been informed of the result of this expedition."

The expedition was a failure. About two months

after it was first reported that Mason had been seen near Cole's Creek, James May came to Greenville, Mississippi – a place formerly called Hunston, some twenty-five miles in a northeasterly direction from Natchez, and now extinct – and gave an account of his recent contact with Mason. James May, it will be recalled, was among the rough characters who were driven out of Henderson County, Kentucky, about the time Mason made his departure from there for Cave-in-Rock. May's past career was not yet known by the citizens to whom he made this report. *The Palladium*, ever reliable but sometimes late, in its issue of September 8, 1803, says:

"By a gentleman from Natchez, we are informed that about the 25th or 26th of July, a man by the name of James May, came to Hunston, near Natchez, and made oath before a magistrate, that sundry articles of property and money, which he then delivered up, he had taken from the notorious Samuel Mason, after shooting him in the head just above the eye. May had been robbed and taken by Mason on his passage down the river, and had joined that party. A few days after which, the company hearing a firing of guns, Mason ordered his party, May excepted, to hide the horses. May he directed to hide a skiff. He took his gun with him, and on his return, whilst Mason was counting his money to divide with the party, he shot him, put the money and property on board the skiff, and conveyed it to Hunston.

"A letter from Natchez, published in the Natchez paper, confirms the above account. A letter to a gentleman in this town from his correspondent at Natchez dated the 25th instant, makes no mention of the above circumstance, but says: 'The Masons have removed

to Mississippi where they have of late committed many
robberies, but no murders that I have heard of.' "

No complete file of any of the newspapers published in Natchez from 1800 to 1805 has been found.
The few stray copies, located in various large libraries,
contain nothing about Mason's career. All are too late
or too early to embrace any current news pertaining to
him. Thus it was without success that an effort was
made to verify, by "the Natchez paper" which "confirms the above account," the statement regarding
May's appearance in Greenville in July, 1803, or to
draw on any Natchez paper for any contemporary reports relative to Mason.

There is nothing in history or tradition to indicate
what action was taken by the authorities after they received James May's report. He evidently left Greenville, but for what purpose can only be surmised. It
is highly probable that, after May presented the
"money and property" he claimed he had taken from
Mason as evidence of his having shot the outlaw for
whom a reward was offered, he was soon convinced
that he had produced no positive evidence at all. Judging from what took place a few months later, he left for
the purpose of bringing in Mason, dead or alive.

May probably had been "robbed and taken" by Mason for the same purpose that John Setton had been
detained – to be used as a witness upon whom he might
try to shift the Mason robberies. If so, May's pursuit
of Mason for the offered reward was stimulated by a
spirit of revenge. He sallied forth, reconnoitered,
and returned; but he did not return to Greenville, nor
alone. He appeared at Natchez and was accompanied
by John Setton. Setton shortly thereafter was recognized as one of Mason's band and both men were taken

and committed to jail some time during the latter part of October. When they were arrested Setton, as shown by later records, claimed he came to Natchez for the purpose of turning state's evidence. *The Kentucky Gazette,* of November 22, 1803, briefly touches on the situation as it was about a month before that paper went to press:

"A letter from a gentleman at Natchez, to his correspondent in this town, dated 20th October, contains information that the men who robbed Mr. Elisha Winters, on his way from New Orleans, have been taken and committed to jail; so that there is a probability of his getting his money. They had in their possession sundry articles taken from the party who were robbed near Bayou Pierre. One of the robbers has turned state's evidence against the rest; and says that if he can be suffered to go out with a guard, he will take them where all the papers were hid and a number of other things with some money. The place is not more than two days' ride, and application has been made to the governor for the above purpose, which will doubtless be granted."

The hunt for Mason was now continued with even greater enthusiasm. Besides the militia stationed at Natchez and Fort Gibson many men were on watch for the notorious outlaw and his band. The woods were full of robber-exterminating and reward-seeking soldiers and civilians. Mason's capture was inevitable. May and Setton evidently formed a pursuing party of their own. According to one tradition, the two men discovered Samuel Mason near Rodney, Jefferson County, Mississippi, and, according to another, they found him near Lake Concordia, Louisiana, not far from Natchez. They gained Mason's confidence and succeeded in convincing him that they had returned in order to follow him as their leader. Then it was that Mason met the fate he had himself invited.

Monette says: "Two of his band, tempted by the large reward, concerted a plan by which they might obtain it. An opportunity soon occurred, and while Mason, in company with the two conspirators, was counting out some ill-gotten plunder, a tomahawk was buried in his brain. His head was severed from his body and borne in triumph to Washington, the seat of the territorial [Mississippi] government." Daniel Roe, in a letter published in *The Port Folio,* August, 1825, states that the two men "took Mason's head to Natchez in the bow of a canoe, rolled up in blue clay, or mud, to prevent putrefaction." Resuming Monette's account: "The head of Mason was recognized by many, and identified by all who read the proclamation, as the head entirely corresponded with the description given of certain scars and peculiar marks. Some delay, however, occurred in paying over the reward, owing to the slender state of the treasury. Meantime, a great assemblage from all the adjacent country had taken place, to view the grim and ghastly head of the robber chief. They were not less inspired with curiosity to see and converse with the individuals whose prowess had delivered the country of so great a scourge." [30]

[30] Under what circumstances Mason was trapped by May and Setton and whether or not he really knew by whom he was snared has not been ascertained. Mrs. William Anthony, in her letter to Draper, states that on one occasion when Mason and his party were crossing the Mississippi River, May was acting as ferryman and "Mason said the others might all go over first and he would remain till last. When all were over but Mason, May returned for him, and as Mason was alone with his bag of money, May killed him and took the head to Natchez."

Audubon, in one of his *Journals* under the head of "Regulators" gives another version: "At last a body of Regulators undertook, at great peril, and for the sake of the country, to bring the villain to punishment. . . One day

One version, which first appeared in print about 1876, has it that "Many fully identified the head by certain marks thereon, except his wife who as positively denied it. . . The Governor had sent his carriage for her expressly to come down and testify . . . and many believed Mason fled the country and died in his bed in Canada. . . Mason's family [probably his wife and youngest son] then resided in this county, not far from old Shankstown, and his wife was generally respected as an honest and virtuous woman by all her neighbors, and one of her sons was a worthy citizen of Warren County not many years ago." This is quoted in Claiborne's history from a "Centennial Address" delivered by Captain W. L. Harper, of Jefferson County, Mississippi. In 1891 Robert Lowry published a statement in his *History of Mississippi,* without citing any authority, that "One of Mason's gang killed an innocent man, cut off his head, carried it to the Governor of Mississippi and claimed the reward."

May, as already seen, claimed that he had been a victim of Mason and, a few months previous, had declared he could find and capture the notorious robber. Setton, on the other hand, having expressed a desire to

---

as he was riding a beautiful horse in the woods he was met by one of the Regulators, who immediately recognized him, but passed him as if an utter stranger. Mason, not dreaming of danger, pursued his way leisurely, as if he had met no one. . . At dusk, Mason, having reached the lowest part of a ravine, no doubt well known to him, hoppled (tied together the forelegs of) his stolen horse, to enable it to feed during the night without chance of straying far, and concealed himself in a hollow log to spend the night. The plan was good but proved his ruin. The Regulator, who knew every hill and hollow of the woods, marked the place and the log with the eye of an experienced hunter, and as he remarked that Mason was most efficiently armed, he galloped off to the nearest house where he knew he should find assistance. This was easily procured, and the party proceeded to the spot. Mason, on being attacked, defended himself with desperate valor; and as it proved impossible to secure him alive he was brought to the ground with a rifle ball. His head was cut off, and stuck on the end of a broken branch of

turn state's evidence, admitted having been connected
with the outlaw. The situation was interesting, for it
was an unusual one. The head, having been identified
as Samuel Mason's, the two heroes of the occasion went
before a judge to make an affidavit and to get an order
on the governor for the payment of the reward. "But
just as the judge was in the act of making out a certificate," writes Claiborne in his *History of Mississippi,*
"a traveler stepped into the court room and requested
to have the two men arrested. He had alighted at the
tavern, had repaired to the stable to see his horse attended to, and there saw the horses of the two men who
had arrived just before him. He recognized the
horses (principally because each had a peculiar blaze
in the face) as belonging to parties who had robbed
him and killed one of his companions some two months
previous on the Natchez Trace, and going into the
court house, he identified the two men."

Suspicion was immediately aroused. This declaration not only showed that May, who complained of
being robbed, was a robber himself, but it also indicated
that the "reformed" Setton as well as the "victimized"
May, had committed at least one robbery since they
left Greenville in search of Mason. Who are May and
Setton, and where do they come from, and what have
they been doing for a living? Such questions were
asked. Absolutely nothing was known about May. As
to Setton, their information was limited to the report
that he had been "badly treated" by Mason; some may

a tree, by the nearest road to the place where the affray happened. The
gang soon dispersed, in consequence of the loss of their leader, and this
infliction of merited punishment proved beneficial in deterring others from
following a similar predatory life."

Such may have been the end of one of the sons of Mason. There is nothing
in history or tradition connecting this act of the Regulators with the career
of Samuel Mason.

have known that he had traveled under assumed names, but evidently none yet suspected he was Little Harpe.

The next step in the development of their careers is given in one of Draper's manuscripts written after an interview with Colonel John Stump, who was born in 1776: "In the winter of 1803-4 old Captain Frederick Stump, commanding a company under Colonel George Doherty, went as far as Natchez to aid in taking possession of Louisiana. There Captain Stump, by invitation of Governor Claiborne, an old friend, made his quarters, and was present when Setton and May came with Mason's head to claim the reward of one thousand dollars. The Governor told them to call at a stated time and the check would be ready for them. After they had gone Captain Stump said he believed that Setton was really Little Harpe. . . The description of Little Harpe so well corresponded with Setton's appearance that it was agreed to arrest them both. . . It was proclaimed at the landing of Natchez that it was believed that Wiley Harpe was taken, and if any Kentucky boatman had any personal knowledge of him, they were desired to examine the prisoner. Five boatmen recognized him and gave in their evidence to that effect. Some of them were witnesses in the Harpe case when they broke from the Danville jail. Said one of these boatmen before seeing him: 'If he is Harpe he has a mole on his neck and two toes grown together on one foot.' And so it proved, and the fellow with such positive proof against him shed tears." [121]

Shortly after this, John Bowman, of Knoxville, Tennessee, called in to see the two men. He recognized Little Harpe. "Little Harpe denied the name, but Bowman persisted and said, 'if you are Harpe you have a scar under your left nipple where I cut you in a difficulty we had at Knoxville.' Bowman tore the man's shirt open and there was the scar." [26]

Up to this time, Little Harpe, under the names of John Taylor, John Setton, and Wells, had succeeded in concealing his identity. He now realized that even though he turned state's evidence against the Masons, the history of his own terrible career in Tennessee and Kentucky and at Cave-in-Rock was too well and widely known for him to expect any mercy, no matter how important his revelations regarding the Masons might be. At New Madrid he had a narrow escape from being identified. After he and the Masons were captured and taken to the Spanish prison, it was rumored that one of the prisoners was "a fellow who calls himself Taylor but who is supposed to be that notorious villain and murderer Harpe." A statement to that effect was written in a letter dated January 24, 1804, and published six weeks later in *The Western Spy*. But, as already seen, he had sworn before the New Madrid court, as John Setton, that he had met a man by the name of Harpe who had been killed and, when further questioned, declared that he knew nothing regarding the whereabouts of Little Harpe. Although his identity was now well established, he, in self-defense, persisted in denying the name. Escape was his only hope.

Nothing was then known about James May's past other than his recent acts connected with the beheading of Mason and his attempted apprehension of the Mason band. These acts in themselves exposed him as a man of such a treacherous character that he could expect no mercy nor any reward. On the other hand, should he be identified as one of the men who had been driven out of Henderson County, Kentucky, and be accused of Cave-in-Rock murders and robberies, then nothing but the severest punishment that could be inflicted upon him might be expected. With him, as with Little Harpe, escape was his only hope. And both escaped.[31]

How Little Harpe and May escaped is not known. While at Natchez they may have been indicted for Mason's murder. If so, having killed Mason in compliance with the governor's proclamation to capture the outlaw dead or alive, they were acquitted. William Darby, then living near Natchez, writes that the two prisoners "learning their danger fled from Natchez, but were taken in Jefferson County, Mississippi, and confined in jail and in due time, tried and convicted. . ." They were tried before the Circuit Court in Greenville, in January, 1804, as is shown by the few existing entries made in the now mutilated docket book of that court. No record of the court proceedings was found, although a careful search was made.

The first entry found in the docket book is dated Friday, January 13, 1804. The court was presided over by Peter B. Bruin, David Ker, and Thomas Rodney, who were among the best known men in Mississippi. It is an interesting fact that when Aaron Burr was arrested the following year on Cole's Creek, near Greenville, he was tried in Washington, Mississippi, before two of these same judges, the third, Judge Ker, having died of pneumonia contracted while serving at the trial of Harpe and May. William Downs, as foreman of the grand jury, brought in "an indictment of robbery" against each of the prisoners: "The Territory against James May" and "The Territory against John Setton."

---

[31] All the early records prove beyond a doubt that John Setton and Wiley Harpe or "Little" Harpe were one and the same man. A few of the later writers confuse May and Setton and, apparently as a result of a superficial knowledge of the careers of these outlaws, state that Wiley Harpe had assumed the name of one May.

Little Harpe, alias Setton, and his co-worker May were represented by Mr. Breazeale and Mr. Parrott. These attorneys evidently made every possible effort to save their clients. A plea of "not guilty" had been entered. Then followed much sparring over technicalities. They first attempted to quash the indictment; they next claimed the court did not have jurisdiction; and finally presented a petition for a writ of *habeas corpus*. But all these contentions were overruled.[32] "And for trial (each) put himself upon the country and General Poindexter, Attorney General." Each was tried by separate jury, James May being the first, and each was found guilty. Then the two attorneys came forward with "a plea of former acquittal," but the court rendered a decision that "the plea of former acquittal is not sufficient in law to be considered a sufficient bar to this indictment." This plea of "former acquittal" leads one to infer that when Mason's head was brought to Natchez both men were tried there and elsewhere for murder, and having been "acquitted" of that charge they, in all likelihood, argued that they were therefore also acquitted of highway robbery which was incidental to the murder.

As already stated, the record of the proceedings containing all these and other details of the case cannot now be found. There is nothing to indicate who the witnesses were, except Elisha Winters, who was "allowed the compensation allowed by law for his attendance at this term and for traveling to and from said court one thousand miles." Among the few available

---

[32] The counsel for the defense evidently objected to the jurisdiction of the court, claiming that the alleged "robberies by Mason's men" did not occur within the bounds of Mississippi Territory. The question of jurisdiction is commented on in two of the letters written in 1804 by Thomas Rodney to Caesar A. Rodney. [52]

GALLOWS FIELD, JEFFERSON COUNTY, MISSISSIPPI
Here, in 1804, two Cave-in-Rock outlaws were hanged
(From a drawing by J. Bernhard Alberts, made in 1917)

pages of the docket book bearing on this case is one containing two entries dated February 4, 1804. They show that the sentence passed was in the same words for each prisoner. James May's is the first on the record, and is immediately followed by Little Harpe's:

"John Setton who has been found guilty of robbery at the present term was this day set to the bar and the sentence of the court pronounced upon him as follows, that on Wednesday the eighth day of the present month he be taken to the place of execution and there to be hung up by the neck, between the hours of ten o'clock in the forenoon and four in the afternoon, until he is dead, dead, dead. Which said sentence the Sheriff of Jefferson County was ordered to carry into execution."

On Wednesday afternoon, February 8th, Little Harpe and James May were taken from the jail to a field about a quarter of a mile north of the village of Greenville. There, on what has ever since been known as "Gallows Field," they received their well deserved reward, but not the one they had planned to procure. They paid, with their lives, what was, considering the atrocity of their crimes, a light penalty.

In pioneer days the official executioner usually prepared a gallows by fastening one end of a long beam or heavy pole in the forks of a tree and placing the other end similarly in another tree. On this cross timber he tied the rope with which the condemned man was to be hanged. The prisoner, as a rule, was put on a wagon, his coffin serving as a seat, and driven to the place of execution. Upon his arrival the same wagon and coffin on which he rode were used as the platform and trap of his gallows. After the suspended rope was properly looped around his neck the condemned man was made to stand erect on his coffin. When all details had been attended to the horses were rushed forward, leaving the human body hung suspended in the air. In some instances the gallows was a frame-work with a platform in which a trap door was built.

In the hanging of Harpe and May the procedure was somewhat unusual even for a frontier country. Two ropes were tied to a heavy pole placed high between two trees. The two men walked from the jail to the gallows. Each with his hands tied behind him was made to mount a ladder; his feet were then bound and the noose fastened around his neck. When the ladders were dropped the two bodies fell as far as the suspended rope permitted, and thus each was "hung up by the neck" until, as prescribed by law, he was "dead, dead, dead." [54]

The news that Samuel Mason had at last been killed was a great relief to the country. The fact that Little Harpe and James May were actually hanged was a matter of equally widespread interest. *The Guardian of Freedom,* February 20, 1804, published the following, which was copied by a number of papers, including *The Kentucky Gazette* of a week later:

"Extract of a letter from a gentleman in Mississippi Territory to his friend in this town (Frankfort) dated February 8, 1804: 'There have been two of Sam Mason's party – which infested the road between this country and Kentucky – in jail at Greenville for trial. They were condemned last term and executed this day. One of them was James May; the other called himself John Setton but was proved to be the villain who was known by the name of Little or Red-headed Harpe, and who committed so many acts of cruelty in Kentucky.' "

The Palladium, March 3, published a news item dated Natchez, February 9, 1804: "Setton and May were executed at Greenville yesterday between three and four o'clock, pursuant to their sentence. We are informed that Setton made some confession at the place of execution which has a tendency to implicate several persons not heretofore suspected as parties concerned with Masons in their depredations. May complained of the hardship of his fate; said he had not been guilty of crimes deserving death and spoke of the benefit he had rendered society by destroying old Mason."

The hanging of Little Harpe and James May for highway robbery was a fulfillment of the written law of pioneer times as well as the unwritten law of frontier communities. But many of the enraged citizens felt that the law of pioneer justice had not been satisfied for the known and unknown murders committed by these two offenders. There is nothing in history or tradition to indicate that an attempt was made to lynch the two condemned outlaws. But the lynch spirit evidently raged. In the words of Franklin L. Riley, an authority on early Mississippi history: "After their execution on the Gallows Field their heads were placed on poles, one a short distance to the north and the other a short distance to the west of Greenville, on the Natchez Trace." [105]

How long these gruesome warnings to highwaymen stood along the road and what finally became of them is not known. Each doubtless met with a fate befitting a head so ignoble. It is not probable that they were ever interred in the grave with the two headless bodies. Tradition has it that the two bodies were placed in a box and buried in a new grave yard about one hundred yards east of the Greenville jail and court house and about the same distance north of the hotel in the central part of the village.

This new grave yard was on the Natchez Trace and contained less than half a dozen graves. Tradition says that an effort was made by a number of people who had kinsmen buried in it to influence the officials to bury elsewhere the decapitated remains of these despised desperadoes. Their request was not granted, and the burial was held late on the night of the execution within a few yards of where stood one of the head-surmounted poles. The next day the indignant men who had opposed this as a burial place for the two villains, exhumed their dead and removed the remains about a half mile south of Greenville and there began a new burying ground which today is known as Bellegrove Church Yard.[33]

What attempts were made to collect the reward offered for the capture of Mason? What became of the Masons? It is probable these questions can never be fully answered. The court records showing the total expense involved in the trial and transportation of the Masons, and in the trial and execution of Little Harpe and James May, have not been found. These expenses were paid by the territorial and federal governments. One of Governor Claiborne's letters [113] shows that in January, 1806, one Seth Caston "exhibited demands for one hundred dollars for apprehending and bring-

---

[33] Greenville, originally called Hunston, was an important town on the old Natchez Trace. It lay about twenty-five miles northeast of Natchez, and was a thriving village as early as 1798, when the United States took possession of Mississippi Territory. A number of the state's wealthiest and most aristocratic pioneers lived in or near the town. In 1825 the seat of justice was moved from Greenville to Fayette and soon thereafter the old town passed out of existence. The site of old Greenville has been under cultivation for many years. The court house and the jail stood in what is now known as "Courthouse Field."

The city of Greenville, Mississippi, on the Mississippi River, which was established long after old Greenville became an extinct town, is a thriving place of more than 10,000 inhabitants.

ing to justice" these two notorious outlaws. There is nothing indicating the character of Caston's claim; nor is there anything to show whether or not he received any money. Harpe and May were entitled to the reward offered in Governor Claiborne's proclamation; it doubtless would have been granted to them in full had they not proven that above all other rewards they best deserved that which they received on the gallows.

Neither history nor tradition tells what became of the Mason family after Samuel Mason met his fate and Little Harpe and James May received their reward. Samuel Mason's wife, who evidently did not approve of her husband's lawlessness – at least not in her later years – made her home, as we have already seen, not far from old Shankstown, in Jefferson County, Mississippi. There, according to Claiborne, the historian, she was "generally respected as an honest and virtuous woman by all her neighbors, and one of her sons [probably Magnus or Samuel Mason Jr.] was a worthy citizen of Warren County." Monette says that "the Mason band being deprived of their leader and two of his most efficient men, dispersed and fled," and thus terminated the greatest terror to travelers which had infested the country.[34]

In the meantime, the headless bodies of Little Harpe and James May continued to lie in their double grave near the Natchez Trace. As time rolled on the narrow Trace widened and, as roads frequently do, it wore deeper into the slight elevation over which it led. About the year 1850 this widening and deepening process reached the fleshless bones in the solitary grave, and

---

[34] What became of Mason's men is not known. A frontier rowdy named Edward Rose is described in Washington Irving's *Astoria*. Lyman C. Draper wrote on the fly-leaf of his copy of this book that "Rose was probably one of Mason's gang."

the two skeletons, protruding piece by piece from the road bank, were dragged out by dogs and other beasts until the highway widened beyond the grave and the burial site became part of the ditch along the Natchez Trace.

Some twenty years ago, upon straightening out a part of the Natchez Trace, the small section of the old road of which the burial place was a part, was discarded as a highway, and today the old road bed, including the site of the grave, is a mere jungle of briars and brush.

Thus the last vestige of these two villains disappeared on the very highway upon which they had committed so many crimes, and possibly on the very spot where one of their victims breathed his last. The ocean of time has closed over every one of the personal relics of all these enemies of society, but the waves that their activities started still carry on as ripples of human interest.

Coiners at the Cave

The Cave had been used for religious purposes, as a haven in time of distress, as an inn and as a decoy house for murder and robbery. Through the widely scattered references to it in early books of travel and in magazines and newspapers we find also occasional indications that it had been, at different times and for short periods, the workshop and headquarters of counterfeiters. There are, indeed, few details concerning its occupation by bandits and criminals of any description; this is the veil of mystery that shrouds it in enduring interest. The knowledge that distinct facts about definite crimes committed there can never be obtained has challenged the imagination of various writers. Facts about the counterfeiters who used it are much less in evidence than facts about those following other forms of crime; probably because counterfeiting must of necessity be more secret than other crimes.

There is nothing to indicate that any of the counterfeiters of Cave-in-Rock were guilty of robbery by force or of murder. The part they played in outlaw river life was in the purchase of goods from passing boats and the payment for these goods in counterfeit coin and currency. Not until it was too late would the receivers of such money discover they had been duped. For this reason the counterfeiters could not long use the Cave at one time. There were, as far as is known, only three counterfeiters identified with the Cave. Two of these were among the first lawbreakers to convert the place into a workshop for a nefarious trade; the other was among the last of its outlaws.

Dr. Frederick Hall, who went up the Ohio in 1839, states in his *Letters from the East and from the West* that "this noted cavern is styled Counterfeiters' Cave." He further comments that "in times gone past, never to revert, it was inhabited by counterfeiters, robbers, and murderers." Charles Augustus Murray, in his *Travels in North America,* writes of his trip down the Ohio in June, 1835. He says that the current report of the country at the time of his visit to the Cave, was that when this den of thieves was finally broken up "it contained great quantities of gold, silver, silks, and stuffs, and false money, with an apparatus for coining."

It is not known what disposition was made of the coining tools and false money referred to by Murray. Nor is it known what became of any of the apparatus and illegal money left behind by the Cave's other counterfeiters. The person who expresses the opinion that an "upper cave" exists, is likely to add that great quantities of good and bad money are hidden in the undiscovered cavern. The counterfeiters probably carried away all their coin and coining apparatus. The only trace of suggestive evidence preserved today indicating the former occupancy by counterfeiters is the half of a double die or mold which was found many years ago in the vicinity of the Cave. It has been cherished as a possible relic of the counterfeiting regime there.

This die was seemingly hidden near the Cave by one of the men who had used it for the purpose of making counterfeit half-dollars and the large five-dollar gold pieces of those days. It is a double plate of iron four and three-quarter inches long and two and one-quarter inches wide, welded together. The upper plate is one-

IMPLEMENTS AND WEAPONS USED BY THE OUTLAWS
Counterfeiter's mold, knife blade, iron tomahawk, and stone idol found in
vicinity of Cave-in-Rock, and a flint-lock pistol of the style used about 1800

eighth of an inch thick and in it are cut two discs, each being one and one-half inches in diameter and having a gap at the top, opening to a funnel shaped "feeder." It is said that a particular local clay or some other suitable material was placed in the circle and into this pliable matrix the impression was made of one side of a genuine half-dollar, or of an old style five-dollar gold-piece, which was of about the same size. This formed, when hardened, a more or less durable mold for one side of the new coin. In like manner another mold was prepared in the other half of the coining apparatus for the other side of the counterfeit piece. The two parts of the mold were then placed in proper position and the hot metal poured into the cavity through the funnel-like opening. This process doubtless produced, as a rule, a more or less crude imitation, but since many of the genuine coins of an earlier date were somewhat crude and were still in circulation, the counterfeiters experienced comparatively little trouble in imitating the old pieces.

Among the early counterfeiters who made the Cave their headquarters for a time was Philip Alston, who looms large in the romance and gossip of the latter part of the eighteenth and early part of the nineteenth centuries. He was a gentleman by birth, education, and early association. He comes down to us handsome in figure and grand in manner, wearing broad-cloth, ruffles, and lace. He had an air of chivalry to women and of aloofness, superiority, and mystery to men. He was the "Raffles" of pioneer days and legend paints him in high colors.

Alexander C. Finley, in his *History of Russellville and Logan County, Kentucky* – a unique publication from the standpoint of its style – says Philip Alston was driven out of the South and settled in Logan County about 1782. A few years later "his thirst for counterfeiting again returned." But "feeling insecure" Alston moved from place to place in western Kentucky. "About 1790 he crossed over the Ohio and became the fast friend and disciple of the notorious counterfeiter Sturdevant [Duff?] at the Cave-in-the-Rock. But he did not reside here long before he came to himself and wondered how he, the gentlemanly Philip Alston, although an elegant counterfeiter, could have become the companion of outlaws, robbers, and murderers . . . and so he returned to Natchez." [35]

[35] Finley says Philip Alston was born in South Carolina and in early manhood became "a full grown counterfeiter." After living in Natchez and "attaining to the highest respectability . . . his avaricious eye rested on a golden image of the Savior, in the Catholic Church, . . . and he went immediately and counterfeited some coins from it." He fled from Natchez to Kentucky and settled in Logan County, where he established a salt works and store at Moat's Lick. While running these he managed the Cedar House, a tavern near Russellville. He also farmed, preached, and taught school, and incidentally "flooded the country with spurious money." Thus he became, "not only the first farmer, manufacturer, and merchant, but he established the first depot of exchange and the first bank, and also the first mint in western Kentucky." About 1788, "the whole people rose up in their majesty and banished him." He next appeared in Livingston and Henderson counties and then fled to Cave-in-Rock. After a short stay at the Cave he returned to Natchez where "he found his old enemies, who became his fast friends. He rose in the estimation of the Spaniards until he was appointed an *empresidio* of Mexico, when in the midst of his success and returning fortune death stepped in and sealed his fate."

Finley, who never cites authorities, states that "Peter Alston, Philip Alston's youngest son, became an outlaw and robber, and joined Mason's band at Cave-in-the-Rock and was allied to the Harpes, and with one of the Harpes was executed at Washington, Mississippi . . . for the killing of his chief, Mason, for the reward." No records have been found that contradict any of Finley's statements, except the one to the effect that Peter Alston killed Samuel Mason.

Nancy Huston Banks in her novel *'Round Anvil Rock* presents Philip Alston as a kind but mysterious gentleman who, although generally trusted by the community, is regarded by some with suspicion because of his frequent absences and ever-replenished supply of imported cloth, laces, and jewelry. In the novel Alston refers to Jean Lafitte as "my resepected and trusted friend," and admits that he, Alston, makes business trips to Duff's Fort, near

It is quite likely that a counterfeiter named Duff had been making use of the Cave long before the time of Philip Alston's short stay at the place. He may be regarded as Cave-in-Rock's first outlaw. Neither history nor tradition has preserved Duff's Christian name. One version suggests that he may have been the John Duff who met George Rogers Clark on the Ohio, near Fort Massac in June, 1778, and who, after some bewilderment, showed General Clark the way to Kaskaskia. It is not improbable that the two were one and the same man. At any rate, very little is known of John Duff, the guide, or of Duff the coiner.

Governor Reynolds in *My Own Times* and Collins, in his *History of Kentucky* devoted only a few lines to Duff, and these lines pertain to his death. The author of *A History of Union County, Kentucky,* prints some five pages on his career, based on traditions gathered in 1886. Duff apparently lived the latter part of his life in or near Cave-in-Rock and procured his lead and silver along the Saline River and in other sections of southern Illinois. He evidently operated a counterfeiter's den in different places. According to tradition, there were at least three places known as "Duff's Fort:" one was at Cave-in-Rock, another at Caseyville, Kentucky (near the mouth of Tradewater River, fourteen miles above the Cave) and a third in Illinois, at Island Ripple on Saline River (thirteen miles above its mouth and about twenty-eight miles, via river to the Cave). Like all outlaws of his and other times, Duff was obliged to shift his headquarters. It is probable that some of the localities in which he lived no longer have any traditions regarding his activities there.

Cave-in-Rock, although "it was no longer a secret that regular stations of outlawry were firmly established between Natchez on the one side and Duff's Fort on the other."

In 1790, Philip Alston, as stated by Finley, fled to the Cave and became a "fast friend and disciple" of Duff. Collins, in his chapter on Crittenden County, Kentucky, says that Duff lived near the mouth of Tradewater River in 1799 and then, or shortly thereafter, was killed by Shawnee Indians and that "there was reason to believe some one residing at Fort Massac had employed the Indians to commit the crime." Governor Reynolds briefly states that Duff was killed "near Island Ripple in the Saline Creek, and was buried near the old salt spring," and that "it was supposed the Indians were hired to commit the murder." Just where he was killed cannot be ascertained with any certainty after a lapse of so many years. There are two or three coves or small caves on Saline below Island Ripple, each of which is known as Duff's Cave, and each has a local tradition to the effect that Duff was killed in it.

The compiler of *A History of Union County, Kentucky,* is the only writer who has gathered any Duff traditions, and since he confined his research to the stories told in and near Caseyville, his life of this Cave-in-Rock outlaw does not branch into the many and varied claims made in local traditions of other sections. Nevertheless, his sketch of this pioneer and counterfeiter is one that might be accepted as typical of what would be found in the other localities in which Duff had made his headquarters. In sum and substance the story runs as follows:

Duff lived in a house called "Duff's Fort," which stood near what later became the old site of the Christian Church in Caseyville. Here he dispensed a rude but cordial hospitality. On the bluff above was his meadow. The overhanging cliff near his house furnished a shelter for his horses. The shallow cove in which they stood is now almost filled with alluvial soil deposited by the little brook which flows near. His household consisted of his wife and a faithful black slave named Pompey, who would risk anything or undergo any hardship for his master.

It is said that Duff was a brave man and a good strategist; he was seldom found at a disadvantage. He often had narrow escapes in his encounters with the officers of the law and the people living in the vicinity. On one occasion, when he was closely pursued by his enemies, he ran towards his home. There he found his wife at the river doing the family washing. Near her was a large iron kettle, in which she was boiling clothes. Without hesitation Duff upset the kettle, rolled it into the stream, where it was quickly cooled, and lifting the kettle over his head, he plunged into the water. The river was low at this point, enabling him to wade most of the way to the farther bank. Before he reached the Illinois shore, however, his pursuers appeared on the Kentucky side and opened fire. Their aim was well directed. Several of the bullets struck the kettle, but rebounded without injury to the man beneath. On reaching the dry land he took the kettle from his head. Holding it behind him as continued protection, he ran for safety. The pursuers increased their fire. More bullets rained upon the impromptu shield – but Duff escaped unhurt to the shelter of the woods.

On another occasion when sorely pressed he took refuge with a Mrs. Hammack, who was an old-time Methodist living in that part of the country. She treated him so kindly that he decided to let her have a glimpse of his hidden treasures. On the appointed day he blindfolded her and his wife and led them by a very circuitous route to a cave. After they were in the mys-

terious cave he removed the bandages from their eyes
and, by the light of torches, the two women were enabled to see the large quantities of counterfeit silver
and gold coins in boxes and chests stored by Duff. He
then replaced the bandages and took the two women
back to Mrs. Hammack's house. Mrs. Hammack's impression was that the cave ran into the side of a cliff but,
notwithstanding many efforts, she was never able to
retrace her steps to the place. Mrs. Duff related, after
her husband's death, that he had taken her from their
home to the cave on another occasion and in the same
manner. He then promised her that he would some
day show her the way to his cave, but explained at the
time that he could not then do so, for his enemies might
torture her into a disclosure of his location when he
was in it. His intentions were frustrated by his sudden
death. There are three different accounts of Duff's
death given by local tradition.

One version has it that he was killed by some of the
citizens of the county, near the bluff where he quartered
his horses. According to this account, a number of men
were pursuing him and when he showed fight they were
obliged to shoot him. Another says he was killed by
Indians with whom he had quarreled about a dog fight.
The following is the version most widely accepted:

Duff, three of his associates, and his slave Pompey,
while in Illinois securing white metal, were surprised
by about six soldiers sent from Golconda, Illinois, or
some other point below Cave-in-Rock. The counterfeiters were captured and taken down the river in a
boat. Handcuffs were placed upon all the white prisoners. Pompey had not been manacled because the
soldiers carried only four sets of irons and, furthermore, they presumed the negro cared little whether

his master was doomed. Near Cave-in-Rock they stopped for dinner. When they landed, all the soldiers went ashore except one who was left in charge of the prisoners and the boat. After stacking their arms near the boat, they went into the Cave to build a fire and prepare the meal.

One of the prisoners whispered to Duff that he found he could slip his irons off. Pompey hearing this, passed a file to him and, taking advantage of the absence of the guard, who went ashore for a few minutes, he filed away at Duff's fetters and soon succeeded in breaking them. At a signal, Pompey sprang upon the guard and tied him to a tree and then proceeded to liberate the two men chained in the boat. Duff and the other unfettered prisoner immediately seized the stacked arms and rushed upon the men in the Cave who, having no side arms, were forced to an unconditional surrender.

Some of the soldiers were tied and others secured with irons and all thrown into the boat and set afloat. They drifted down the river and, as they were floating opposite the fort from which they had been sent, they were ordered to stop, but of course could not do so. They were fired upon a number of times before the commander discovered their helpless condition. He then sent out a skiff and brought them ashore. In the meantime, Duff and his companions had made their way up the river to the Saline and had got safely home again.

The inglorious outcome of this expedition greatly incensed the commander of the fort and he was determined upon revenge. He accordingly hired a Canadian and three Indians to go up the river to Duff's Fort and kill him. They were to ingratiate themselves into the good graces of the counterfeiter and watch their oppor-

tunity to kill him. If they succeeded they were to
return and receive a reward.

They arrived in Duff's neighborhood and camped
below his house. The Canadian soon became friendly
with Duff, who did not suspect the object of his presence, and was invited to his house. The genial hospitality of the counterfeiter was fatal to the Canadian's
plan, and each day he found himself less inclined to
carry out his murderous scheme. Meanwhile the Indians were becoming impatient. One evening they
informed the Canadian that they had concluded to kill
Duff the next day, whether he helped or not. He then
decided to put Duff upon his guard.

The next morning, although Duff was drinking
rather heavily, the Canadian disclosed the plot to him.
Duff, seizing a stick, rushed from the house, swearing
he would whip the Indians with it and drive them off.
He met them coming towards his house, painted and
armed for a conflict. Pompey, recognizing the danger
his master was facing, rushed to him with a loaded gun,
but before it could be used the Indians shot Duff and
his slave. "The leader having fallen," says the author
of *A History of Union County, Kentucky,* in concluding his account of Duff, "the rest of the gang were
speedily dispersed." [36]

About a generation after the days of Duff there appeared upon the scene a man named Sturdevant, whose

---

[36] Duff secured metal from the veins of lead ore on the Saline and, as it
contained a little silver, he separated the silver from the lead as best he
could and made counterfeit coins. In this connection the author of *A History
of Union County, Kentucky,* further comments:

"The traditions of Duff's great wealth have acted upon many of the
citizens of Caseyville much as the tales of Captain Kidd's plunder affected
the inhabitants of Long Island. Youthful imaginations have been inflamed
with thoughts of the fabulous wealth stored away in some cavern along the
Caseyville cliffs. Many a ramble has turned into a search for the caves in
that vicinity, but so far as the public knows, none of them has ever eventu-
ated in any discoveries."

counterfeiting career continued in the Cave-in-Rock country until 1831. In the mean time the flatboat pirates who had used the Cave as their headquarters had disappeared and the mysterious Ford's Ferry band was drifting towards its dispersement.

The identity of Sturdevant is as vague as that of Duff. Tradition has it that Sturdevant did not counterfeit money in the Cave but that, beginning about 1825, and for a short time thereafter, he used the "House of Nature" as a "Banking House of Exchange." There he met his confederates and exchanged, at an agreed rate, some of the counterfeit money he made in his fortified home nine miles below the Cave. Judge James Hall, in his *Sketches of the West,* published in 1835, devotes two pages to Sturdevant. His is the best of the few published accounts. It is well worth quoting in full:

"At a later period [that is, after Mason's time] the celebrated counterfeiter, Sturdevant, fixed his residence on the shore of the Ohio, in Illinois, and for several years set the laws at defiance. He was a man of talent and address. He was possessed of much mechanical genius, was an expert artist and was skilled in some of the sciences. As an engraver he was said to have few superiors; and he excelled in some other branches of art. For several years he resided at a secluded spot in Illinois, where all his immediate neighbors were his confederates or persons whose friendship he had conciliated. He could, at any time, by the blowing of a horn, summon some fifty to a hundred armed men to his defense; while the few quiet farmers around, who lived near enough to get their feelings enlisted and who were really not at all implicated in his crimes, rejoiced in the impunity with which he practiced his schemes. He was a grave, quiet, inoffensive man in his manners,

who commanded the obedience of his comrades and the
respect of his neighbors. He had a very excellent farm;
his house was one of the best in the country; his domestic arrangements were liberal and well ordered.

"Yet this man was the most notorious counterfeiter
that ever infested our country and carried on his nefarious art to an extent which no other person has ever attempted.   His confederates were scattered over the
whole western country, receiving through regular channels of intercourse their supplies of counterfeit bank
notes, for which they paid a stipulated price – sixteen
dollars in cash for a hundred dollars in counterfeit bills.
His security arose, partly from his caution in not allowing his subordinates to pass a counterfeit bill, or to do
any other unlawful act in the state in which he lived,
and in his obliging them to be especially careful of their
deportment in the *county* of his residence, measures
which effectually protected him from the civil authority. Although all the counterfeit bank notes with which
a vast region was inundated were made in his house,
that fact could never be proved by legal evidence. But
he secured himself further by having settled around him
a band of his lawless dependents who were ready at all
times to fight in his defense; and by his conciliatory
conduct, which prevented his having any violent enemies.   He even enlisted the sympathies of many reputable people in his favor. But he became a great nui-
sance from the immense quantity of spurious paper
which he threw into circulation; and although he never
committed any acts of violence himself, and is not
known to have sanctioned any, the unprincipled felons
by whom he was surrounded were guilty of many acts
of desperate atrocity; and Sturdevant, though he escaped from the arm of the law, was at last, with all his

confederates, driven from the country by the enraged people, who rose, almost in mass, to rid themselves of one whose presence they had long considered an evil as well as a disgrace."

Governor Reynolds notes that in 1831 Sturdevant's fort was attacked by some Regulators, and that one Regulator and three counterfeiters were killed, and "the suspected gang broken up."

James A. Rose in his article on "The Regulators and Flatheads in Southern Illinois" says: "Regulators descended on the Sturdevant stronghold only to find that their movements had been spied upon and that they were expected. A number of shots were exchanged; finally a charge was made on the stockade and the door broken down. They found, however, that a small piece of artillery was trained on the stairway leading to the Sturdevant stronghold, and a halt was called and reinforcements asked for. During the night Sturdevant and his band of criminals managed to make their escape. This is one of the earliest records of the citizens of this region taking the law into their own hands."

Sturdevant was never again heard of in that or any other locality. What became of him is not known. This attack on his headquarters ended forever counterfeiting in the Cave-in-Rock country.[36a]

[36a] Sturdevant's stockaded fort stood on the long bluff immediately above what later became the town of Rosiclare, Illinois, and commanded a good view of the Ohio. Dr. Daniel Lawrence, of Golconda, saw the ruins of the Sturdevant house as late as 1876. The place had then been in a dilapidated condition for some time, but enough remained to show that in its day it was a substantial log structure, a story and a half high, with three rooms on the ground floor, including a log L on the north side. Digging into some of the old logs, he discovered many small holes made by bullets. A new stone quarry was in operation at the time of his visit and he was present when a blast blew out of a crevice a set of dies for making counterfeit half dollars. The foreman took the plates home for souvenirs, but their whereabouts is now unknown.

The Ford's Ferry Mystery

After Mason left Cave-in-Rock other outlaws still continued to use the cavern as a temporary stopping place or headquarters. An outlaw's stay at any place is of necessity short. Mason, in 1797, had lived there longer than any other. Those who followed him were more or less migratory. Residents in the vicinity were in no way implicated in the various acts that made the Cave so notoriously dangerous, until the mysterious Ford's Ferry band began its robberies. Since 1834, when that organization ceased its operations, the Cave has never been identified with outlawry.

To what extent James Ford, the owner of Ford's Ferry – a crossing place on the Ohio two and one-half miles above the Cave – was connected with this organization was not revealed in his day nor since, and it is not at all likely that it will ever be determined. He is more frequently discussed in tradition, and his life is the subject of a greater variety of opinions than that of any other man connected with the tragedies of the Cave-in-Rock country. According to one version, "Jim Ford was as black as some have painted him," and, according to another, his connection with the mysterious band had the effect of preventing bad men from committing more crimes than they would have if his influence had not acted as a restraint.

A careful study of the few written records and the many varied oral traditions pertaining to Ford, indicates that when he reached the prime of life conditions

had undergone many changes. Outlaws were no longer
in a position to carry on their depredations with the
freedom that attended the earlier days. Population
had increased, and with that increase came a better
reign of law. The line between law-abiding and law-
breaking citizens was rapidly widening. For about ten
years, ending in 1833, Ford apparently stood between
the two, and kept in close touch with both. By ming-
ling with the upright citizens he held in some measure
the respect of the community, and by acting as one of
the leaders of the highwaymen he reaped a share of
their booty. In serving the two opposing classes he
faced, and finally met, the fate common to such men.

His education and appearance, and his public activities, gained for him the confidence of the community
and the standing of a trustworthy man, which he held
until toward the close of his life. Before he died many
of his fellow-citizens began regarding him with more
or less suspicion, and he soon became a man of mystery. After his death his career was extensively discussed throughout the lower Ohio valley. Our account
is confined principally to court records and oral traditions. These old records, as far as known, have not
been cited heretofore by anyone attempting to tell the
story of James Ford.

Tradition has it that James Ford was born some time
during the latter part of the Revolution. His father,
it is said, was a Revolutionary soldier and moved with
his son to western Kentucky about 1803. Thus he appeared in the Cave-in-Rock country about half a dozen
years after the Masons and Little Harpe had gone
south, but was living in the neighborhood when "Jim
Wilson" and some of the other outlaws were holding
forth at the Cave. His home was a half-mile southwest

of what is now the village of Tolu, Crittenden County, Kentucky. It was a mile from the Ohio and the head of the notorious Hurricane Island, about eight miles below Ford's Ferry and five miles below Cave-in-Rock. Ford owned a number of good farms in what was then northern Livingston, now Crittenden County. So well was he known along the lower Ohio that Samuel Cuming's *Western Navigator,* published in 1822, designates the river landing near his home as "Major Ford's." The old court records preserved at Smithland show that he was a justice of the peace in 1815 and held the office a number of times thereafter, and that practically every suggestion made before the county court "on motion of James Ford" was carried. He frequently served as appraiser and administrator of estates. Through these and other acts of trust he gained the prestige of a desirable citizen. The improvement of roads was encouraged by him, especially those leading to Ford's Ferry.

One of the most interesting chapters of the mystery surrounding Ford's Ferry may be found in a book of personal reminiscences and local traditions of Cave-in-Rock and its vicinity disguised as historical fiction and called *Chronicles of a Kentucky Settlement.* Its author, William Courtney Watts, who possessed an excellent education, was a very successful man of international business experience, born at Smithland, Kentucky, near Cave-in-Rock. Much of his information came directly from his father and other pioneer settlers.

Among the men who figure in the romance, and whom Watts personally knew, was Dr. Charles H. Webb, of Livingston County, of which Smithland is the seat. Dr. Webb married Cassandra Ford, the daughter of James Ford. He related the story of his life to Watts and thus contributed a chapter to history

that stands alone. There exists in more or less abundance printed data relative to some of the methods employed by the bands of robbers at Cave-in-Rock to
entice boats to land at the Cave and get possession of
victims. All these, however, are, as already observed,
stories based on statements made, not by men who spoke
from actual observation, but by persons who had heard
others relate another man's experience. In Dr. Webb
we actually touch hands with a well-known and highly
respected citizen who was lured to the Cave by some of
the tricks suggested – tricks regarding which few lived
to tell the tale and of which nobody else left any direct
authoritative account.

Dr. Charles H. Webb and his brother John, both
young men, left South Carolina in 1822 for Philadelphia and shortly thereafter set out for the West in
search of fortune, with St. Louis as their destination.
At Cave-in-Rock, on their way down the Ohio, they
met their great adventure and were separated as the
narrative records. Dr. Webb, having lost all, settled
at Salem. There he subsequently met and knew Watts.
The two became fast friends when Watts, much the
younger of the two, had grown up. It was from Dr.
Webb, in the flower of his middle age, that Watts had
this story:

"My brother and I descended the Ohio River from
Pittsburgh to Louisville in a flatboat, and after remaining a few days in Louisville we again started on another
flatboat, intending to go on it as far as the mouth of the
Ohio River or near there. . . The boat, a 'broad-
horn,' was in charge of one Jonathan Lumley, who
owned a large proportion of the cargo which consisted
of corn, provisions, and whiskey. With Mr. Lumley
were three other stout young men as hands, making,

with my brother and myself, who had agreed to work our way for food and passage, six persons on board.

"Day after day as we floated along, the better I got acquainted with my companions and the more I found that, under a rough exterior, they were warm-hearted, generous, and confiding fellows, equally ready for a jig or a knock-down, for a shooting match or a drinking bout, for a song or a sermon.

"I was playing on my flute as our boat was nearing Cave-in-Rock, and when within full view of the high rocky bluff, at the base of which is the entrance of the Cave, we observed a woman on the top of the bluff hailing us by waving a white cloth, whereupon our captain, as we called Mr. Lumley, ordered us to pull in close to shore, within easy speaking distance, so as to learn what was wanted.

"Presently a man came from the entrance of the Cave, and called out: 'Hey, Cap! have you enny bacon or whiskey on board?'

" 'I – yie!' shouted back our captain.

" 'Won't yer land? We're short on rations here, an' want ter buy right smart!' said the man.

" 'Goin' to the lower Mississippi!' answered our captain, 'and don't want to break bulk so high up.'

" 'But, Cap, we'ud be mi'ty obleeged ef you'd lan'. An' we've got a woman here and a boy who want passage down ter the mouth er Cumberlan'. They've bin waitin' a long time, an'll pay passage.'

" 'All right then,' replied the captain, 'I'll land; but let them come aboard at once.'

"And land we did some two hundred yards below the Cave, when the captain and three others – my brother being one of them – went ashore and walked up to the entrance. After waiting for more than an hour, and

none of our men returning, I asked my remaining
companion to go up to the Cave and see what was detaining them. Another hour passed away; the sun had
gone down, and night, with clouds, was rapidly coming
on.

"I began to feel uneasy, and to add to my uneasiness,
a large dog which we had on board began howling most
dismally. Presently, by the dim twilight, I saw three
men approaching the boat from the Cave. At first I
thought them a part of our crew, but I was soon undeceived, for they came on board, and with pistols drawn,
demanded my surrender. Resistance was useless; my
arms were soon bound behind my back, and I was told
that if I made any row my brains would be blown out.
I asked about my friends but was only told that they
were 'all right,' that the captain had 'sold the boat and
cargo,' and that what little information they had given
was 'enough' for me 'to know.'

"I was then blindfolded, and when my money had
been taken from me, I was assisted – I should say lifted –
into a skiff, into which two of the three men, so I
thought, entered. I begged to know what had become
of my brother, and told them that he and I were passengers on the boat and no part of the crew proper. I did
this hoping that if they knew we were passengers and
had no direct interest in the boat and cargo they would
think us less likely to return to the Cave and molest
them. But the only answer I got was that the 'fewer
questions' I asked the better it would be for me, 'by a
d – – – sight.'

"The skiff was then rowed away – in what direction I
could not tell, but in some five minutes there was a
pause in the rowing, and soon a slight jar as of two
skiffs coming together, followed by a conversation in

low tones, the purport of which I could not catch. Very soon, however, one of the men approached me and whispered in my ear. There seemed to be a remnant of mercy in the intonations of his words, rather than in the words themselves. He said: 'We're goin' ter vi'late orders a little, an' turn yer loose here in the middle er the river. An' the furder yer float away frum here 'fore yer make enny noise, the better for yer by a d — — — sight. Yer'd better lay low an' keep dark till mornin' comes.' The speaker then slackened the cords that bound my arms, after which he again whispered: 'Yer ken work 'em loose when we're gone, say in 'bout an hour, but not sooner, er yer may get inter trouble. An' don't yer never come back here to ax enny questions, or yer'll fare worse, an' do nobody enny good.'

"The man then left me seated in the stern of the skiff, and I could tell from the motion and the rattling of a chain that a second boat was being pulled along side it, into which the man stepped, leaving me alone. I strained my ears to catch the slightest sound, but I could neither hear the click of oars nor the dip of a paddle; the latter, however, might have been used so noiselessly as to be unheard. I was therefore in doubt. I thought possibly the other boat might be floating close to me and that I was being watched. This brought to my mind the man's caution not to try to free my arms for an hour. I therefore, remained quiet for about that length of time. No sound reached me except the moaning of the night winds among the forest trees that lined each shore, the occasional barking of wolves, and the weird cry of night-fowls – particularly the blood-curdling hooting of great owls. . .

"After a long and painful effort I succeeded in releasing my arms and freeing my eyes from the bandage.

Looking around I found the heavens overcast: the night was so intensely dark that I could see only a dim outline of the shore. I discovered there were neither oars nor paddle in the skiff, but I was floating some two or three miles an hour, and it might be many hours before I would pass any habitation. I therefore made up my mind to lie down in the skiff, try to get some sleep and await the coming of morn. But the distant growling thunder was creeping nearer and nearer; flash after flash lit up the heavens, followed by almost deafening discharges that rolled, crashed, and reverberated along the river and among the forests, which moaned and groaned under the pressure of the rising wind. The waves in the river were momentarily increasing, and were dashing my little skiff about in a way that was alarming. . .

"I knew if the downpour continued for many minutes my skiff would fill and sink. There was but one way to bail it out – to use one of my thick leather shoes as a scoop. I worked manfully while the rain lasted, which, fortunately, was not for more than an hour.

"The long night finally passed, but the heavens were still overcast. I peered along both banks – looked, hoping to see smoke curling above some cabin chimney – but there was no sign of human habitation. Occasionally I raised my voice to its highest pitch – gave a loud halloo – but no answering voice was returned. However, about an hour later, I saw an island ahead of me; it was evidently inhabited, for notwithstanding the leaden aspect of the skies, I could see smoke ascending from among the trees. I used my hands as paddles as vigorously as I could so as to drift against the head of the island, and in this I succeeded. Having secured my boat, I soon found the cabin, and was kindly received by a Mr. Prior and his wife who gave me a good breakfast. I told them of my misfortune, and they expressed much sympathy for me. Mr. Prior, who seemed to be an honest and intelligent man, told me that he was one of the earliest settlers in those parts. He said he had often heard of the depredations of the Wilson gang about the Cave and that I was lucky to have escaped with my life. He advised me to stop at Smithland, at the mouth of the Cumberland River, where I might obtain assistance and directions as to what was best for me to do. Mr. Prior then made me a paddle out of a clapboard, and bidding him and his kind wife goodbye I returned to my skiff, pushed off, and that evening arrived in Smithland."

At Smithland young Webb was directed to Salem, "which then contained a population, white and black, of about two hundred and fifty." There, in turn, he was advised by Judge Dixon Given to consult Colonel Arthur Love relative to the best method of gaining information regarding his brother who had been captured at the Cave. Colonel Love, a highly esteemed citizen, lived a few miles from the home of James Ford, who was suspected by many of being a leader of the Cave-in-Rock band. No crime, however, had ever been traced to Ford "with sufficient clearness to cause his arrest and trial." On his way to Colonel Love's farm Webb fell from his horse and sprained his ankle, and it so happened that Cassandra Ford, daughter of James Ford, found the helpless young man lying in the road. She took him to her home, and he soon discovered he was in the house of the very man he dreaded most. But his fears rapidly vanished, for his rescuer had become very much attached to him and he to her. He was shown the flute of which he had been robbed near the Cave. The mother and daughter revealed to him the fact that they, like many of their neighbors, felt somewhat suspicious that James Ford was, in some way, connected with the notorious crowd at the Cave. Ford, who was away from home much of his time, did not return until about a week after the crippled man was admitted. Then Webb saw "the masterful, self-willed, dreaded, and almost outlawed man." He gave a description of him as he appeared at that time:

"He was about six feet in height, and of powerful build, a perfect Hercules in point of strength; but he has now grown too corpulent to undergo much fatigue. His head is large and well shaped; his sandy brown hair, now thin, is turning gray, for he must be fully fifty years old; his eyes, of a steel-gray color, are brilliant and his glance quick and penetrating; his nose rather short and thick; his upper lip remarkably long, his mouth large, and his lips full and sensuous. He has a broad, firm, double chin, and his voice is deep and sonorous. His complexion is very florid, and he converses fluently. On the whole, when in repose, he gives one the idea of a good natured, rather than a surly, bulldog; but, if aroused, I should say he would be a lion tamer."

When Webb's foot was sufficiently healed to permit his leaving the Ford home he took his flute and crutches and returned to Salem. Shortly thereafter he made the first of his many calls on Miss Ford. In the meantime, learning that his brother had been allowed to depart from the Cave unhurt, he wrote letters to various places and finally located him. Later he "went to Fort Massac on a flatboat and from there walked to St. Louis," where he found his brother established in business. The two spent several months together in the city and, according to the story as related in *Chronicles,* it was during his absence from Kentucky that Ford, the "almost outlawed man," passed beyond the reach of law.

It was at Ford's Ferry that many emigrants going to the Illinois country crossed the Ohio. In Ford's day the ferry at Shawneetown and another at Golconda also were thriving and the three were, in a sense, rivals.

A river crossing with the reputation of having the best roads leading to and from it was usually given the preference. Ford, realizing this, placed sign-boards at a number of road crossings, and cards in some of the taverns, advertising the highway to his ferry. What was known as the Ford's Ferry Road extended, in Kentucky, some eight miles south of the ferry and, in Illinois, about twelve miles north of it. That part of it in Kentucky running north from Pickering Hill to the ferry, a distance of four miles, was well maintained by the county through Ford's influence. The road leading from his ferry into Illinois was an equally important one, but its condition depended solely upon his interest and efforts in the matter. He attempted to persuade the local authorities in Illinois to change the old Low Water Road running through the bottoms to Pott's Hill, a distance of twelve miles, to one over higher ground. Failing in this effort, he, at his own expense, opened up a new road ever since known as Ford's Ferry High Water Road.

Thus with about twenty miles of comparatively good road through a densely wooded country and with a first class ferry, and by proper advertising, he succeeded, as one man expressed it, "in having things come his way." Many people, it is true, were molested at the ferry and along the highway leading to and from it; but such misfortunes were then likely to befall any traveler at any place. If a robbery occurred along the Ford's Ferry Road, the news of the hold-up invariably ended with the report that "Jim Ford found the robbers and ran them out of the country." And so, for many years, the Ford's Ferry Road and Ford's Ferry maintained the reputation of being "safe again." In the meantime, strangers continued to travel over it, and many fell into the well-set trap.

At the foot of Pickering Hill, near Crooked Creek, newcomers frequently met, as though by chance, some "strangers" who explained that they were on their way to Illinois. The unwary emigrants continued their travel accompanied by persons who seemed honest men. The "strangers" soon gained their confidence, and if, by the time Ford's Ferry was reached, the desirability and possibility of a hold-up had not been ascertained, the united party crossed over into Illinois. At Potts' Hill, or before reaching that wayside tavern on the south hillside, the newcomer was either robbed or permitted to continue his journey unmolested. It is said that many a traveler who was found weak and destitute by the "strangers" was given money and other help by them. On the other hand, the traveler who exhibited evidence of wealth and prosperity almost invariably met his fate along the road, at the ferry or at Potts' Hill.

Billy Potts was the strategist on whom the highwaymen relied as their last and best man to dispose of any encouraging cases that had not been settled before they reached his house. Potts, by one means or another, succeeded in persuading the selected travelers to remain all night at his inn. His log house was large and comfortable and stood near a good spring which, then as now, offered an abundant supply of water for man and beast. Tradition says many a man took his last drink at Potts' Spring and spent his last hour on earth in Potts' house. Human bones are still turned up by plowmen in the Potts' Old Field, and since there is nothing to indicate that they are the remains of Indians, the conclusion is they represent some of the victims of the mysterious Ford's Ferry band. The log house occupied by Billy Potts is still standing. Many years ago it was converted into a barn. On its floor and walls there can still be seen a number of large dark spots. Tradition has it that they are stains made by human blood. Some of the old citizens living in the neighborhood insist that they are as distinct today as they were more than half a century ago, notwithstanding the ravages of time.

There are many traditions of mysterious murders attributed to the Ford's Ferry highwaymen. Every one is a fearsome tale and has evidently undergone many changes since it was first told. Some seem to have more versions than they are years old. None, so far as is now known, can be verified by documentary or other positive evidence. All these tales are apparently based on facts but it is also evident that each is much colored by fiction. A version of the tradition pertaining to Billy Potts and his son is here retold:

A traveler was riding north on the Ford's Ferry Road one day, and after crossing the ferry was overtaken by the son of Billy Potts. Young Potts expressed a delight at having found a man with whom he could ride and thus not only pass the time away more pleasantly, but also travel with greater safety. After going a few miles young Potts gained sufficient information to convince him that the man was well worth robbing. When they reached a point along the road where a hold-up could be made with the least danger of exposure, Potts pulled out his pistol, forced the man to throw up his hands and

then proceeded to rob him. While Potts was in the
act of taking his victim's money, two farmers living in
the neighborhood happened upon the scene. Not being
in sympathy with the gang of highwaymen and having
recognized young Potts, they informed others what they
had witnessed and reported the robbery to the authorities. Ford, so runs the story, realizing that one of his
men had been detected and that much evidence could
be produced to convict the guilty one, advised him to
leave for parts unknown, and thus not only save himself but also shield his confederates from further suspicion. The young man left, and a few days later,
rumors emanating from the gang, to the effect that
young Potts had been driven out of the country by Jim
Ford, circulated freely. The disappearance of Potts
substantiated the report, and Ford received the credit
for ridding the community of an undesirable citizen.

Young Potts wandered around for several years, in
the meantime growing a beard and gaining in weight.
He evidently changed in appearance to such an extent
that he felt confident no one – not even his mother –
would recognize him, and that he could return home
without the least fear of detection. He reached Pickering Hill on his homeward journey and there met a
number of "strangers" who informed him that they
were resting preparatory to resuming their travel to
the Illinois country. Potts recognized in these men his
old companions in crime, but none suspected who he
was. He rode with them to Ford's Ferry, in the meantime keeping the men in ignorance as to his identity.
When they reached the Ohio he saw that active preparations were being made to rob him and, if necessary,
to murder him. He then revealed his identity. But it
was only after producing considerable proof that he

convinced the men that he was their long gone accomplice. A great rejoicing followed.

Early in the evening young Potts started alone over Ford's High Water Road to his father's house, where he arrived shortly after dark. He found his father and mother at home and, as he had anticipated, was not recognized by them. He decided to attempt to conceal his identity until late in the night, for he concluded that if before making himself known he could impress his father with the fact that his wandering boy had accumulated money, the surprise which he was soon to give him would be even greater. With this double surprise in view, young Potts displayed a large roll of money and whispered to his unsuspecting host that he knew he was in a safe place for the night. The two men had chatted in the candle lighted room for an hour or more, when the guest asked for a drink of water. Out into the dark they walked and down to the Potts Spring, a distance of some three hundred feet. The young man getting down on his knees, leaned over the rock-lined spring. While in the act of drinking he was stabbed in the back, under the left shoulder blade, and instantly killed.

The murderer took the money from his victim's pocket, but failed to find anything to indicate who he was, from where he came, or to what place he intended to go. Old Potts dug a shallow grave and in it buried all evidence of the crime. He returned to the house, and after reporting to his wife that he had "made a good haul," retired for the night.

The next morning some of the Ford's Ferry gang rode to Potts' Hill to celebrate the return of their friend. Before they had an opportunity to explain the object of their coming, Potts recited the details of how he had disposed of an "easy" man the night preceding. One of them then began the story of how they had met the young fellow and how, when they were at the point of carrying out their intention of robbing and killing him, he made himself known and proved beyond doubt that he was young Potts, their former associate. But before the account was finished old Potts and his wife accused the crowd of concocting this story and cursed the men for plotting against them. But, persisting and giving every detail of what happened during the time the victim was in their presence, the men created doubt in the minds of Potts and his wife, though Potts asserted that in his opinion the man he had killed was not his son, but perhaps a friend in whom his son had confided to such an extent that he was able to convince them that he was young Potts himself.

At this point of the discussion Mrs. Potts recalled that her son had a small birthmark under one of his shoulder blades, but which shoulder blade she could not remember. Upon learning this, the men, hoping to find such evidence as would convince the parents of the identity of their son, repaired to the grave. It was shallow and the soil loose. In a little while the body was uncovered. Without waiting for it to be taken from the grave, Potts bent forward and began to rip the clothing from the corpse. The back showed no mark on the right side. The bloody wound made by the dagger that had pierced the heart was then examined. It revealed the presence of the remembered birth mark. . .

It was at Cave-in-Rock that the Ford's Ferry band met to discuss some of its plans and operations and to divide the spoils. This rendezvous was two miles from the road on which the highwaymen operated, and there-

ENTRANCE TO THE CAVE AND LOWER END OF CAVE-IN-ROCK BLUFF

(From an original photograph made in 1917)

fore sufficiently distant to avoid discovery by anyone traveling over that land route. It was conveniently reached by a boat from Hurricane Island or from Ford's Ferry. Furthermore, it was an ideal hiding place in which to lie in wait for flatboats going down the river.

What went on at these meetings was never revealed to any one not a member of the organization. The tragic story of Billy Potts and his son is one of the few secrets that leaked out, and it was not divulged until long after Potts died and the organization had ceased to exist. No arrests were made and for a long time no local citizens were suspected; for, as already stated, every reported robbery was soon followed by the news that the crime had been committed by a traveling highwayman, who had since been driven out of the country.

In time suspicion began to point toward a number of local men whose incomes were out of proportion to their labor, and whose frequent and long absences were accounted for by them in contradictory ways. Vincent B. Simpson, who lived on the Kentucky side of the Ohio and ran the ferry boat at Ford's Ferry, and Henry C. Shouse, who lived on the Illinois shore at Cedar Point almost opposite, were among those suspected of being implicated in some of the depredations and were regarded as two of the men responsible for the circulation of counterfeit money. Both were apparently on intimate terms with James Ford, whose two sons were also suspected of being involved in some of the lawlessness which was then increasing rapidly. Ford owned Ford's Ferry and the ferry house near it. The ferry, however, was run by Simpson, who occupied the house.

After carefully concealing its acts for many years, the clan began drifting to the inevitable. A lack of trust among the men themselves and the increasing danger of their work indicated that sooner or later something would occur to end its career. The end came in 1834. Strange to say, it was brought about, not through a dispute over the division of spoils or a wholesale arrest of its members, but was due more directly to a lawsuit regarding a slave than to any other cause known to the public. Tradition is vague regarding this litigation, but the court records reveal sufficient data from which to glean the cause of the beginning of the end of the Ford's Ferry mystery.

The Circuit Court Records of Livingston County contain the proceedings of a suit entitled "Ford versus Simpson" which began in September, 1829, and continued nearly two years. James Ford's petition recites that on January 7, 1829, he bought from Vincent B. Simpson a slave named Hiram, for the sum of eight hundred dollars. Simpson guaranteed him to be "a good blacksmith, sound and healthy," but the negro died soon after the sale, at the age of thirty-four. Ford set forth that the man was "no blacksmith and no labourer and was labouring under a disease called hernia," and that he was worth only two hundred and fifty dollars at the time of the sale. In consequence of the loss of time and work resulting from the purchase of the negro, Ford sued for one thousand dollars damages. Simpson tried, through various witnesses, to prove that the slave was a good mechanic and a healthy negro, but failed to establish any of his claims. Ford, on the other hand, produced many men who upheld him and gave much testimony to prove that Simpson had practiced a fraud in making the sale. The case dragged through the courts until March 9, 1831, when, by agreement of the attorneys, the suit was ordered dismissed, "each party paying their own costs."

This was a victory for Ford, for rumor had it that he and Simpson were equally implicated in certain robberies. Ford had proved Simpson a deceitful man and could now cite the Hiram transaction as an example of his unreliability. Ford was prepared, should Simpson reveal any of their secrets and "try" to implicate him; he was fortified against any accusation, true or false, that Simpson might make. In the meantime, Simpson continued to run Ford's Ferry. Whether or not Ford attempted to remove him is not known. It is probable that each feared the other, and that each was awaiting the other's first damaging act. Ford and his two grown sons evidently foresaw the possibility of serious trouble.

These two sons were Philip and William M. Ford (whose ages, in 1831, were respectively thirty-one and twenty-eight years). He had one daughter, the Cassandra who, February 5, 1827, married Dr. Charles H. Webb, as previously noted. The daughter was an accomplished and highly respected woman, and is so represented in Watt's *Chronicles*. Her husband was all his life a model citizen. Ford's first wife, it is said, was a Miss Miles, whose brother at one time ran a ferry where the village of Weston, Kentucky, now stands. After the death of his first wife, Ford, January 15, 1829, as shown by Livingston County marriage records, married Mrs. Elizabeth Frazer, a widow with three daughters. Mr. Frazer and his family, so runs the story, were coming down the Ohio in a flatboat and chanced to stop at Ford's home. Mr. Frazer became ill while there, and a few days later died. In the course of a short time

Ford married the widow, and from that union was
born, in 1830, one child, James Ford Jr.

Trouble was brewing. What preparations were made
by Ford and his two sons to meet the uncertain develop-
ments is not known. A perusal of the wills recorded in
Livingston County reveals the fact that Philip Ford
made a will on November 21, 1831, and that within
seven months thereafter wills were also made by his
brother and father. Philip Ford died two days after
he had prepared his will. One tradition has it that he
died of yellow fever, but that is not at all likely to be
true. The document was not recorded until June, 1833.
It shows he was a widower and a man of some means.
He designates his father and brother-in-law, Dr. Webb,
as administrators. He bequeathed some of his estate to
his father, sister, and brother William, but the greater
part to his only child, Francis Ford, then a small boy.
Among the items were seven slaves, two of whom,
"Irene, a woman, and Kitty, a girl," were to be retained
and the other five sold "at nine months credit, the proceeds to go for the whole use and benefit of my son."
Another item reads: "My gold watch I wish Doct.
Charles H. Webb to take charge of until my son comes
of age and then to go to my son Francis Ford." As requested in this document, he was "buried by the side of
where my beloved wife is buried and in a decent manner." The inscription on his gravestone reads:

"To the memory of Philip Ford who was born November 25th,
1800, departed this life November 23d, 1831."

A year later William died and was buried beside his
brother. Tradition ascribes his death to cholera. Be
that as it may, there is nothing to indicate that he "died
with his boots on," although he might have met that
fate had he survived a few years longer. The graves of

the two brothers are on the Ford Old Place about one mile southwest of Tolu. Each is marked with a dressed stone box grave cover, which, before the collapse a few years ago, was about six feet long, three feet wide and three feet high, the top being a well carved slab bearing an inscription. The inscription on the grave of Ford's second son can be interpreted in more than one way:

"To the memory of William M. Ford, who departed this life on the 3d day of Novr. 1832, aged 28 years. Whose benevolence caused the widow and orphant to smile and whose firmness caused his enemies to tremble. He was much appresst while living and much slandered since dead."

William also left a will. It is dated June 1, 1832. The official records show that it was recorded July 27, 1832, a little more than three months before he died. Tradition has forgotten how William's "firmness caused his enemies to tremble" and by what means he was "much appresst while living and much slandered since dead." Nor is there any tradition regarding the identity of the widows and orphans who, through his benevolence, were caused to smile. His will, however, throws some sidelights on his career as a father. The document does not refer to a wife, living or dead. One tradition has it that at the age of twenty-two he married a girl by the name of Simpson, but that name does not appear among the three mothers of his children referred to by him. He first bequeaths all his estate to his two sons, one of whom was, in 1832, seven years old, and the other seven months. After stating the name of the mother of each, he adds: "both of said children I acknowledge to be my sons." But in the event of the death of both boys before they reached the age of twenty-one, he gives two thousand dollars to the young daughter of a certain woman he mentions, and be-

queaths practically all the residue of his estate to his
uncle, Richard Miles.

It is said that the inscription placed on the grave of
William was dictated by James Ford. Beginning a
short time before the death of his two sons, many accu-
sations against William and his father gained wide
circulation. Ford evidently hoped that such an inscription on the tomb of the "appresst" and "slandered" son
would have the effect of a voice from the grave and do
much toward subduing undesirable true and false reports that might continue to circulate after his death.
Tradition says James Ford requested his wife to place
an inscription of a similar character on his grave,
hoping it would, to a considerable extent, prevent the
community from attributing all the lawlessness to him
and none to the mysterious Ford's Ferry band, of which
he was openly accused of being the leader. Mrs. Ford,
in all probability, would have carried out this wish had
she not died so soon after her husband. Be that as it
may, nothing marks the grave of James Ford nor that
of his wife. If small stones were erected over them
they have long ago disappeared, as have some of the
other headstones that once stood in the same graveyard.
The spot pointed out as the one where James Ford was
buried is a few feet from William's grave and is now,
and long has been, covered by a briar patch.

Paying the Penalty

After the death of his two sons James Ford was, in a sense, obliged to stand alone and face, as best he could, any and all reflections upon his reputation. According to one tradition, some of the law-abiding citizens continued to regard him as an innocent victim of treacherous associates. It appears that among the members of the Ford's Ferry crowd there were only a few whom he dared trust. Henry C. Shouse was one of them and he, with two others, as is shown later, played an important part in the closing act of the mysterious band.

From the time of the lawsuit between Ford and Simpson each lay perdu awaiting the action of the other. Each realized, so runs the tradition, that the other "knew too much." One morning, shortly after the death of Ford's second son, Shouse approached Simpson at Ford's Ferry and tried to arouse the ferryman's anger and lead him into a fight. Simpson, suspecting a hidden motive, quietly withdrew. A few days later Shouse accused Simpson of treachery, claiming, among other things, that Simpson had circulated a report to the effect that "some one will soon turn state's evidence, and certain robbers, counterfeiters, and murderers will then quit business for good." A lively fight followed; both men were badly bruised, but neither was victorious.

Thus did Shouse, greatly influenced by others, make and set his trap for Simpson. Simpson, sensing the situation, immediately prepared for any defense that firearms might afford him. These strained relations between the two men, each watching the other, continued for about a week. On June 30, 1833, Simpson went in his boat from Ford's Ferry down to Cave-in-Rock and, upon his return, stopped at Cedar Point and walked up to the home of Shouse. Whether Simpson had gone there to kill Shouse or to attempt to bring about a reconciliation is an unsettled question. He had reached a point in Shouse's yard when, without warning, some one, firing from the second story window of Shouse's log house, shot him in the back, inflicting a wound of which he died next morning.

News that Simpson had been shot spread fast. Shouse was, of course, immediately accused of the murder. Those most familiar with the general state of affairs suspected that James Mulligan and William H. J. Stevenson, both of whom lived near by, were accessories. A search was made in the neighborhood, but not one of the three men could be found. The law-abiding citizens on both sides of the Ohio recognized in the death of Simpson the removal of a man who, either through a selfish motive or for the good of the public, contemplated revealing secrets the exposition of which would have led to the extermination of a band of men who had disturbed the community for many years. Pursuing parties were sent out and messengers and letters dispatched in every direction in an effort to capture the three fleeing men and bring them back for trial and punishment.

In the meantime, the situation and its causes were taken under consideration by certain citizens not in any of the posses. Most versions have it that a few days after Simpson had been killed a small number of men who chanced to gather at the home of his widow, took up, in secret, the question of avenging Simpson's death. It is said that no definite decision was reached by them, but that each trusted the vengeance to fate itself. However, three men were appointed to ride to Ford's residence and ask him to come to Simpson's in order that he might be prepared to join the crowd which was, early the next morning, to appear before the grand jury and give testimony as to the killing.

On their way the messengers met Ford near the Hurricane Camp Ground. After hearing their mission he stated he was then riding to the ferry to learn the latest news and offer his services. The messengers, accompanied by Ford, rode back to Simpson's, where they arrived about sundown. A few minutes later Ford and a dozen or more men present were invited to take supper, but all declined, apparently for the reason that they were occupied discussing their plans for the next day. After night had fallen the invitation was again extended. About half the number then went into the kitchen to eat, and the rest stood in the open passage that ran between the two rooms of the log house. Ford, accepting a chair, leaned it against the log wall and sat down. The men, one by one, stepped out of the passage, leaving Ford comfortably seated alone in the dark. While in this position a man handed him a letter, in the meantime standing to one side and holding a lighted candle over Ford's head, seemingly for the purpose of throwing light on the paper. Ford was engaged in reading the letter when someone concealed behind a rose bush in the front yard, shot him through the heart, the bullet lodging in the log wall against which he was leaning. Ford fell on the floor dead. The body was immediately carried out in the yard and preparations were soon begun to send it to his home.

Placed in a rude box, on a wagon drawn by two oxen, Ford's body was taken to the Ford farm and there prepared for burial, which took place a day or two later. According to tradition, the only persons present at the funeral were his wife, his daughter and her husband, two of his neighbors and about half a dozen slaves. A terrific storm suddenly came up while the little procession was marching from the house to the family graveyard, a distance of about a quarter of a mile. The slaves were in the act of lowering the coffin when a crash of thunder frightened one of them so badly that he dropped the rope with which he was helping to lower the corpse, and ran away. The head of the coffin struck the bottom of the grave and wedged the box into an angular position. Attempts were made to pry it to a level, but without success. While the storm was raging the remaining slaves, with all possible haste, filled the grave. After completing the mound, these superstitious negroes ran to their cabins and from that date "saw things" that have not been seen since, but have entered into many traditions pertaining to the Fords. For example: Some of them *saw* "Jim Ford land in Hell head foremost."

The names of the man who held the candle and the one who fired the shot that killed Ford were never revealed, then or thereafter. It is said that no investigation of the assassination was ever made, and, furthermore, that if official proceedings had been attempted, no evidence of any kind could have been procured.

Ford was suspected to be the leader, adviser, and protector of the so-called Ford's Ferry band, but whether or not he was actually all these was never positively proved. Had his wife lived a little longer, she in all probability, would have carried out his suggestion to erect a monument over his grave. If so, the inscription would have followed, more or less, the lines prepared by him as his son William's epitaph. There would have been some truth in words to the effect that James Ford had not only rendered much assistance to widows and orphans, but also to the poor and destitute, and that his "firmness caused his enemies to tremble." As to how he was "appresst while living" it is impossible to determine now. That he was "much slandered since dead" is true, judging from some of the tales told about him even to this day.

One of these improbable stories is that Ford punished a slave by placing the man's head in a vise and while it was thus fastened cut off the negro's ears and pulled out his teeth.

Another is to the effect that after the Ford's Ferry men had murdered and robbed a flatboatman they learned from papers in his pocket that his name was Simmons. They buried their victim on the hill near the Ferry. Soon thereafter it was noticed that many persimmon sprouts began to shoot up out of the grave and the ground near by. Although grubbed out a number of times they reappeared each succeeding spring. Ford, seeing that the matter was viewed as an evil omen and working on the superstition of some of his men, ordered the remains taken up and ceremoniously lowered into the river below Cave-in-Rock, "where," as one man expressed it, "Simmons couldn't sprout any more." But the sprouts continued to sprout on the hill overlooking Ford's Ferry and today "the old 'simmons thicket" helps perpetuate this old tale.[37]

---

[37] The *Chicago Times* published an article July 17, 1879, entitled "Hell on the Ohio," which, in 1888, was republished in *The Life of Logan Belt,* a book by Shadrack L. Jackson, who then lived in the village of Cave-in-Rock. This distorted account of Ford is here reprinted as an example of

There is an absurd but widespread tradition that
James Ford had acquired, through his "frolics at the
ferry," a vast fortune consisting of "dozens of farms,
hundreds of slaves, and barrels of money" and that in
his will he not only named every man connected with
the robber band, but gave each a slave or mule. This
story, like many of the others, is absolutely without
foundation. His will, recorded August 5, 1833, indicates that he was not a man of more than ordinary
wealth. It was written in his own hand. It contains
many errors in composition and spelling and, like many
other early documents, is sparsely punctuated. It is
nevertheless evidence that his practical education was
far above most of his contemporaries, though his scho-

one of the many absurd and almost groundless stories that have gained
wide circulation:

"Not far from Cave-in-Rock is Ford's Ferry, which gets its name from
a man who was one of the noted criminals of pioneer history. He lived on
the Kentucky side about two miles above Cave-in-Rock and was ostensibly
a farmer, owning a large tract of land. He also kept a hotel. Ford was
always surrounded by a gang of desperate men, highwaymen and murderers,
and, while nothing was ever proved on him, he was looked upon as equal
to his companions in guilt. He was a robber of flatboats and of emigrants.
Dead bodies were found near his house, and isolated and freshly made
graves were discovered in that neighborhood. Men were known to start
West with a little money, to locate, and were never after heard of. Their
friends would inquire, follow them to Ford's and there lose all traces of them.
It was one of his habits to cut down trees and obstruct the road to rival
ferries, until the owners would be compelled to quit and leave, thinking
retaliation only a means of provoking death. But Ford brought on himself
the penalty of his lawlessness.

"An old feud existed between him and the father-in-law of a man named
Simpson, and Ford killed his enemy. Simpson gathered a crowd of friends
and went armed to Ford's house for the purpose of killing him. They found
him on the Illinois side loading a boat. He knew at once why they had
come, begged for his life and appealed for protection to one of their number,
Jonathan Brown by name. Brown was touched by the appeal and inter-
ceded for the terrified man. The plea was so far successful that the crowd
waited two or three hours, but when darkness came, they took him out and
shot him dead when he was begging hardest to be spared. It is said that
none of the crowd proper did the shooting, but that Simpson compelled his
negro to do the deed."

lastic training was slight. His penmanship was good, as can be seen by his signature here reproduced.[38]

Tradition has it that Ford had been buried only a few days when the report reached Ford's Ferry that Shouse, Mulligan, and Stevenson, who were accused of having killed Simpson, had been overtaken. The three had started for Texas, but were arrested in Arkansas. Shortly after the guards and their charges started on their return the captives tried to escape. Each prisoner was then placed astride a horse and his feet tied under the animal. In due time they were landed in the jail at Equality, Illinois, then the county seat of Gallatin County.[39]

The court records show that the Gallatin County grand jury at its September term, 1833, indicted Shouse for the murder of Simpson, with Mulligan and Stevenson named as accessories to the crime. The original indictment is still preserved. The greater part of the document is a repetition of old and verbose legal phraseology, reciting what is summed up in the following extracts:

---

[38] It may be proper here to record that descendants of James Ford, like the descendants of other crude but strong pioneer stock, rose to deserved prominence in the business and social life of several western cities. The family is scattered, but the respect its members command and the success they have achieved bears testimony to the strain of ability and energy inherent in the blood. It leads also to deeper consideration of one of the theories in the Ford's Ferry mystery, that James Ford was perhaps a victim of circumstances growing out of his peculiar personality in a dangerous surrounding.

[39] The crime was committed in that part of Gallatin County which in 1839 (when Hardin County was formed out of parts of Gallatin and Pope counties) became the eastern portion of Hardin. Previous to the organization of Hardin, Cave-in-Rock was a "corner" at the southern extremity of the line separating the two original counties.

"That . . . not having the fear of God before their eyes, but being moved and seduced by the instigations of the Devil on the thirtieth day of June . . . with force and arms . . . in and upon one Vincent B. Simpson, in (violation of) the peace of God and of the people of the said State, feloniously, wilfully, and of their malice aforethought, did make an assault, and that the said Henry C. Shouse, with a certain gun called a rifle, of the value of ten dollars, then and there charged with gun powder and a leaden bullet . . . did shoot off and discharging said rifle gun, so loaded . . . did wound the said Vincent in and upon the left side of the back bone near the shoulder blade, inflicting a mortal wound in and through the body . . . of which said mortal wound said Vincent did languish and languishing did live until the first day of July . . . and of said mortal wound did die. . . And that the said James Mulligan and the said William H. J. Stevenson, then and there, feloniously, wilfully, and of their malice aforethought, were present, aiding, helping, abetting, comforting, assisting, and maintaining the said Henry C. Shouse, the felony murder aforesaid to do and commit."

A careful perusal of the court records and documents leads to the discovery of these facts: The case was called for trial a few days after the indictment had been found. Fifteen witnesses had been summoned; all were ready to give testimony for the state, but none for the defense. After considerable discussion by the attorneys, a change of venue to Pope County was granted, and the case was docketed for trial at Golconda in November. Beginning November 21, 1833, and continuing six days, Shouse's attorneys, Fowler and Gatewood, made every effort to secure a postponement, claiming technical errors committed by the court. Failing in this, they presented the fact that Mulligan had died in jail and Stevenson had escaped, and on that ground succeeded in deferring the trial until the May term following. There is nothing to indicate the circumstances of the death of the one, nor the escape and disappearance of the other.

On May 21, 1834, the case was again presented and the attorneys argued for further delay, but failed. Shouse stood trial, and after a two days' hearing the jury was instructed to consider the evidence. There is nothing in the written records showing for what motive Shouse killed Simpson. In fact, the records contain little other than stereotyped legal phrases relative to postponing the case. They throw practically no light on the evidence heard. No summaries of the testimony have been found. Shouse denied his guilt. The name of Ford does not appear in any of the documents. Tradition says that Shouse not only did not betray Ford, but shielded him whenever an opportunity presented itself.

After the jury had retired, one William Sharp appeared on the scene and begged to be heard. Shouse's attorneys prepared a written avowal of what Sharp's statement would contain and presented it to the judge with an argument that in view of the new evidence by a material witness the case be retried, regardless of the verdict of the present jury. This was overruled. This document is the only one from which can be gathered any suggestion as to the character of evidence probably employed by the defense. Its plea was that "Shouse expects to prove by said witness (Sharp) that the deceased Simpson told him about a week before his death that he had some short time before collared the defendant Shouse and dared him to cut, that he in-

tended then in a few days to take his pistol and go over
to Shouse's house and settle him." This was a plea of
self-defense. But, as already stated, this motion was
overruled. The jury, after due deliberation, found
Shouse "guilty as charged."

According to most traditions, Simpson had more
knowledge of the criminal conduct of the Ford's Ferry
outlaws than it was safe for one man to have. It was
rumored that a large reward was about to be offered for
evidence leading to the conviction of any member of
the band, and Simpson's confederates feared he would
be tempted to betray them. Shouse, it seems, was
selected – or volunteered – to see that "dead men tell no
tales."

No man of his time was more familiar with the details of the Shouse murder trial than William Courtney
Watts. He furnished the following statement to a
representative of the Louisville *Courier-Journal* which
published it March 27, 1895:

"Shouse was one of the ring-leaders of the notorious
Ford gang and it is generally believed that Ford depu-
tized him to kill Simpson. It was observed that after
Shouse was sentenced to be hanged, his attorney, Judge
Wyley P. Fowler, spent a large part of his time in the
cell of Shouse. It finally leaked out that Shouse was
dictating to Judge Fowler a history of the robber band
to which he had belonged and that his statements implicated some of the wealthiest and most prominent citizens in Livingston County. At that juncture Judge
Fowler received a number of anonymous letters in
which writers threatened his life in the event of his
ever making public the communications made to him
by Shouse. By the advice of friends Judge Fowler
spent the succeeding winter in Frankfort. Upon his

return Mr. J. W. Cade, the circuit clerk, asked Judge Fowler if the Shouse history had been destroyed. He replied: 'No good could come of its publication. It would cast a shade upon the reputation of some of Livingston County's most esteemed citizens.' Nothing further was ever heard of the manuscript and it is believed that Judge Fowler destroyed it."

It is said Judge Fowler's notes were based on the dictations the doomed Shouse intended for the public, and on such reports as were being openly discussed among the people. Judge Fowler, however, having been Ford's attorney for a number of years and having represented Shouse in his last trial, recognized that any statement he made would be considered as based on confidential information received by him as an attorney, and that, in consequence, he would be unjustly condemned.

What Shouse's history and confession contained was the subject of much speculation for a generation or two. There is an impression among some people living in the lower Ohio River valley that Judge Fowler's alleged manuscript on the history of the robber band still exists. Inquiry recently made among his descendants resulted in learning that many years before his death in 1880, he, in the presence of an intimate friend, destroyed all his data on the subject. Judge Fowler never permitted any one to see his notes and seldom discussed the matter. It is said that on one occasion when he was asked whether or not the Ford's Ferry band was a branch of the clan led by John A. Murrell, he left the impression that it had at one time made some preparations to work in conjunction with the great western land pirate and his band of negro stealers.

More or less has been written by historians and novelists about John A. Murrell, but no writer connects him with Cave-in-Rock or Ford's Ferry. *The History of Virgil A. Stewart,* a book on the life of Murrell, compiled by H. R. Howard and published in 1836, gives an incomplete list of Murrell's associates. Among the four hundred and fifty names there recorded there is none familiar to persons now living near Cave-in-Rock. Tradition says that Shouse made a few trips between the Cave and Marked Tree, Arkansas, to meet Murrell or some of his representatives for the purpose of delivering and receiving messages pertaining to ne-gro stealing and the disposition of counterfeit money. But whether or not the Ford's Ferry band was ever part of the John A. Murrell clan will remain, in all prob-ability, one of the Ford's Ferry mysteries.[40]

On June 7, 1834, Judge Thomas C. Brown sent a writ to Joshua Howard, Sheriff of Pope County: "Where-as . . .   Judgment hath been given in our said court that the said Henry C. Shouse shall be hanged by the neck until he is dead and that execution of said judgment be made and done on Monday the ninth day of June A.D., 1834, between the hours of twelve of the clock at noon and four of the clock in the evening of the same day, at some convenient place in the vicinity, not more than one-half mile from the town of Golconda in said county, in the usual manner of inflicting punish-

---

[40] The fact that the names Murrell and Mason sound somewhat alike is sometimes the cause of confusion. For example, occasionally one hears that Little Harpe cut off the head of Murrell, whereas Harpe was hanged when Murrell was four or five years old.

On a map of the Ohio, compiled 1911-14 under the supervision of the Ohio River Board of Engineers on Locks and Dams, Cave-in-Rock is erroneously designated Merrell's [sic] Cave.

One absurd tradition has it that James Ford's first wife was a sister of Murrell, and another is to the effect that both Ford and his wife were related to Mason, Murrell, and the Harpes.

ment in such cases. . ." And on June 9 Shouse paid the extreme penalty.

Tradition has it that on the day of the hanging thousands of people came to Golconda from Gallatin and Pope counties, Illinois, and from Livingston County, Kentucky, and other sections, to see the first legal hanging in the county and to witness the death struggle of a Ford's Ferry and Cave-in-Rock outlaw. Even to this day, a large crowd in that section of the country is measured as being "as big as the one when Shouse was hanged." The execution took place in the creek bottom immediately north of the town limits, at a spot where the slopes of the hills converge to form a natural amphitheatre. About two o'clock in the afternoon Shouse was placed on an ox-cart and driven to the scaffold that had been built by erecting two heavy timbers with a cross beam over them. Between these two upright posts the cart was placed, and into it the condemned man's coffin was then shoved, thus serving the purpose of a platform and trap. Shouse's hands were tied behind his back; he was blindfolded and made to stand erect upon his coffin. The suspended rope was looped around his neck; the oxen pulled the cart forward and Shouse fell.

Thus terminated the career of one of the members of the mysterious Ford's Ferry band, and with it passed away forever bloodshed and robbery at Cave-in-Rock.

The Cave in Fiction

Historical novels, with some exceptions, present the past in a more interesting manner than do the formal histories which are intended as chronicles of actual facts. It has been said, on the one hand, that "truth is stranger than fiction," and on the other that "fiction is often more truthful than fact." Fiction is undoubtedly more truthful in the presentation of the manners and social life of the period portrayed than is formal history. The history of Cave-in-Rock and the careers of the outlaws identified with the place is not only stranger than fiction, but is besprinkled with many tragic and melodramatic scenes which, although almost unimaginable, are actually true. For more than a century fiction writers have used the Cave as a background for stories. These authors by freely discarding the leading facts and drawing on their own imaginations wrote stories less original than might otherwise have been produced.

No effort has been made to compile a more or less complete collection of works of fiction pertaining to the Cave. The stories and poems commented on in the course of this chapter are only such as were incidentally found while in search of history. Although this fiction has very little of facts for a basis, and most of the scenes are far from probable, nevertheless it necessarily stands not only as Cave-in-Rock literature, but also as a contribution to the good, bad, or indifferent literature of America. The fact that more than one edition was published of the Cave-in-Rock novels here referred to indicates, to some extent that they represent some of the types of stories then in demand.

Stories dealing with mysterious murders and highway robberies have always found many enthusiastic readers. It seems that every decade of the nineteenth century produced at least one new tale of Cave-in-Rock. And in our own times the writings of some well-known living authors show that the Cave is still supplying material for fiction.

In Irvin S. Cobb's story "The Dogged Under Dog," (originally published in the *Saturday Evening Post*, August 3, 1912, and shortly thereafter printed in Cobb's book entitled *Back Home*) one of the characters, recalling some of the rough men who lived near the Cave when that country was still new, says Big Harpe and Little Harpe were run down by dogs and killed and that "the men who killed them cut off their heads and salted them down and packed them both in a piggin of brine, and sent the piggin by a man on horseback up to Frankfort to collect the reward."

Nancy Huston Banks in *Oldfield*, 1902, devotes a few pages to Cave-in-Rock, the Harpes, and a character she calls "Alvarado," a mysterious Spaniard who frequented the lower Ohio valley and who was suspected of having been a comrade of Jean Lafitte. Mrs. Banks, in her next historical novel, *'Round Anvil Rock*, 1903 (in which Philip Alston is one of the leading characters) refers to that section of Kentucky lying opposite the Cave as having been the "Rogues Harbor."

The Harpes, Masons, and the Cave are introduced in *The Ark of 1803*, by C. A. Stephens. This book for boys, published in 1904, is intended as a picture of romances and tragedies incidental to early navigation on the Ohio and Mississippi. It serves that purpose

VIEW OF CAVE-IN-ROCK AND VICINITY, 1833

It shows a landscape interesting in itself but false to the actual scene

(Reproduced from Charles Bodmer's drawing)

fairly well, although practically no statement made by the author regarding the Harpes and the Masons is in accordance with history or tradition.

Our earliest item relative to fiction pertaining to the Cave was found in a review published in *The Port Folio*, February, 1809, of Thomas Ashe's *Travels in America Performed in 1806*, printed in London in 1808. The critics in Ashe's day, and ever since, declared the writer of *Travels* a literary thief, bone thief, and infamous prevaricator and ridiculed his work on the ground that it was filled with incredible stories grafted onto authentic incidents and actual facts. This general condemnation gave the new book a wide circulation for a few years. The editor of *The Port Folio* devotes a dozen pages to his "entire contempt both of Mr. Ashe and his work."

Most of the travelers who appeared after Ashe's day and examined the Cave detected in his sketch a combination of facts and fiction that helped spread the name and history of this interesting and picturesque rendezvous of outlaws. Many a visitor still goes to the place expecting to explore the "upper cave" but soon discovers that its size has been wildly exaggerated by Ashe. His account of the Cave is one of the longest ever written and will always be of curious interest no matter from what standpoint it may be read, other than history. The reproach to Ashe is that he gave the hoax out as veritable facts encountered in his travels and never corrected this impression or acknowledged his purpose. About half of what he says concerning the Cave is at least highly probable; the remainder is wholly fictitious.

A casual investigation of the stories published after outlawry terminated at Ford's Ferry, brought to light two novels and a long poem in which the Cave serves as a background. Viewed from the standpoint of today their plots have the consistency of a dime novel. Browsing in the field of fiction also led to the discovery of the one time celebrated romance of *Harpe's Head*.

Harpe's Head, by Judge James Hall, was first published in America in 1833, and the following year was printed in London under the title of *Kentucky, A Tale.* It was later republished in America in Judge Hall's volume, *Legends of the West. Harpe's Head* is the only novel in which the notorious Harpes are introduced as characters. It is a story of a small emigrant family traveling from Virginia to western Kentucky over the route then endangered by the Harpes. All the characters are fictitious, except the two outlaws and their wives. No reference is made to their career at the Cave.

The romance is written in a dignified and graceful style. *Atkinson's Casket* for November, 1833, in its comments on the book says "it has some masterly scenes," and quotes one in full – a Virginia barbecue. Among other interesting sketches of pioneer times woven into *Harpe's Head* is one of "Hercules Short" or "Hark Short, the Snake Killer," a half-witted boy who performs extraordinary feats and who labors under the impression that he is a son of Big Harpe. On one occasion "Hark" remarks that his mother told him, "If anybody was to rake hell with a fine-comb they would not find sich a tarnal villain as Big Harpe."

Edmund L. Starling, in his *History of Henderson County, Kentucky,* 1887, says: "The history of the Harpes in this portion of Kentucky, has long ago, and repeatedly found its way into the histories of Kentucky and other states, in pamphlets and the newspapers of the country, and at one time was even dramatized for the American stage. But it was so desperate and appalling to all rational sensibilities that it was abandoned by the drama." I did not find any pamphlets or dramas regarding the Harpes.

The earliest novel found using Cave-in-Rock for a background is *Mike Fink, A Legend of the Ohio,* by Emerson Bennett, who for a time was a well-known writer of thrilling romances. This melodrama was first published in Cincinnati in 1848, and although now a somewhat rare book, it ranked, judging from the number of editions issued, among widely-read stories of the middle of the last century. Its popularity was not due to any high literary merit, but to its wild and extravagant plot. The greater part of the story deals with bloody battles between a band of outlaws and the flatboat crew and passengers led by Mike Fink. Practically all the action takes place in or near the Cave, and for that reason "A Legend of Cave-in-Rock" would have been a more appropriate subtitle.

Shortly after *Mike Fink* was put into circulation there appeared in the *Alton* (Illinois) *Courier,* 1852, a prize serial entitled *Virginia Rose,* by Dr. Edward Reynolds Roe. Having gone through a pamphlet edition, this Cave-in-Rock story was published in book form in 1882 under the title of *Brought to Bay,* and in 1892 the same story was republished and its title changed back to *Virginia Rose.* Dr. E. R. Roe – not E. P. Roe with whom he is sometimes confused – was a citizen of Illinois, practiced medicine and wrote a number of books. He died in Chicago in 1893 at the age of eighty. He lived in Shawneetown a few years, beginning in 1843, and it is said he prepared the greater part of this manuscript while residing there.

The book has no preface and the presumption is that
all the characters are fictitious. The story deals with
the career of a girl, Virginia Rose, who was kidnapped
in Shawneetown by her father, the leader of the Cave-
in-Rock outlaws. He takes her to the Cave, and it so
happened that shortly thereafter the New Madrid
earthquake of 1811 occurs. The citizens of Shawneetown, suspecting that the stolen Virginia Rose may have
been taken to the Cave, so runs the story, organize a rescuing party. Upon their arrival at the Cave, they, to
their great surprise, find the place abandoned. Boxes
and barrels were scattered around, their contents undis-
turbed, and the general appearance indicated that the
place had been abandoned suddenly.

In the words of the author: "Remnants of a feast
which had never been eaten were lying upon a table;
lamps were hanging around burnt out for want of
oil. . . The hatchway overhead, which communi-
cated with the room above was not closed . . . but
the avenues which led from it to the inner cave had disappeared. The rock had fallen from above in vast
masses and closed all connection between the upper
cave and the outer world forever. . . What was a
hill back of the cave bluff now appeared to be a hollow
or depression, as compared to the ground around it. . .
The outlaws had met their fate – they had perished in
the earthquake [except the leader and his daughter
who were on the Mississippi at the time] perhaps in the
midst of gay festivities, perhaps in the hour of music
and dancing! Who could say? Not a soul was left to
tell the tale. The men who had come to execute vengeance could not now avoid sympathy for the dead."

Thus did the author of *Virginia Rose* make the New
Madrid earthquake wipe out the Cave-in-Rock's "inner

cave" or "upper cave" that had been "discovered" and is so extravagantly described by Thomas Ashe!

Between recorded history on the one hand and stories of fiction on the other stands the book *Chronicles of a Kentucky Settlement,* 1897, by William Courtney Watts. It is a historical romance based solely on local tradition. Although this work is somewhat faulty in its general construction, and may be, at times, somewhat crude in its literary style, it is, nevertheless, one of the most faithful historical sketches of early Kentucky.

The leading characters are Joseph Watts and Lucinda Haynes, who were first thrown together in 1805 when children on their way from North Carolina to the West, Joseph going to Tennessee and Lucinda moving with her parents to Kentucky. A few years later Joseph Watts began a search for Miss Haynes and found her near Salem, Kentucky. After a courtship such as none but lovers in a new country could experience, they were married and became the parents of the author who tells their story. Among other characters is Charles H. Webb, who gave Watts an account of his capture at Cave-in-Rock and escape from the outlaws and who later married the daughter of James Ford.

The gloomiest tragedy in the book concerns the unfortunate Lucy Jefferson Lewis, sister of Thomas Jefferson, whose two sons killed a slave on their farm near Smithland, Kentucky, and cut up the body in an attempt to conceal their crime. One of the Lewis brothers committed suicide on his mother's grave and the other escaped after he had been arrested for murder and placed in jail. All the characters in *Chronicles* are presented under fictitious names.[41]

It is probable that every person who saw the land-

---

[41] An exhaustive search through the fiction printed during the first part

scape of which the opening of the Cave forms a part had his sense of romance and poetry stirred by the sight. To what extent attempts were made to express this emotion in the form of poetry or verse is not known. Only one poem has been found – "The Outlaw," by Charles H. Jones, of Cincinnati. It comprises about one thousand two hundred lines, published in 1835 in a neatly bound booklet called *The Outlaw and Other Poems.* In the October, 1835, issue of the *Western Monthly Magazine,* of Cincinnati, Judge James Hall devotes two pages to a eulogistic review of the book, encouraging the young poet in his work. A more enthusiastic reviewer might have called this an epic of Cave-in-Rock.

In his introductory note Mr. Jones briefly refers to the then well-known fact that the Cave had been for many years the resort of a band of outlaws all of whom were finally either killed or driven out by the Rangers. As to his authorities he states that "the ravages of the robbers are still fresh in the recollection of many of the inhabitants of the lower Ohio valley."

About one-half of the poem is an "effervescence of

of last century probably would result in finding all the Cave-in-Rock tales referred to by early writers.

Henry R. Schoolcraft visited the Cave in 1818 and in his *Personal Memoirs* commented that "as a scene of a tale of imaginative robber-life it appeared to me to possess great attractions." Later in his book entitled *The Indian in His Wigwam* he adds: "The Cave's associations of the early robber era . . . have been commemorated by the pen of fiction of Charles Brockden Brown." In 1834 Charles Fenno Hoffman writes that "its peculiar form has suggested one of the most agreeable tales to an admired Western writer." Edmund Flagg, in *The Far West,* written in 1836, states that murdering and boat robbing perpetrated at the Cave by Samuel Mason and his band "has suggested a spirited tale from a popular writer."

Judge James Hall wrote for a number of magazines. Among his articles may be one on the outlaws at Cave-in-Rock, or a story in which he pictures the activities of the Harpes, the Masons, and others during their stay there. My search for any of his Cave sketches has been fruitless.

poetic fancy," with here and there a real gem. The plot is dramatic. The story begins in Virginia. Our hero shoots his successful rival in love immediately after the wedding ceremony. Believing he has killed the groom and that the shock has proven fatal to the bride, he flees to the wilds of the West. He drifts down the Ohio, joins the band of outlaws at the Cave and soon becomes their leader – The Outlaw.

One "dark tempestuous night" a flatboat passing the Cave is attacked by the robbers; a fierce and bloody combat follows. The Outlaw discovers among the passengers the very girl who had discarded him for another – and still alive. He stabs her in the heart and then –

> "He raised her body from the floor,
>   And hurled it to the foaming wave,
> Her white robe red with streaming gore,
>   A fitting shroud for such a grave."

The battle continues. The Outlaw kills man after man, when to his surprise he finds himself facing the very man he thought he had killed in Virginia. The two recognize each other instantly. They draw daggers and The Outlaw is slain. And the boatmen, so runs the story, exterminate the band of robbers at the Cave.

> "The morning breaks, the fight is o'er,
> Peace smiles again upon the shore.   .   .
> Yon arching cave is lonely now,
> The tenants of its holds have fled,
> Or on the hill-top's rocky brow
> Are sleeping with the dead.   .   .
>
> No more those cavern's walls will ring
> With sounds of mirth and rioting,
> And peacefully along the tide,
> The laden barks will slowly glide;

Their crews no more will deem they see
A robber's form in every tree,
And grasp their rifles and prepare
For deeds of blood and carnage there;
But as they pass along the shore,
Will pause and rest upon the oar,
And tell of many a bloody tale,
The legends of yon gloomy vale;
And travelers, with curious eyes,
Will view its chambers in surprise,
And scarce believe that where they stand,
Was heard the clash of brand on brand,
And yonder yawning cavern's gloom
The Outlaw's dwelling — and his tomb;
But rather all they hear they'll deem
A fable, or a fairy dream."

Bibliography

Manuscript Sources

EXECUTIVE JOURNAL, May 25, 1796 to October 23, 1799, and Appendix, Governor James Garrard. Archives of Secretary of State, Frankfort, Kentucky. [1]

CRIMINAL PROCEDURE AGAINST SAMUEL MASON and companions begun January 11, 1803, Port of New Madrid. MS in French. Department of Archives and History, Jackson, Mississippi [2]

LETTER FROM NICHOLAS MARIA VIDAL, in Spanish, dated New Orleans, March 3, 1803, to Governor W. C. C. Claiborne. Department of Archives and History, Jackson, Mississippi. [3]

LETTER FROM DR. JOHN SIBLEY, dated Natchez, February 18, 1803, to his son Samuel Hopkins Sibley. Sibley Letters, Vol. I, Missouri Historical Society, St. Louis. [4]

COURT OF QUARTER SESSIONS RECORDS, September 1798-March 1802. Danville District Court Records, September 1796-1800. Also Filed Documents. Stanford, Lincoln County, Kentucky. [5]

COURT OF QUARTER SESSIONS RECORDS, Vol. I. Also Filed Documents, Henderson, Henderson County, Kentucky. [6]

LOGAN DISTRICT COURT RECORDS, Vol. I. Russellville, Logan County, Kentucky. [7]

GREENVILLE COURT DOCKET, 1803-1804. Fayette, Jefferson County, Mississippi. [8]

LIVINGSTON COUNTY COURT RECORDS, 1810-1836. Livingston County Circuit Court Records, Books G and H. Smithland, Livingston County, Kentucky. [9]

LIVINGSTON COUNTY WILL BOOKS, A and B. Livingston County Deed Book B. Livingston County Marriage Register, 1822-1839. Smithland, Livingston County, Kentucky. [10]

POPE COUNTY CIRCUIT COURT RECORDS, Book B. Also Filed Documents. Golconda, Pope County, Illinois. [11]

DRAPER MSS (Wisconsin State Historical Society). [12]

A Draper's Notes: 2s 187.
B Draper's Notes: 3s 27, 28.

c Draper's Notes: 3s 37, 38.
d Draper's Notes: 5s 70-72.
e Draper's Notes: 30s 114-129.
f Draper's Notes: 30s 183-193.
g Draper's Notes: 30s 306-311.
h Draper's Notes: 30s 312-316.
i Draper's Notes: 31s 55, 56.
j Draper's Frontier Wars MSS: 1u 65-79.
k Draper's Kentucky MSS: 2cc 34a.
l Draper's Kentucky MSS: 29cc 75, 76.
m Draper's Pittsburgh and Northwest Virginia MSS: 7nn 16.
n Draper's Shepherd Papers: 1ss 91.
o Draper's Virginia MSS: 6zz 61.

Printed Sources

ALLEN, WILLIAM B. History of Kentucky (Louisville, 1872). 411-417. [13]

AMERICAN PIONEER, Cincinnati. *See* 65, 66.

ASHE, THOMAS. Travels in America Performed in 1806 (London, 1808). 250-265. [14]

ATKINSON'S CASKET, a monthly, Philadelphia, November, 1833: Review of James Hall's Harpe's Head, A Legend of Kentucky. [15]

AUDUBON, JOHN JAMES. Audubon and his Journals, by Maria R. Audubon (New York, 1900). vol. ii, 232, 233. [16]

BACON, M. E. Memories of Bold River Pirates kept alive by Cave on the Ohio. Courier-Journal, Louisville, October 6, 1907. [17]

BAILY, FRANCIS. Journal of a Tour in the Unsettled Parts of North America, 1796-1797 (London, 1856). 247. [18]

BECK, LEWIS C. A Gazetteer of the States of Illinois and Missouri (Albany, 1823). 98, 99. [19]

BLOWE, DANIEL. View of the United States of America (London, 1820). 577. [20]

BODMER, CHARLES. Maximilian Atlas. *See* 84.

BREAZEALE, J. W. M. Life as It Is (Knoxville, 1842). 126-151. [21]

BROWN, SAMUEL R. The Western Gazetteer (Auburn, New York, 1817). 29. [22]

CAROLINA GAZETTE, a weekly, Charleston, South Carolina. News item: October 24, 1799. [23]

CASKET MAGAZINE, Philadelphia. *See* 15, 37.

CHARLEVOIX, P. F. X. DE. History of New France (Paris, 1757): Map dated 1744. [24]

CINCINNATI LITERARY GAZETTE, a weekly. Editorial: May 28, 1825. [25]

CLAIBORNE, J. F. H. Mississippi as a Province, Territory and State (Jackson, 1880). 226, 227, 530, 531. [26]

CLAIBORNE, Gov. W. C. C., Official Letters. *See* 113.

COLLINS, LEWIS. Historical Sketches of Kentucky (Maysville, Kentucky, and Cincinnati, 1847). 352-354. [27]

COLLINS, RICHARD H. History of Kentucky (Covington, also Louisville, 1874 and 1882). Vol. i, 25; vol. ii, 345-352, 476, 482, 695, 757. [28]

COLLOT, GEORGE H. VICTOR. A Journey in North America (Paris, 1826). vol. i, 185-187 and Atlas. [29]

CRAMER, ZADOK. The Ohio and Mississippi Navigator (Pittsburgh), 1803, 1806, 1814, 1818. [30]

CRITTENDEN PRESS, Marion, Crittenden County, Kentucky, August, 1893: The Cave-in-Rock, a Rendezvous of Cut-throats and Robbers. [31]

CUMING, FORTESQUE. Sketches of a Tour to the Western Country (Pittsburgh, 1810); in Thwaites, Early Western Travels, vol. iv, 267-274. [32]

CUMINGS, SAMUEL. The Western Navigator (Philadelphia, 1822). Map no. 14. [33]

CUTLER, JERVIS. A Topographical Description of the State of Ohio, Indiana Territory and Louisiana (Boston, 1812). 60. [34]

DANIELS, WILSON. Steamboating on the Ohio and Mississippi before the Civil War. Indiana Magazine of History, Bloomington, June, 1915. [35]

DARBY, JOHN F. Personal Recollections (St. Louis, 1880). 84-97. [36]

DARBY, WILLIAM. Notes on Western Border Life. Casket Magazine, Philadelphia, July 1834. [37]

DAVIDSON, REV. ROBERT. An Excursion to the Mammoth Cave and the Barrens of Kentucky (Lexington, 1840). 21. [38]

Dow, Lorenzo. History of Cosmopolite or Lorenzo's Journal (Cincinnati, 1849). 7th ed., 344.   [39]

Drake, Samel G. Book of the Indians of North America (Boston, 1833). 61.   [40]

Draper, Lyman C. King's Mountain and Its Heroes (Cincinnati, 1881). 224.   [41]

Draper, Lyman C. A Sketch of the Harpes. Western Literary and Historical Magazine, a monthly, Louisville, September, 1842.   [42]

Dunbar, Seymour. A History of Travel in America (Indianapolis, 1915). vol. i, 299-300, vol. ii, 649-650.   [43]

Ellicott, Andrew. Journal of Andrew Ellicott 1796-1800 (Philadelphia, 1803). 21.   [44]

Evans, Estwick. A Pedestrious Tour of Four Thousand Miles (Concord, New Hampshire, 1819); in Thwaites, Early Western Travels, vol. viii, 281.   [45]

Evansville Courier Company. History of Union County, Kentucky (Evansville, Indiana, 1886). 376-380.   [46]

Everybody's Magazine, New York. *See* 126.

Fiction. *See* chapter "The Cave in Fiction."

Filson Club. *See* 106, 123.

Finley, Alexander C. History of Russellville and Logan County, Kentucky (Russellville, 1878, 1879, and 1890). Volume First three pamphets comprising five books: Book i, 1878; Books ii and iii, 1879; Books iv and v, 1890.   [47]

Flagg, Edmund. The Far West, or A Tour Beyond the Mountains (New York, 1838); in Thwaites, Early Western Travels, vol. xxvi, 71-77.   [48]

Flint, Timothy. History and Geography of the Mississippi Valley (Cincinnati, 1832). vol. i, 332.   [49]

Flint, Timothy. Recollections of the Last Ten Years (Boston, 1826). 83.   [50]

Folk-Lore, Journal of American, Boston. *See* 93.

Forman, Samuel S. Narrative of a Journey Down the Ohio and Mississippi in 1789-1790 (Cincinnati, 1888). 36, 37.   [51]

Gratz, Simon. Letters of Thomas Rodney to Caesar A. Rodney. Pennsylvania Magazine of History and Biography, Philadelphia. July and October, 1919.   [52]

GUARDIAN OF FREEDOM, a weekly, Frankfort, Kentucky. News
item: February 29, 1804. [53]

GUILD, JOSEPHUS C. Old Times in Tennessee (Nashville, 1878).
92-99. [54]

HALL, FREDERICK. Letters from the East and from the West
(Washington, 1840). 163. [55]

HALL, JAMES. Story of the Harpes. Port Folio, Philadelphia,
April, 1824, and August, 1825. [56]

HALL, JAMES. Letters from the West (London, 1828). 91-94,
266-268, 272. [57]

HALL, JAMES. Harpe's Head, A Legend of Kentucky (Philadelphia,
1833); Kentucky, A Tale (London, 1834); Harpe's Head, in
Legends of the West (Cincinnati, 1855). [58]

HALL, JAMES. Review of The Outlaw and Other Poems, a booklet, Charles A. Jones, published in Cincinnati, 1835, Western
Monthly Magazine, Cincinnati, October, 1835. [59]

HALL, JAMES. Sketches of History, Life and Manners in the West
(Philadelphia, 1835). vol. ii, 71, 89-90. [60]

HALL, JAMES. Romance of Western History (Cincinnati, 1857).
353-355. [61]

HANNA, CHARLES A. Wilderness Trail (New York, 1911). vol.
ii, 126. [62]

HARPER, LILLIE DuPUY. Journal of Colonel Daniel Trabue. Colonial Men and Times (Philadelphia, 1916). 141-146. [63]

HARRIS, THADDEUS M. Journal of a Tour into the Territory
Northwest of the Allegheny Mountains 1803; with appendix
(Boston, 1805). 373, 374. [64]

HILDRETH, SAMUEL PRESCOTT. History of a Voyage from Marietta
to New Orleans in 1805. American Pioneer, vol. i, Chillicothe,
Ohio, January and April, 1842. [65]

HILDRETH, SAMUEL PRESCOTT. Extracts from B. Van Cleve's
Memoranda. American Pioneer, vol. ii, Cincinnati, Ohio, January, 1843. [66]

HOFFMAN, CHARLES FENNO. A Winter in the West (New York,
1835). vol. ii, 121. [67]

HOUCK, LOUIS. History of Missouri (Chicago, 1908). vol. ii,
143. [68]

HOUGH, EMERSON. Story of the Outlaw (New York, 1907). 36-
73. [69]

HOWARD, H. R. History of Virgil A. Stewart and His Adventure in Capturing and Exposing the Great Western Land Pirate [John A. Murrell] (Philadelphia, 1836). [70]

HOWE, HENRY. Historical Collections of the Great West (Cincinnati, 1852). 181-185. [71]

HULBERT, ARCHER BUTLER. Ohio River, a Course of Empire (New York, 1906). 196-198. [72]

ILLINOIS STATE HISTORICAL SOCIETY. *See* 75, 108.

INDIANA STATE HISTORICAL SOCIETY. *See* 35.

JACKSON, SHADRACH L. Life of Logan Belt, the Noted Desperado of Southern Illinois (Cave-in-Rock, Illinois, 1888). 57,58. [73]

JAMES, EDWIN. Account of an Expedition from Pittsburgh to the Rocky Mountains, from Notes of Major Stephen H. Long (Philadelphia, 1823); in Thwaites, Early Western Travels, vol. xiv, 80, 81. [74]

JENNINGS, JOHN. Journal from Fort Pitt to Fort Chartres in the Illinois Country, March 8, 1766-April 6, 1766; in Illinois Historical Collections, 1916, vol. xi, 167-177. [75]

KELLOGG, LOUISE PHELPS. Frontier Retreat on the Upper Ohio 1779-1781. Wisconsin Historical Society, Collections, 1917, vol. xxiv, Draper Series vol. v, 413, 427, 429, 494. [76]

KELLOGG, LOUISE PHELPS. *See* 76, 130, 131.

KENTUCKY ACTS, Passed at the Seventh General Assembly for the Commonwealth (Frankfort, 1799). 199. [77]

KENTUCKY ACTS, Passed at the Ninth General Assembly for the Commonwealth (Frankfort, 1801). 19. [78]

KENTUCKY GAZETTE, a weekly, Lexington. News items: January 2, March 28, April 25, August 15, September 5, 1799; September 14, 1801; May 3 and 17, November 22, 1803. [79]

LESUEUR, CHARLES ALEXANDRE, in America, by Adrien Loir (Le Havre, France, 1920). [79A]

LONG, C. W. Bloody History of a Graveyard. Evening Post, Louisville, November 2, 1905. [80]

LOUISVILLE COURIER-JOURNAL. *See* 17, 94.

LOUISVILLE EVENING POST. *See* 80.

LOWRY, ROBERT, and William H. McCardle, History of Mississippi (Jackson, 1891). 504, 505. [81]

MARSHALL, HUMPHREY. History of Kentucky (Frankfort, 1824). vol. i, 159, vol. ii, 470. [82]

MASSEY, STEPHEN L. James' Traveler's Companion (Cincinnati, 1851). 168, 169. [83]

MAXIMILIAN, PRINCE OF WIED-NEUWIED. Voyage in the Interior of North America, 1832 to 1834 (London, 1843); in Thwaites, Early Western Travels, vol. xxii, 202. Bodmer's Atlas. [84]

MISSISSIPPI DEPARTMENT OF ARCHIVES AND HISTORY. *See* 2, 3, 105, 114.

MISSOURI HISTORICAL SOCIETY, St Louis. *See* 4.

MONETTE, JOHN W. History of the Discovery and Settlement of the Valley of the Mississippi (New York, 1848). vol. ii, 352, 353. [85]

MURRAY, CHARLES AUGUSTUS. Travels in North America, 1834-1836 (London, 1839). vol. i, 165. [86]

MURRELL, JOHN A., Life of. *See* 70.

NATIONAL HISTORICAL COMPANY. History of Caldwell and Livingston Counties, Missouri (St. Louis, 1886). 711. [87]

NEVILLE, MORGAN. Mike Fink, the Last of the Boatmen. The Western Souvenir for 1829, edited by James Hall. (Cincinnati, Ohio, 1829). 107. [88]

NUTTALL, THOMAS. Journal of Travels into the Arkansa Territory, 1819 (Philadelphia, 1821); in Thwaites, Early Western Travels, vol. xiii, 71. [89]

PALLADIUM, a weekly, Frankfort, Kentucky. News items: May 2 and 9, August 15 and 22, 1799; August 12, 1802; May 5, July 14, September 8, 1803; March 3, 1804. [90]

PARRISH, RANDALL. Historic Illinois, the Romance of the Earlier Days (Chicago, 1905). 293, 401, 402, 446. [91]

PENNSYLVANIA HISTORICAL SOCIETY. *See* 52.

PERRIN DU LAC, F. M. Travels Through the Two Louisianas in 1801-1803 (Paris, 1805); in Richard Phillips' Collection of Travels, vol. vi, 43. [92]

PERROW, EBER CARLE, Songs and Rhymes from the South. Journal of American Folk-Lore, Boston, April-June, 1912. [93]

POOL, A. H. T. Smithland, One of Kentucky's Most Picturesque Towns. Courier-Journal, Louisville, March 27, 1895. [94]

PORT FOLIO, a monthly, Philadelphia, February, 1809: A Criticism by "C." of Thomas Ashe, Travels in America. [95]

PORT FOLIO, Philadelphia. *See* 56, 95.

PRIEST, JOSIAH. American Antiquities and Discoveries in the West (Albany, 1833). 138-144. [96]

PURCELL, MARTHA GRASSHAM. The Sister of the Sage of Monticello Sleeps in Kentucky's Soil. D. A. R. Souvenir, Lexington, Kentucky, October, 1908. [97]

PURCELL, MARTHA GRASSHAM. Stories of Old Kentucky (Cincinnati, 1915). 153-155. [98]

RAFINESQUE, CONSTANTINE S. Ichthyologia Ohiensis (Lexington, Kentucky, 1820). Reprint, Cleveland, 1899. 52. [99]

RANKIN, JOHN. Letters on American Slavery (Boston, 1833). 62-65. [100]

REYNOLDS, JOHN. My Own Times (Belleville, Illinois, 1855). Reprint, Chicago, 1879. 46, 114. [101]

REYNOLDS, JOHN. Pioneer History of Illinois (Belleville, 1852). 72, 239. [102]

RICHARDS, J. ADDISON. Romance of American Landscape (New York, 1854). 195, 197-200. [103]

RICHARDSON, JACOB. Going West in 1820. In Hyde Parke Historical Record (Massachusetts) 1904, vol. iv, 54. [104]

RILEY, FRANKLIN L. Extinct Towns and Villages of Mississippi. In Publications of the Mississippi Historical Society, 1902, vol. v, 346. [105]

ROBERTSON, JAMES R. Petitions of the Early Inhabitants of Kentucky to the General Assembly of Virginia, 1769 to 1792. Filson Club Publications No. 27 (Louisville, 1914). 141. [106]

RODNEY, THOMAS, letters of. *See* 52.

ROOSEVELT, THEODORE. The Winning of the West (New York, 1889). vol. i, 173. [107]

ROSE, JAMES A. Regulators and Flatheads in Southern Illinois. In Transactions of the Illinois State Historical Society for the Year 1906 (Springfield, 1906). 109. [108]

ROTHERT, OTTO A. History of Muhlenberg County, Kentucky (Louisville, 1913). 93, 435-448. [109]

ROTHERT, OTTO A. History of Unity Baptist Church, Muhlenberg County, Kentucky (Louisville, 1914). 3. [110]

ROTHERT, OTTO A. Local History in Kentucky Literature (Louisville, 1915). 9. [111]

ROWLAND, DUNBAR. Encyclopedia of Mississippi History (Madison, Wisconsin, 1907). [112]

ROWLAND, DUNBAR. Official Letter Books of W. C. C. Claiborne. 1801-1816 (Jackson, Mississippi, 1917). vol. i, 9, 45, 61, 91-94; vol. ii, 40; vol. iii, 245. [113]

ROWLAND, MRS. DUNBAR. Marking the Natchez Trace. In Publications of the Mississippi Historical Society, 1910. vol. xi, 345-361. [114]

ST. LOUIS REPUBLIC, October 29, 1911: Lower Illinois Cave Long a Nest of Pirates. [115]

SAFFORD, WILLIAM H. Blennerhassett Papers (1891). 186. [116]

SCHOOLCRAFT, HENRY R. Indian in His Wigwam (New York, 1848). 23. [117]

SCHOOLCRAFT, HENRY R. Personal Memoirs (Philadelphia, 1851). 26, 27. [118]

SCHULTZ, CHRISTIAN. Travels on an Inland Voyage in the Years 1807 and 1808 (New York, 1810). vol. i, 201, 202. [119]

SEALSFIELD, CHARLES. Americans as They Are (London, 1828). 76. [120]

SMITH, T. MARSHALL. Legends of the War of Independence and of the Earlier Settlements in the West (Louisville, 1855). 318-377. [121]

SPALDING, MARTIN J. Sketches of the Early Catholic Missions in Kentucky (Louisville, 1844). 175, 176. [122]

SPEED, THOMAS. Wilderness Road. Filson Club Publications No. 2 (Louisville, 1886). 17-51. [123]

STARLING, EDMUND L. History of Henderson County Kentucky (Henderson, 1887). 26, 31-33, 95, 104, 105, 523-529, 796. [124]

STEELE, MRS. ELIZA R. Summer Journey in the West (New York, 1841). 216. [125]

SWAIN, JOHN. The Natchez Trace. Everybody's Magazine, New York, September, 1905. [126]

TENNESSEE GAZETTE, a weekly, Nashville, Tennessee. News item: April 27, 1830. [127]

THWAITES, REUBEN GOLD. On the Storied Ohio (Chicago, 1903). 273, 274. [128]

THWAITES, REUBEN GOLD, Editor, Early Western Travels, 1748-1846 (Cleveland, 1904-1908), 32 vols. vol. iv, Cuming; vol. viii, Evans; vol. xiii, Nuttall; vol. xiv, James; vol. xxii, Maximilian; vol. xxvi, Flagg. Also editor of Withers's Chronicles. [129]

THWAITES, REUBEN GOLD, and Louise Phelps Kellogg. Frontier Defense on the Upper Ohio, 1777-1778; Wisconsin Historical Society, 1912. Draper Series vol. iii, 21-68.   [130]

THWAITES, REUBEN GOLD, and Louise Phelps Kellogg. Revolution on the Upper Ohio, 1775-1777. Wisconsin Historical Society, 1908. Draper Series, vol. ii, 254, 255.   [131]

TRABUE, DANIEL, Autobiography of. *See* 63.

TRIPLETT, FRANK. History, Romance and Philosophy of Great American Crimes and Criminals (St. Louis, 1884). 223-250. [An unreliable book.]   [132]

TRIPLETT, ROBERT. Roland Trevor, or the Pilot of Human Life (Philadelphia, 1853). 201   [133]

VENABLE, W. H. Beginnings of Literary Culture in the Ohio Valley (Cincinnati, 1891). Biographies of Timothy Flint and James Hall, 323-385.   [134]

VIRGINIA STATE LIBRARY. List of the Revolutionary Soldiers of Virginia (Richmond, 1912). 301.   [135]

WATTS, WILLIAM COURTNEY. Chronicles of a Kentucky Settlement (New York, 1897).   [136]

WESTERN LITERARY AND HISTORICAL MAGAZINE, Louisville. *See* 42.

WESTERN MONTHLY MAGAZINE, Cincinnati. *See* 59.

WESTERN MONTHLY REVIEW, [Timothy Flint, Editor,] Cincinnati, January, 1830: Colonel Plug, the Last of the Boat-wreckers.   [137]

WESTERN SPY AND HAMILTON GAZETTE, a weekly, Cincinnati. News items: September 3, 1799, March 9 and May 4, 1803.   [138]

WHEELING GAZETTE, (West Virginia), a weekly, December 10, 1829: The Robber of the Wilderness, reprinted from The Natchez Galaxy. (Draper MSS. 29cc 75-76).   [139]

WISCONSIN STATE HISTORICAL SOCIETY. *See* 12, 76, 130, 131.

WITHERS, ALEXANDER S. Chronicles of Border Warfare (Clarksburg, Virginia, 1831). Edited by Thwaites (Cincinnati, 1895). 224-228.   [140]

WOODS, EDGAR. Albemarle County in Virginia (Charlottesville, 1901). 236, 237, 251, 254.   [141]

WORTHEN, A. H. Geological Survey of Illinois (Springfield, 1866). vol. i, 354.   [142]

YOUNG, JACOB. Autobiography of a Pioneer (Cincinnati, 1858). 95-97.   [143]

LIBRARIES used in the preparation of this book.

Chicago: J. Christian Bay's Private, Chicago Historical Society, John Crerar, Newberry, and University of Chicago. *Cincinnati:* Cincinnati Public, Historical and Philosophical Society of Ohio, and Young Men's Mercantile. *Frankfort:* Kentucky State Historical Society, and State Library. *Jackson:* Mississippi Department of Archives and History. *Lexington,* Kentucky: Lexington Public. *Louisville:* Young E. Allison's Private, Filson Club, Louisville Free Public, and R. C. Ballard Thruston's Private. *Madison:* Wisconsin State Historical Soceity. *New Harmony,* Indiana: Workingmen's Institute. *New Orleans:* Gaspar Cusach's Private, Howard Memorial, Louisiana Historical Society, State Museum, and Thomas P. Thompson's Private. *St. Louis:* Missouri Historical Society. *Springfield:* Illinois State Historical Society. *Washington:* Library of Congress.

Index

Index

Robert A. Clark is the president of the Arthur H. Clark Company.

Shawnee Classics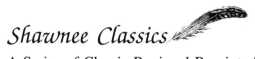
A Series of Classic Regional Reprints for the Midwest

"Black Jack"
John A. Logan and Southern Illinois
     in the Civil War Era
James Pickett Jones

A Woman's Story of Pioneer Illinois
Christiana Holmes Tillson
Edited by Milo Milton Quaife